How to Reread a Novel

How to Re-read a Novel

Matthew Clark

Louisiana State University Press
Baton Rouge

Published by Louisiana State University Press
lsupress.org

Designer: Andrew Shurtz
Typeface: Martina Plantijn

Library of Congress Cataloging-in-Publication Data

Names: Clark, Matthew, 1948– author.
Title: How to reread a novel / Matthew Clark.
Description: Baton Rouge : Louisiana State University Press, [2024]
    | Includes bibliographical references and index.
Identifiers: LCCN 2023007825 (print) | LCCN 2023007826 (ebook)
    | ISBN 978-0-8071-8070-9 (paperback) | ISBN 978-0-8071-
    8009-9 (cloth) | ISBN 978-0-8071-8078-5 (pdf) | ISBN 978-0-
    8071-8077-8 (epub)
Subjects: LCSH: Fiction—History and criticism. | Literary form.
    | Narration (Rhetoric)
Classification: LCC PR823 .C54 2024 (print) | LCC PR823 (ebook)
    | DDC 823.009—dc23/eng/20230522
LC record available at https://lccn.loc.gov/2023007825
LC ebook record available at https://lccn.loc.gov/2023007826

to Reva, who is always by my side through thick and thin

Contents

How to Reread a Novel

Introduction

A good novel is a tremendously intricate creation. Imagine a large old-fashioned mechanical clock housed in a transparent casing. If you stand in front of the clock, you will see two or three hands pointing to numbers arranged on the face in a circular array perhaps with smaller demarcations between the numbers. That's all that most people will want to see, because all they want from the clock is an indication of the time. But if you step behind the clock and look through the transparent casing, you can see a multitude of gears and springs and bearings and escapements, and you can watch the moving parts move at various speeds in various directions in various ways. Some of the parts, however, are hidden, and you would have to take off the casing and disassemble the works to see how the whole thing fits together to make a functioning clock. Perhaps only a few professional watchmakers would want to take the mechanism apart, but many people like to step behind the clock to watch at least what they see of the works. I don't want to push the analogy too far, but in a sense a novel is something like a clock. It has a face that it turns toward the public, and most people will be content to read what that public face presents. Others, however, will want to step behind the case to get a look at the mechanism. The aim of this book is to provide an account of some of the mechanisms of the novel.

According to Frank Kermode (1981, 84), "it is not uncommon for large parts of a novel to go virtually unread; the less manifest portions of its text (its secrets) remain secret, resisting all but abnormally attentive scrutiny." A reader will register the high points, but the rest of the text will remain in the background. A similar statement could be made about music: many audiences will pay attention to the melodies, but not to the secondary voices, or the patterns of repetition, or the key relationships. But musical attention can be taught, for example in ear-training lessons, and a good listener will hear more. Likewise, a good reader will be able to pay attention to more of what is going on in a novel. One important goal of this book is what could be called a kind of narrative ear-training.

The devices used by novelists probably have their effect even if readers never notice or name them. Some readers may even feel that dissection will ruin the effect. I have no complaint with these people, but they should not read this book. Some people, however, will enjoy watching the gears move, and a few will want to take the novel apart to see its gears and springs and bearings. If this is what Kermode would call "abnormally attentive scrutiny," so be it.

The big themes of a novel are probably apparent on first reading, but it usually takes a second or third reading to notice all the mechanisms and devices used by the writer. Thus a first-time reader of Jane Austen's *Emma* probably won't realize right away that Frank Churchill and Jane Fairfax have a romantic understanding—that they are, in fact, engaged. Frank and Jane keep this information secret from the other characters in the novel, and Jane Austen keeps it secret from the reader. I'm not sure when an attentive first-time reader would catch on. Mr. Knightley certainly becomes suspicious, but Emma herself is deluded until the news becomes public. The second-time reader, however, the reader who is in on the secret, will notice that Austen has very carefully supplied hints almost as soon as Frank and Jane are introduced; moreover, there are moments in the story which make sense only in light of this secret engagement.[1] Austen has been very clever in planting hints, and there is a pleasure that comes from seeing her cleverness—on second reading.

There are many other kinds of second-reading pleasure. Keywords, for instance, only become evident in the process of reading. To stay with *Emma,* the first time the reader sees the word "elegant" in the novel it may not make much of an impression, but by the fifth or sixth time it occurs it may begin to stand out, and by the end of the book, the reader will probably realize that elegance is an important theme in the story. The second-time reader can then be on the lookout from the beginning. A first-time reader may enjoy Austen's style without thinking much about how her sentences are constructed. A second-time reader may notice the deployment of various kinds of parallel structure, such as antithesis and tricolon.

Some of the effects of second-time reading can be experienced only on the second reading. I would suggest, however, that part of learning to be a good reader is developing the ability to reread, so to speak, on the first reading. A good reader can develop a kind of sense of what to be looking for, and that sense can be activated very quickly, even on a first reading. The more you read, the more you get a feel for the kinds of things writers are likely to do, the more you will notice even on first reading; and the more you read a particular writer, the more you get a feel for that writer's particular bag of tricks. But this sense of what to look for should never become closed: the reader should always be on the lookout for new kinds of delight. Every novel has the potential to reveal something new.

My interests are primarily practical rather than theoretical, but theory often lurks in the background of nontheoretical discussions, so it seems appropriate to set out a few fundamental principles of language and literature that will guide the discussion of texts. First, language is an activity: it is something that we do, and we do it with our bodies. Second, language is dialogue: it is an interaction between at least two people—even if, when you're talking to yourself, those two people happen to be the same person. Third, language is a representation of the world, or what we think about the world, and especially about other people and what they do. Language evolved the way it did because it improves our way of dealing with the world and with each other.

Most language occurs face to face. When we talk with someone, language involves the whole person—tone of voice, facial expressions, gestures, the eyes, the hands, everything. Writing pulls away from this totality of language, more or less. The extreme form of abstracted language might be a mathematical proof, which in a way is spoken by no one to no one. Literary language, which is my concern here, takes advantage of the decoupling of the usual face-to-face situation to create new and different kinds of meanings.

Some theorists in recent decades have suggested that language does not refer to anything outside language. Some of these theorists base their questioning of reference on what they take to be linguistics, for instance, the theory of the sign proposed by Ferdinand de Saussure. Any interpretation of Saussure which calls reference into question is simply incorrect. Saussure certainly knew that language refers to the world. In his account, reference is indirect: a sign is composed of a signifier and a signified, and both of these are mental entities: so the word "tree" is related to the mental image of a "tree," rather than to the tree itself. Saussure is probably right about signification. But the mental images that we have in turn refer to the world. Indirect reference is still reference. Reference can be very complex; it can, for instance, include mistakes about the world or lies or fictions or fantasies. But just because reference is complex, that doesn't mean it doesn't happen. Language, however, is not a picture of the world.

Language is an action people have developed to make meaning, for themselves and for each other. I take the meaning of meaning rather broadly. There are levels of language, and different kinds of meaning at different levels. Words have certain kinds of meaning, while sentences have other kinds of meaning. Very roughly, nouns can be used to talk about objects or concepts as if they were objects; verbs can be used to talk about states of being or actions; prepositions can talk about how nouns are related to each other; and so on. Most words don't function on their own—they function in, and partly take their meaning from, the utterances in which they occur and the circumstances in which they occur. Ordinarily we don't say that a word is true or false; we might say that it is appropriate in its context, or that it is ambiguous, or the wrong word for the intended meaning of the utterance.

When words combine to form a sentence, then we might say that the sentence is true or false. But meaning is not limited to sentences with truth-value; an imperative sentence is neither true nor false, but it certainly has meaning; likewise a hope or a wish or a promise, and so on. Meanings like these are well analyzed by speech act theory. At the level of sentences I would also include shades of meaning such as emphasis or the introduction of the speaker's subjectivity with a word like "please": "Close the door" versus "Close the door, please."

Linguistic structures larger than the sentence also have meanings, and these meanings are different from the mere summation of sentences. Only a few of these structures above the sentence have been identified, named, and analyzed. The syllogism, for instance, is a structure with a kind of meaning: we can say that a syllogism is valid or invalid. But there are many other meaningful structures of roughly the size of a syllogism— a knock-knock joke, for example. A syllogism is valid or invalid, while a joke makes us laugh or falls flat.

The hierarchy of language structures reaches all the way from words to sentences to paragraphs to chapters to episodes to whole books, and there are kinds of meaning appropriate to every level. As a general rule, meaning at one level does not easily translate into meaning at another level: the meaning of a sentence doesn't translate into the meaning of a word, and the meaning of a whole story doesn't translate into the meaning of a sentence. One of the goals of this book is to develop some provisional ideas about narrative meanings at various levels—what kinds of meanings they are and how we can best talk about them.

One way to begin thinking about a story is to pose three questions: How is it constructed? What does it represent? What does it mean? These three questions apply to what can be called the synthetic aspect, the mimetic aspect, and the thematic aspect. I borrow these terms from rhetorical narratology, especially as formulated by James Phelan and Peter Rabinowitz, but I have adapted them to fit my own analytical practice.[2] Here is a brief description of these terms as I use them.

Every narrative can be considered from these three aspects, the synthetic, the mimetic, and the thematic; these aspects are simultaneous and interdependent. Every text can be seen as synthetic, mimetic, and thematic. Synthetic analysis concerns all kinds of verbal construction, from sentences to whole plots. Mimetic analysis concerns the representation of characters and worlds constructed in a narrative, realistic or not. Thematic analysis concerns all kinds of meaning imparted by or derived from a text, direct and indirect, intended by the author or not.

The reader will quickly notice that I often use the names of rhetorical figures. Some rhetorical terms, such as metaphor and simile, are familiar; others may not be: isocolon, anaphora, congeries, and so on.[3] There is nothing particularly difficult about these terms; they are certainly easier than the technical terms in most fields. The great advantage of rhetorical terminology is that it makes it easy to notice features of writing and then to talk about them with some precision. Some readers may suppose there are too many terms—the traditional handbooks list something over two hundred—but probably only about fifty are used a lot. My own feeling is that we could use more terms—in particular, we lack terms for compositional features larger than a sentence—so I will suggest a few.

The reader may notice that I rarely make judgments about the books I discuss. I am interested in how novels are written, not in how they should be written. I like many different kinds of writing, including some kinds that are not usually thought of as literature in the higher sense, and I favor no particular school—modernist, postmodernist, classical, realist, unnatural, whatever. Of course I have preferences, and I rarely discuss books I don't like.

These, then, are the fundamental principles that underlie the following discussion. In general, theory will take a backseat to practical questions, but some theoretical discussion will be necessary; when I do discuss theory it is always as a prelude to an analysis of how writers use the techniques of narrative to make meaning. Throughout the emphasis is on practical criticism; the result is a provisional system of narrative analysis.

Chapter 1 begins with a discussion of the physicality of language as reflected in style and rhetorical figures; this chapter also challenges the idea of transparent prose. Chapters 2 and 3 examine the fundamental narrative roles taken by the storyteller and the story listener. Chapter 4 examines the meaning or function of some selected rhetorical figures. Chapter 5 considers aspects of rhetorical prose in Charles Dickens, Anne Brontë, and Toni Morrison. Chapter 6 turns to the tropes, particularly metaphors and similes, in the work of Homer, Raymond Chandler, and Henry James. This volume is part of a larger project; a companion volume is planned which will deal with larger narrative structures.

I

The Language of Fiction

Language and Reference

Language, in our first experience of it, consists of speaking and listening to other people speak; speaking itself grows out of noises that are not yet speech. Speech is physical. In order to learn how to speak, a child has to learn how to control the breath and how to control the volume of the voice—how to shout and how to whisper and everything in between. The child also has to learn to move the tongue around in the mouth and to shape the mouth itself in order to produce the various sounds of whatever language it is learning to speak. As a listener, the child has to learn how to perceive and interpret the physical speech actions of other people speaking. What does it mean when a person speaks loudly? What does it mean when a person whispers? Which of the many vocal sounds I hear count as part of the language? The physical side of speaking is also reinforced by physical play that is often associated with early speech: bouncing, singing, clapping, and so on. All of this belongs to the practical side of language use.

Some modern linguistic theories tend to regard language as primarily abstract and cognitive. Language is seen as having to do with mental entities, signs or signifiers or the like, which perhaps get transferred from one person's mind to another person's mind; and grammar consists of a set of complex abstract rules, most of which are unknown to the people who use them. I don't mean to say that these theories are wrong; I do mean to say that what comes first is physical, bound up with the body and with actions of the body. The physical aspect of language is fundamental, and the traces of this physical practice are often retained even when language becomes abstract and elaborated.

The physicality of language persists, for instance, in the rhymes and rhythms of songs and most poems. Good oratory is physical. Martin Luther King's most famous speech, the "I Have a Dream" speech, uses the physicality of language to great effect. Some of this physicality can be seen even on the page—the repetitions of the phrase "I have a dream" create a rhythm that is apparent even to a silent reader—but the speech as a whole can be appreciated only if you hear King's voice: the rise and fall of the pitch, the speeding up and the slowing down at crucial moments, and the quaver he gives to key words—all of these are effective because they are physical. But the physicality of public speech can also be a danger, as we see from the history of demagoguery.

The physicality of language also persists in many works of literature. Here is the beginning of "How the Whale got his Throat," the first story in Rudyard Kipling's *Just So Stories:* "In the sea, once upon a time, O my Best Beloved, there was a Whale, and he ate fishes. He ate the starfish and the garfish, and the crab and the dab, and the plaice and the dace, and the skate and his mate, and the mackereel and the pickereel, and the really truly twirly-whirly eel" (1987, 7). All of these words mean something: all the various marine creatures that the Whale eats really are marine creatures, the words represent things in the world, but the particular words in this list are selected and arranged because of the physicality of the words. If we were to try to translate this passage into another language, French, for example, we could just find the French words for starfish and garfish, and the French words for crab and dab, and so on, and put them in the same order in the French sentence. But I think we would agree that such a translation would not really represent what Kipling is doing, because the words would not form rhyming pairs. A different translation would find French words for marine life that also rhyme in pairs, no matter if they matched up with Kipling's original list. I'm not proposing any general law of translation here; each translator has to make decisions in each particular case, but the problem I think tells us something about language and how language is used in literature.

As Kipling's story goes on, the whale swallows a Mariner, who finds a way to make the whale disgorge him:

> But as soon as the Mariner, who was a man of infinite-resource-and-sagacity, found himself truly inside the Whale's warm, dark, inside cupboards, he stumped and he jumped and he thumped and he bumped, and he pranced and he danced, and he banged and he

clanged, and he hit and he bit, and he leaped and he creeped, and he prowled and he howled, and he hopped and he dropped, and he cried and he sighed, and crawled and he bawled, and he stepped and he lept, and he danced hornpipes where he shouldn't, and the Whale felt most unhappy indeed. (1987, 9)

The words in this pattern of rhyme and rhythm are verbs instead of nouns, but they also refer to reality, they are not nonsense, and they are appropriate to the (imaginary) situation—they designate the kinds of things that might make a whale uncomfortable. But again, they are chosen and arranged for their physicality: a single verb shows up in two different forms—"leaped" and "lept," in the phrases "he leaped and he creeped" and "he stepped and he lept"; clearly the form of the past tense is chosen to match the other verb in the phrase. A rhetorician would note the figure isocolon—which means equality of phrase length—as all the verb phrases here are two syllables long; and the figure homoioteleuton, which means "similar endings," or as we would say in English, rhyme. Isocolon and homoioteleuton are two of the most obvious of the rhetorical figures.

But these passages are not just about the sounds of the pairs of words. The first passage is a great catalog of various kinds of fishes—rhetoricians call this kind of heaping up of words a "congeries," which is just the Latin word for "heap." The suggestion of this congeries is that the whale eats every kind of marine creature there is, so it's not surprising that he would eventually eat a mariner. The second passage is a different kind of congeries, this time a congeries of verbs. The point of this great heap of verbs is to show just how much trouble the mariner is causing for the whale. It wouldn't do just to say, "He jumped" and stop there; the more verbs there are, the greater the discomfort.

The *Just So Stories* are intended for children, but the kind of physicality of language we find there can also be found in books intended for adults. The following passage from Samuel Beckett's *Watt* uses the same kinds of rhyme and rhythm used by Kipling: "Personally of course I regret everything. Not a word, not a deed, not a thought, not a need, not a grief, not a joy, not a girl, not a boy, not a doubt, nor a trust, not a scorn, not a lust, not a hope, not a fear, not a smile, not a tear, not a name, not a face, no time, no place, that I do not regret, exceedingly" (1959, 46). And later in the same paragraph: "The whacks, the moans, the cracks, the groans, the welts, the squeaks, the belts, the shrieks, the pricks, the prayers, the kicks, the tears, the skelps, and the yelps. And the poor old lousy old earth, my earth and my father's and my mother's and my father's father's and my mother's mother's and my father's mother's and my mother's father's and my father' mother's father's and my mother's father's mother's and my father's mother's mother's" (46). This goes on for a good while longer. If you try to read this out loud, the words tend to become sounds in the mouth rather than signs of anything beyond themselves. The world represented by the language has become the sounds of the language. The point of these passages is partly the physicality of the words, but I think the passage also fits into a larger project of Beckett's novel, a project which calls into question the relationship between language and the world.

These passages from Kipling and Beckett are extremes, but some of the same effects can be seen in less extreme examples. The following passage comes from Vladimir Nabokov's novel *Bend Sinister* (1974, 53–54). Here some academics in an unspecified (and fictional) Eastern European country are being asked to sign copies of a declaration in support of a dictatorial regime that has just taken power. The narrator gives a little detail about the reactions of some of the signatories, but then ends with a general description: "The rest sighed and signed, or did not sigh and signed, or signed—and sighed afterwards, or did neither the one nor the other, but then thought better of it and signed." The words here certainly have not lost their meaning; the whole passage is leading up to the moment when the hero of the story, Adam Krug, alone of these academics, refuses to sign the declaration. Nabokov is telling a story about people and what they do and don't do, but he is also constructing a world of words. At the very end of the story, the narrator reveals the essential artifice of the narration, as the characters—Krug and the dictator he calls the Toad—disappear from the story; the "I" at the end is the storyteller: "He saw the Toad crouching at the foot of the wall, shaking, dissolving, speeding up his shrill incantations, protecting his dimming face with this transparent arm, and Krug ran towards him, and just a fraction of an instant before another and better bullet hit him, he shouted again: You, you—and the wall vanished, like a rapidly withdrawn slide, and I stretched myself and got up from among the chaos of written and rewritten pages, to investigate the sudden twang that something had made in striking the wire netting of my window" (200). This moment has been prepared by all the verbal trickery throughout the novel: the patterning of the words gives the physicality of the language a certain reality of its own—and this kind of reality of the fiction or fictionality of the real becomes one of the themes of the whole story.

Here we can introduce some technical terms. A normal sentence operates on two dimensions, or two axes, a horizontal axis and a vertical axis; or we can say that sentence is a chain (the horizontal axis) of choices (the vertical axis). "The whale ate a mariner" is a chain of words and phrases in certain grammatical relationships: first a subject noun phrase, "the whale," then a verb, "ate," and finally an object noun phrase, "a mariner"; and the two noun phrases are made of a determiner, "the" and "a," plus a noun. At each point in the chain, other words could have been chosen; for instance, "A dog chased the cat." Here the axis of combination is the same—subject phrase, verb, object phrase—but there are differences on the axis of selection: the phrase "a dog" has been chosen instead of "the whale," the verb "chased" has been chosen instead of "ate," and "the cat" has been chosen instead of "a mariner." Ordinarily the choices we make are determined by what we want to say about the world—real or imaginary. We chose "the whale" rather than "a dog" because we want to talk about a whale instead of a dog—and so on. The words at one point in the chain don't usually determine the words in any other point in the chain. The word "whale," for instance, doesn't select the word "mariner"; we could just as well have said "the whale ate a lion," if that's what we wanted to represent. What selects "lion" rather than "mariner" is the reference we want to make rather than the other words in the sentence. Of course the words of a sentence are likely to be part of the same general field of reference, so "whale" might be linked to "mariner" more often than it is to "lion," but that's a fact about the world, not a fact about the words.

But sometimes the selection of the words in a sentence is influenced by other words in that sentence—as, for instance, the rhymes in a poem partly determine what words are chosen. As Roman Jakobson says, in technical terms, "The poetic function projects the principle of equivalence from the axis of selection into the axis of combination" (Jakobson 1987b, 71). This just means that the choices at one point in the chain can be influenced by choices made in the rest of the chain. In the first passage quoted above from the *Just So Stories,* we can see that the word "starfish" influences the selection of the word "garfish," the word "crab" influences the selection of the word "dab," and so on. In the second passage, the word "creeped" influences the selection of the word "leaped," while the word "stepped" influences the selection of the word "lept"; and all of these verbs have to be monosyllables. A similar analysis would show the same "poetic" principle at work in the passages from Beckett and from Nabokov.

Jakobson calls this aspect of language "poetic," but the examples we've been reading come from prose. As Jakobson says, "when dealing with the poetic function, linguistics cannot limit itself to the field of poetry" (70). The passages I have quoted from Kipling and Beckett and Nabokov are all prose, but they are also, in Jakobson's terms, poetic.

One might be tempted to propose a sort of continuum of language use, from very poetic poetry on one end to very prosaic prose on the other end, and in the middle some poetic prose and some prosaic poetry. The extreme ends of the continuum, pure prose and pure poetry, would be essentially different, even if hybrids exist; the extremes are the ideal forms, and the hybrids (some would say) are usually not worthy of praise. The essence of poetry would be to call attention to itself as language, but the prose writer should look through the language in order to see the world; the essence of prose would be transparency.

Prose (in this model) is transparent if the choice of words is simply determined by reference: the writer looks out at the world, sees something, and writes down the word that refers to that thing. Furthermore, the grammar of a sentence directly expresses the relationships things have to each other; again, the writer looks at the world and simply writes down what is happening. Thus, according to James R. Sutherland, good prose "allows the writer's meaning to come through with the least possible loss of significance and nuance, as a landscape is seen through a clear window" (Sutherland 1965, 77). Transparency is one of the goals of what Francis-Noël Thomas and Mark Turner call "classic prose"; classic prose is "a medium that will, at its best, be transparent, as if the reader were looking at something through a perfectly clean and undistorting window; the window should not draw attention to itself, and will not unless it is obviously defective in some way" (Thomas and Turner 1994, 36).

Language, however, is not a visual medium; the effects created by prose are vocal and auditory; they are created by sound, and sound can't be either transparent or opaque. Words don't give direct visual information; language does not provide a picture. The best language can do is to name some visual quality; the person who hears that name may then call up some kind of visual image—an image massively less detailed or immediate than what we see through a window.

Richard Lanham is no great fan of the transparent style—"prose style begins in pleasure and not in clarity" (1974, 10)—but he gives a good account of the style he calls into question: "Our ideal prose, like our ideal typography, is transparent: if a reader doesn't notice it, if it provides a transparent window to the meaning, then the prose stylist has succeeded" (Lanham 2003, vii). "Prose must be entirely transparent, poetry entirely opaque. Prose must be minimally self-conscious, poetry the reverse. Prose talks of facts, of the world; poetry of feelings, of ourselves. Poetry must be savoured, prose speed-read out of existence" (2003, 3). Lanham thus poses a set of dichotomies:

poetry is opaque, while prose is transparent;
poetry is self-conscious, while prose is conscious of the external world;
poetry is centered on feelings, while prose is centered on the world;
poetry should be savored, while prose should be speed-read.

Prose is, or should be, transparent precisely because it is not self-conscious, because it is centered on facts and the world, and because it is read too fast to be savored. As soon as prose becomes self-conscious, as soon as it is centered on feelings, as soon as it is savored, it has lost the essence of prose—or so this theory would suggest.

This argument from theory can be linked to an argument from history. According to Ian Watt, early English fiction—fiction before Defoe, Richardson, and Fielding—"was not primarily concerned with the correspondence of words to things, but rather with the extrinsic beauties which could be bestowed upon description and action by the use of rhetoric"—as in John Lyly's *Euphues* or Sir Philip Sidney's *Arcadia* (Watt 1983, 30). But Defoe and Richardson aimed for a style that could achieve "immediacy and closeness of the text to what is being described" (32). "It would appear, then, that the function of language is much more largely referential in the novel than in other literary forms" (33).[1] If prose is simply referential, if it is determined simply by its relation to the world, then we don't need to spend any time thinking about it. As Lanham notes, "All prose style cherishes a single goal and that goal is to disappear" (Lanham 1974, 17).

The history of English fiction, however, shows that novelists draw on the full resources of the rhetorical tradition; writers have never restricted themselves to reference as the sole virtue of prose; rhetoric and reference can coexist, and Jakobson's poetic function can be found in prose. The "poetic" qualities of prose, however, are usually not quite like the poetic qualities of poetry; the poetry of prose is its own, not something borrowed from verse.

But it is simply wrong to claim that good prose must be transparent. The passages I have quoted from Kipling and Beckett are perhaps unusual in their insistence on the physicality of the language, but attention to that physicality can be found in most good prose. Here is the beginning of Katherine Anne Porter's story "Pale Horse, Pale Rider": "In sleep she knew she was in her bed, but not the bed she had lain down in a few hours since, and the room was not the same but it was a room she had known somewhere. Her heart was a stone lying upon her breast outside of her; her pulses lagged and paused, and she knew that something strange was going to happen, even as the early morning winds were cool through the lattice, the streaks of light were dark blue and the whole house was snoring in its sleep" (1964, 141). The rhythms here are not the rhythms of verse, but they are rhythmic in the way prose rhythms can be rhythmic. Prose rhythms are usually more varied than most verse rhythms, with irregular runs of light and strong syllables, but they are nonetheless effective in pointing out particular words and particular sounds.

The test is how the passage reads aloud. There is no single way to read such a passage, but a good reading, I think, would take the emphasis of the first iamb, "In sleep," as well as the emphatic iamb "but not"; a good reading might well slow down at "a few hours since" and "known somewhere." A good reading would probably indicate the repetition of "bed" and "bed," "room" and "room" (in the figure called "conduplicatio"); but the variations in the passage are as important as the repetitions. The phrase "lagged and paused" might lag and pause; the run of iambs in "the early morning winds were cool" is broken by "through the lattice," which I read short/short/long/short (a tertius paeon, or a pyrrhic followed by a trochee); and the iambs of "the streaks of light were dark" are broken by the spondees "dark blue" and "whole house"; the alliteration of "snoring in its sleep" emphasizes the return of "sleep" from the beginning of the paragraph; this kind of return is known as "ring composition." The prose itself is not a script for reading, it doesn't give unequivocal instructions about how it should be read, but it certainly encourages a reading which notes the physical quality of the words and the way they are combined. It is perhaps relevant that the whole passage is about the intermingling of the physical and the emotional.

One might argue that this passage recounts a kind of dream, or half dream, and therefore it does not have to be referential in the way that Watt talks about reference; it is allowed to be centered on feelings and the self rather than the world because that's how dreams work. But the beginning of Earnest Hemingway's *A Farewell to Arms* is no dream, it is fully referential, and it is still poetic—in the way prose is poetic:

> In the late summer of that year we lived in a house in a village that looked across the river and the plain to the mountains. In the bed of the river there were pebbles and boulders, dry and white in the sun, and the water was clear and swiftly moving and blue in the channels. Troops went by the house and down the road and the dust they raised powdered the leaves of the trees. The trunks of the trees too were dusty and the leaves fell early that year and we saw the troops marching along the road and the dust rising and leaves, stirred by the breeze, falling and the soldiers marching and afterward the road bare and white except for the leaves. (1997, 9)

The rhythmic effects here are quite clear; and the rhythm combines with the figure known as polysyndeton, the repetition of conjunctions, which here reduces the sense of causality and increases the sense that one thing just follows another. This prose is very conscious of itself as language, even if it doesn't use the more obvious figures, such as isocolon and homoioteleuton. This passage is referential, but it is also emotional; the emotion is conveyed partly through the physicality of the language.

And here is a descriptive passage from Raymond Chandler's *The High Window:*

Stillwood Crescent Drive curved leisurely north from Sunset Boulevard, well beyond the Bel-Air Country Club golf-course. The road was lined with walled and fenced estates. Some had high walls, some had low walls, some had ornamental iron fences, some were a bit old-fashioned and got along with tall hedges. The street had no sidewalk. Nobody walked in that neighborhood, not even the postman.

The afternoon was hot, but not hot like Pasadena. There was a drowsy smell of flowers and sun, a swishing of lawn sprinklers gentle behind hedges and walls, the clear ratchety sound of lawn movers moving delicately over serene and confident lawns. (1988, 23)

Here we can note, for example, the series of clauses beginning with the word "some," in the figure called anaphora; it is no accident the last of these clauses is the longest. We also note the transferred epithets "serene" and "confident," which modify "lawns" but probably refer to the owners of the lawns, as well as the onomatopoeia in "swishing" and "ratchety." In Watt's terms, the passage is referential: there is nothing to get in the way of the transparent window. And yet the passage is also a constructed piece of rhetoric.

The most referential of the rhetorical figures, I suppose, is congeries— the heap of words I mentioned earlier. A congeries of nouns simply lists the names of a collection of things. Here is a congeries from the beginning of Joseph Conrad's *The Secret Agent;* this is the description of the window of the shop owned, as a cover, by the secret agent, the central character of the novel:

The window contained photographs of more or less undressed dancing girls; nondescript packages in wrappers like patent medicines; closed yellow paper envelopes, very flimsy, and marked two-and-six in heavy black figures; a few numbers of ancient French comic publications hung across a string as if to dry; a dingy blue china bowl, a casket of black wood, bottles of marking ink, and rubber stamps; a few books, with titles hinting at impropriety; a few apparently old copies of obscure newspapers, badly printed, with titles like *The Torch, The Gong*—rousing titles. And the two gas-jets inside the panes were always turned low, either for economy's sake or for the sake of the customers. (2012, 1)

And another congeries from Chandler's *The High Window:*

The hock shop was on Santa Monica, near Wilcox, a quiet old-fashioned little place, washed gently by the lapping waves of time. In the front window there was everything you could think of, from a set of trout flies in a thin wooden box to a portable organ, from a folding baby carriage to a portrait camera with a four-inch lens, from a mother-of-pearl lorgnette in a faded plush case to a single action Frontier Colt, .44 calibre, the model they still make for Western police officers whose grandfathers taught them how to file the trigger and shoot by fanning the hammer back. (1988, 60)

Part of the effect of these lists is the lack of any logical or causal connection in the collection; any one thing is not there because of any other thing. In technical terms the items are joined in parataxis, side by side, rather than hypotaxis, where one item is subordinated to another. A long series in parataxis is a kind of statement about the world: things are not joined according to any pattern, they are just a jumble. And part of the effect of congeries is physical: if you actually read through the whole list, aloud or silently, by the end you feel the weight of the series, and the jumble of items in the world is a jumble of sounds in your mouth. But we will see in chapter 4 that some congeries have a different effect.

The poetic qualities of good prose I think have often been neglected; if prose is supposed to be transparent, if it is supposed to be simply referential, then there is no reason to pay much attention to the poetic quality of the writing; there is something even a little disreputable in taking pleasure in the physical quality of the language. We should be interested in something higher, something more rarefied, such as the ideas or the themes of the story. But if good writers pay attention to the poetic quality of the prose, so should good readers.

One might argue that the passages I have quoted so far are unusual; they were written to call attention to themselves, but most prose, so the critic might say, wants to disappear. I certainly don't mean to suggest that every passage of every novel is equally poetic. There are many passages of good plain style. It is not easy to write a good plain style. (The rhetoricians, who like to have a name for everything, call the plain style *aphelia.*) In its way, plain prose is just as difficult, and just as artificial, as highly figured prose. It's worth paying attention to prose that doesn't call attention to itself to see how it creates its sense of transparency. Here is the beginning of Willa Cather's *A Lost Lady:*

> Thirty or forty years ago, in one of those grey towns along the Burlington railroad, which are so much greyer today than they were then, there was a house well known from Omaha to Denver for its hospitality and for a certain charm of atmosphere. Well known, that is to say, to the railroad aristocracy of that time; men who had to do with the railroad itself, or with one of the "land companies" which were its by-products. In those days it was enough to say of a man that he was "connected with the Burlington." There were the directors, the general managers, vice-presidents, superintendents, whose names we all knew; and their younger brothers or nephews were auditors, freight agents, departmental assistants. Everyone "connected" with the Road, even the large cattle- and grain-shippers, had annual passes; they and their families rode about over the line a great deal. There were then two distinct social strata in the prairie States; the homesteaders and hand-workers who were there to make a living, and the bankers and gentlemen ranchers who came from the Atlantic seaboard to invest money and to "develop our great West," as they used to tell us. (1972, 9–10)

I think it's fair to say that this prose does not call attention to itself in the manner of the previously quoted passages. There is no isocolon, no homoioteleuton, no anaphora. Perhaps we can count one instance of *correctio*—"Well known, that is, to the railroad aristocracy"—where a statement is made and then corrected or qualified. We might note the repetition of the word "grey," which introduces the narrator's judgment in addition to description. We can also note the two short lists, both with asyndeton, the lack of a conjunction; perhaps these would count as small instances of congeries. And we can note the mild crescendo "for its hospitality and for a certain charm of atmosphere"—compare "a certain charm of atmosphere and for its hospitality." But nothing really obtrudes. The easy rhythms read very well without any sense that the order of the words is forced or unusual. Overall there is nothing here to call the reader away from the reference toward the prose itself.

This paragraph has three fundamental tasks. First, it briefly presents a house; second, it situates the house in a time and place; and third, it sketches the social structure of that time and place. Social structure is not something that simply exists, the way a house exists, but the referential style puts them on the same ontological footing. (In the third paragraph we will see that a house also doesn't simply exist.)

This first paragraph begins with the house and then moves to the railroad and the social strata of the prairie, but the next paragraph brings the house back into sight: "When the Burlington men were travelling back and forth on business not very urgent, they found it agreeable to drop off the express and spend a night in a pleasant house where their importance was delicately recognized; and no house was pleasanter than that of Captain David Forrester, at Sweet Water. Captain Forrester was himself a railroad man, a contractor, who had built hundreds of miles of road for the Burlington,—over the sage brush and cattle country, and on up into the Black Hills" (10). Now we have not just a house, but also the owner of the house, himself situated in the social structure.

It would have been possible, even easy, to leave the introduction of the house to the second paragraph. The story then would have started with the railroad and the people connected with it; the first sentence of the second paragraph would make a smooth transition to the house. One can suppose that Cather wanted the house to be in the reader's mind from the outset. In any case, we see the mind of the writer making decisions; the organization of information is not simply transparent.

The third paragraph focuses more closely on the house and the vegetation around it:

The Forrester place, as every one called it, was not at all remarkable; the people who lived there made it seem much larger and finer than it was. The house stood on a low round hill, nearly a mile east of town; a white house with a wing, and sharp-sloping roofs to shed the snow. It was encircled by porches, too narrow for modern notions of comfort, supported by the fussy, fragile pillars of that time, when every honest stick of timber was tortured by the turning lathe into something hideous. Stripped of its vines and denuded of its shrubbery, the house would probably have been ugly enough. It stood close into a fine cottonwood grove that threw sheltering arms to left and right and grew all down the hillside behind it. Thus placed on the hill, against its bristling grove, it was the first thing one saw on coming into Sweet Water by rail, and the last thing one saw on departing. (10–11)

There's a good deal of referential detail here, but also a lot of judgment, as we see in words such as "fussy" and "honest" and "tortured" and "hideous" and "ugly." These are not transparent terms. The house did not just grow, it was made by human hands for human purposes. Nor is the personification of the cottonwood grove simply referential.

The end of the paragraph begins to bring the reader into the picture, and the next paragraph does so more clearly:

> To approach Captain Forrester's property, you had first to get over a wide, sandy creek which flowed along the eastern edge of the town. Crossing this by the foot-bridge or the ford, you entered the Captain's private lane, bordered by Lombardy poplars, with wide meadows lying on either side. Just at the foot of the hill on which the house sat, one crossed a second creek by the stout wooden road-bridge. This stream traced artless loops and curves though the broad meadows that were half pasture land, half marsh. Any one but Captain Forrester would have drained the bottom land and made it into highly productive fields. But he had selected this place long ago because it looked beautiful to him, and he happened to like the way the creek wound through his pasture, with mint and joint-grass and twinkling willows along its banks. He was well off for those times, and he had no children. He could afford to humour his fancies. (11)

The reader now is getting closer to the house, and also learning more about Captain Forrester. The landscape and Captain Forrester are closely linked: a description of the poplars and marsh and pastures is a description of their owner. The writer here is not just looking at the world; she is making decisions about what to look at and what to say about it:

> When the Captain drove friends from Omaha or Denver over from the station in his democrat wagon, it gratified him to hear these gentlemen admire his fine stock, grazing in the meadows on either side of his lane. And when they reached the top of the hill, it gratified him to

see men who were older than himself leap nimbly to the ground and run up the front steps as Mrs. Forrester came out on the porch to greet them. Even the hardest and coldest of his friends, a certain narrow-faced Lincoln banker, became animated when he took her hand, tried to meet the gay challenge in her eyes and to reply cleverly to the droll word of greeting on her lips. (12)

The writer here almost puts the reader into the democrat wagon along with the Captain's guests. We are now at the house itself, and now we reach the goal of the whole journey, Mrs. Forrester—the Lost Lady of the title. We meet her through the reactions of the guests, and one guest in particular; and at the end of the paragraph we see the Lady herself. We have moved all the way from the general social structure of the prairie and the people connected with the Burlington Railroad to a particular house, a particular woman in that house, and finally to her eyes and lips. The following paragraphs, to the end of the chapter, are all about Mrs. Forrester.

Cather's style is as clear and plain as can be. I admire Cather's writing, and I have spent many hours trying to emulate her clarity. Her prose is not, however, transparent. The words are simple, but they are carefully chosen to be read without a bump. The descriptions are detailed, and the details make a point. Judgment goes right along with reference. And the structure of the whole chapter is careful and deliberate. Everything is artificial, in the best sense of the word. The first reading may be so easy and natural that the artifice doesn't reveal itself, but it's there if you want to see it second time through.

Language and Characterization

When language represents the world of things, one kind of reality tries to grasp another kind of reality, and there is an unavoidable gap between the two. But when language represents speech, as it does in dialogue, the gap—almost—disappears. There is still a difference between the spoken word and the written word, and there are also conventions of representation, such as the elimination of hemming and hawing. Still, if language can't be a window to the world, it can be a pretty good approximation of what people say. The physicality of language is often represented in the speech patterns of the characters in a story. Speech fills the mouth, and as the reader reads dialogue, the sounds in the character's mouth fill the mouth of the reader, even if silently. In the following discussion I will be more interested in how a character speaks than in what the character says, though the two are not always easy to separate.

Dickens takes great delight in representing peculiar speech patterns. As early as *The Pickwick Papers,* we find the characteristic speech of Mr. Alfred Jingle: "'Heads, heads—take care of your heads!' cried the loquacious stranger, as they came out under the low archway, which in those days formed the entrance to the coach-yard. 'Terrible place—dangerous work—other day—five children—mother—tall lady, eating sandwiches—forgot the arch—crash—knock—children look around—mother's head off—sandwich in her hand—no mouth to put it in—head of a family off—shocking, shocking!'" (2000, 15–16). Mr. Jingle's characteristic style combines implausible stories, inappropriate affect, unmerited self-assurance, and irrelevant detail—all in a series of disconnected sentence fragments. The style is sufficiently distinctive to identify the speaker by sound even before he is seen: "'Capital game—smart sport—fine exercise—very,' were the words which fell upon Mr. Pickwick's ears as he entered the tent; and the first object that met his eyes was his green-coated friend of the Rochester coach" (90). Mr. Pickwick asks Mr. Jingle how he came to be at a cricket match in Muggleton: "'Come,' replied the stranger—'stopping at Crown—Crown at Muggleton—met a party—flannel jackets—white trousers—anchovy sandwiches—devilled kidneys—splendid fellows—glorious.'" And the narrator adds, "Mr. Pickwick was sufficiently versed in the stranger's system of stenography to infer from this rapid and disjointed communication" that he had become acquainted with the Muggleton cricket team (90).

Another character with a distinctive speaking style is Sam Weller, who joins the story part way through to become Mr. Pickwick's servant. Sam speaks a kind of Cockney dialect; he says "ven" for "when," "pint" for "point," "farden" for "farthing," and so on. He also has characteristic ways of turning a phrase. Here Mr. Pickwick is first offering Sam a job:

> "Now with regard to the matter on which I, with the concurrence of these gentlemen, sent for you," said Mr. Pickwick.
> "That's the pint, sir," interposed Sam; "out with it, as the father said to the child, when he swallowed a farden." (153).

A few chapters later, Sam announces that someone has come to see Mr. Pickwick:

> "Does the person want me, Sam?" inquired Mr. Pickwick.
> "He wants you particklar; and no one else will do, as the Devil's private secretary said ven he fetched away Doctor Faustus," replied Mr. Weller. (187)

Later on, Mr. Pickwick and a party of his friends go hunting, and they stop for lunch: "'Hold on, sir,' said Mr. Weller, invigorated with the prospect of refreshments. 'Out of the vay, young leathers. If you walley my precious life, don't upset me, as the gen'l'm'n said to the driver when they was a carryin' him to Tyburn'" (241). Tyburn was a place where criminals were executed; the joke is that the condemned man is worried he'll be killed in an accident on the way there. Just a page later the lunch is spread out: "'And a very good notion of a lunch it is, take it altogether,' said Mr. Weller, surveying his arrangement of the repast with great satisfaction. 'Now, gen'l'm'n, 'fall on,' as the English said to the French when they fixed bagginets'" (242). There are at least a dozen of these characteristic Wellerisms, all based on the phrase, "as so-and-so said," which serves as a sort of hinge, with the actual situation on one side of the hinge and some odd comparison on the other. Some are based on a double meaning in a word or phrase, while others look at a situation in more than one way; I think they all give a sort of unexpected twist, as they show Sam Weller's somewhat ironic view of the world.

The language in these passages is not simply transparent, because the language itself is (part of) what we are looking at. We are looking at the glass in the window. The visual metaphor, however, doesn't quite capture what's going on. Usually when someone speaks, we are interested in the message spoken more than in the manner of speaking. It can even be rude to pay too much attention to the way someone talks. And yet a person's voice is part of a person's character. We know our friends partly through their characteristic voices, and we come to know the characters in a novel partly through the way they talk.

Dickens is like a comedian doing an impression; he seizes on one or a few traits which both identify and characterize the speaker. The language is a representation and a thing represented, both at once. The voice also has to be at least consistent with the rest of what the person does. Without pushing the analysis too far, we can suppose that Mr. Jingle's fragmented speech pattern is consistent with a kind of social and moral fragmentation; we can't trust the way he speaks or what he says. Samuel Weller's wry sense of humor is expressed both in what he says and how he says it. I think we would have a very different impression of these two characters if their speech patterns were switched, if Mr. Jingle told wry little jokes and Sam talked only fragments.

Throughout his career Dickens showed a delight in devising particular speech patterns for his characters. In *Little Dorrit,* Arthur Clennam has returned to England from many years in China. He becomes reacquainted with his former fiancée, now a widow, Flora Finching, who clearly wants to revive their relationship. Flora talks a lot, but even a small sample (from chapter 13) will show her patterns of speech: "'Oh Mr Clennam you insincerest of creatures,' said Flora, 'I perceive already you have not lost your old way of paying compliments, your old way when you used to pretend to be so sentimentally struck you know—at least I don't mean that, I—oh I don't know what I mean!'" (1980, 192). And just after that:

> "You mustn't think of going yet," said Flora—Arthur had looked at his hat, being in a ludicrous dismay, and not knowing what to do: "you could never be so unkind as to think of going, Arthur—I mean Mr Arthur—or I suppose Mr Clennam would be far more proper—but I am sure I don't know what I am saying—without a word about the old days gone for ever, when I come to think of it I dare say it would be much better not to speak of them and it's highly probable that you have some much more agreeable engagement and pray let Me be the last person in the world to interfere with it though there *was* a time, but I am running into nonsense again." (192–93)

And just after that:

> "Indeed I have little doubt," said Flora, running on with astonishing speed, and pointing her conversation with nothing but commas, and very few of them, "that you are married to some Chinese lady, being in China so long and being in business and naturally desirous to set-

tle and extend your connection nothing was more likely than that you would propose to a Chinese lady and nothing was more natural I am sure than that the Chinese lady should accept you and think herself very well off too, I only hope she's not a Pagodian dissenter." (193)

Flora's speech comes through in the written form; Dickens as narrator mentions commas, marks on a page, to describe Flora's voice. Later on, in chapter 23, the narrator notes, "Even Flora's commas seemed to have fled on this occasion; she was so much more disjointed and voluble than in the preceding interview" (315).

Dickens maintains Flora's style throughout the course of the novel; in chapter 24, for instance, Flora is hinting to Little Dorrit that she and Arthur still have a romantic attachment:

"Ask me not," said Flora, "if I love him still or if he still loves me or what the end is to be or when, we are surrounded by watchful eyes and it may be that we are destined to pine asunder it may be never more to be reunited not a word not a breath not a look to betray us all must be as secret as the tomb wonder not therefore that even if I should seem comparatively cold to Arthur or Arthur should seem comparatively cold to me we have fatal reasons it is enough if we understand them hush!" (332)

The phrase "not a word not a breath not a look" could be the small seed which grew into the passage quoted earlier from Beckett's *Watt*.

Flora is a continuing character; she appears in chapters 13, 23, 24, and 35 of Book the First, and in chapters 9, 17, 23, and 34 of Book the Second; she is in fact one of the last characters to speak. Dickens must have enjoyed writing her speeches, and no doubt he expected that readers would enjoy reading them. In a sense they are referential, because they represent Flora's speech, but they are also language for its own sake.

Jane Austen was particularly skilled in characterization through speech. Here I will look at just one instance from *Emma*. Mrs. Elton, the bride of Mr. Elton, is first introduced midway through the book; Emma, after a few minutes conversation with her, is convinced "that Mrs. Elton was a vain woman, extremely well satisfied with herself and thinking much of her own importance; that she meant to shine and be very superior, but with manners which had been formed in a bad school, pert and familiar; that all her notions were drawn from one set of people, and one style of living; that if not foolish she was ignorant, and that her society would certainly do Mr. Elton no good" (2012, 187). Mrs. Elton's words and actions confirm Emma's conviction. Mrs. Elton's first speech is presented in a mixed narrative form:

> The very first subject after being seated was Maple Grove, "My brother Mr. Suckling's seat"—a comparison of Hartfield to Maple Grove. The grounds of Hartfield were small, but neat and pretty; and the house was modern and well built. Mrs. Elton seemed most favourably impressed by the size of the room, the entrance, and all that she could see or imagine. "Very like Maple Grove indeed!—She was quite struck by the likeness!—That room was the very shape and size of the morning-room at Maple Grove; her sister's favourite room." Mr. Elton was appealed to.—"Was not it astonishingly like?—She could really almost fancy herself at Maple Grove." (187)

And Mrs. Elton continues with further exclamations and comparisons to Maple Grove. Even in this short initial passage we can see a few typical features of her manner—exclamations, repetitions, rhetorical questions designed to elicit agreement, and of course her tendency to refer every situation back to herself. Initial exclamations can be found, for example, in the next few pages: "Oh! yes, I am quite aware of that" (188). "Ah, there is nothing like staying at home, for real comfort" (189). "Ah! that's a great pity" (189). "Oh! no, indeed; I must protest against any such idea" (190). Then a few pages later, "Oh! but dear Miss Woodhouse" (195). "Oh! do not tell *me*." (203). "Oh! she *shall not* do such a thing again" (204). "Oh! my dear; but so much as Patty has to do!" (204). And so on. In these passages the frequent italics denote a kind of overly emphatic tone; a number of these are emphatic first-person pronouns. "Something of that nature would be desirable for *me*" (191). "If *we* set the example, many will follow it as far as they can; though all have not our situations. *We* have carriages to fetch and convey her home, and *we* live in a style which could not make the addition of Jane Fairfax, at any time, the least inconvenient" (195). And this exclamatory habit persists throughout her speeches: "Oh! now you are looking very sly. But consider,—you need not be afraid of delegating power to *me*" (244). "I mentioned no *names,* you will observe" (312).

Mrs. Elton also uses, or misuses, a pretentious Italian epithet for her dear husband: "cara sposo" (192); "cara sposa" (208); and "caro sposo" (245). And she repeats other words as well. She is fond of saying that she has the resources to make up for the lack of society:

> "I honestly said as much to Mr. E. when he was speaking of my future home, and expressing his fears lest the retirement of it should be disagreeable. . . . When he was speaking of it in that way I honestly said that the *world* I could give up—parties, balls, plays—for I had no fear of retirement. Blessed with so many resources within myself, the world was not necessary to *me.* I could do very well without it. To those who had no resources it was a different thing, but my resources made me quite independent." (190)

Later she says, "I assure you we have not a disengaged day!—A woman with fewer resources need not have been at a loss" (200). Speaking of Mrs. Churchill, "perhaps she may not have resources enough in herself to be qualified for a country life. I always say a woman cannot have too many resources—and I feel very thankful that I have so many myself as to be quite independent of society" (212). And later she talks about purchasing a donkey: "In a country life I perceive it to be a sort of necessity; for, let a woman have ever so many resources, it is not possible for her to be always shut up at home" (245–46).

There is more to be said about Mrs. Elton's speaking habits: for instance, her tendency to interrupt, to blithely contradict what she has just said, or to talk and talk and talk.[2] Many of the features of her speech are also found here and there in the speeches of other characters, but no other character uses just this recipe with such frequency. Other characters in *Emma* also have distinctive manners of speaking—Miss Bates, of course—as do characters in other Austen novels—Mr. Collins in *Pride and Prejudice,* for example. A considerable strength of Austen's writing is her ability to express character through speech. Both Austen and Dickens characterize by selecting and exaggerating little features of grammar or style or expression, such as sentence fragments or exclamatory italics, and so on. Dickens seems to give just one or a few traits to any one character. Austen's characterization of Mrs. Elton at least uses a combination of several traits, and perhaps her characters thus seem a little less caricatured than Dickens's characters.

First-time readers will probably get a feeling about Mrs. Elton and the way she talks, but almost certainly they won't notice all the details of her speaking style. Perhaps an impression is enough. Perhaps there's no advantage in noticing the details. The writer's job is to create the effect, that's all. But those who like to re-read may find some pleasure in paying attention to how Austen creates her effects.

2
Narrators

In chapter 1 I explored some preliminary aspects of the language of narrative; that topic will be continued in chapter 4. In this chapter and the next I discuss two other fundamental features of narrative: in this chapter the storyteller, and in the next, the story-listener. I begin with a few definitions and a little theory, but as quickly as possible I move on to discuss how the various positions of the storyteller and the story-listener can be used by writers for specific purposes.

Storytellers and Story-listeners
A story needs a storyteller—and a story-listener. I might say to you, for instance, "Let me tell you what I did today. . . ." These three elements— the storyteller, the story, and the story-listener—constitute the simplest form of narrative, a minimal narrative situation. This minimal situation can be abstracted and elaborated in many ways. I might, for instance, tell a made-up story, intending to entertain or deceive. I might tell a story that was told to me by someone else. I might tell a story in which someone in the story tells a story to someone else in the story. I might write down my story so that someone can read it at another time—someone I have never met, perhaps in the far distant future.

Narrative situations and their complications are among the most highly theorized—and most controversial—aspects of narrative theory. One influential model, based on the work of Wayne Booth, Seymour Chatman, and others, distinguishes six roles in the narrative situation, as shown in this diagram, which I will call Chatman's paradigm (see Chatman 1978, 151):

Real Author	Implied Author	(Narrator)	(Narratee)	Implied Reader	Real Reader

The real author and the real reader are essential to the narrative situation, but they are outside the narrative proper; "in the text, they are 'represented' by substitute agents . . . the 'implied author' and 'implied reader'" (Rimmon-Kenan 1983, 86)—I will have more to say about the implied author and the implied reader below. The narrator is optional, and so Chatman's paradigm places it in parentheses. Plays and movies tell stories, but ordinarily they don't have narrators; most written stories do have narrators, in some sense, but this narrator may be more or less evident in the reading experience. The narratee—also optional, as designated in the diagram—is a figure within the text to whom the story is told. All of these terms require more discussion and explanation.

I begin with the real author, the flesh-and-blood person who tells or writes the story; Samuel Clemens, for instance, is the flesh-and-blood author of *Huckleberry Finn*. Then there is the implied author; this is not a real person, but a figure created by the real author, or by the act of narrating, or by the narrative itself. We might say, for convenience, that the implied author of *Huckleberry Finn* is Mark Twain. Samuel Clemens was a real person, who was born in Missouri, married, had children, earned money, paid taxes, and wrote novels. But in order to write these novels, according to this model, Clemens had to create a sort of second self, whom we can call Mark Twain. This second self, this implied author, is not a real person, he never lived anywhere, never had a family, never paid taxes. This second self is not the narrator of the story—Huck is the narrator—but neither is it the real author. The implied author is no doubt related to the real author, but it is inevitably a selection of the traits of the real author, and the real author and the implied author may even hold different opinions. Furthermore, the implied author of *Huckleberry Finn* is different from the implied author of *Tom Sawyer*—we might call them Mark Twain1 and Mark Twain2—though both books have the same real author. Because the implied author never speaks directly, its characteristics have to be deduced by the reader. It may seem odd that an entity which does not speak is nonetheless part of an act of communication; thus it may be better to think of the implied author as "a set of implicit norms rather than as a speaker or a voice" (Rimmon-Kenan 1983, 88).

The implied author as an independent entity may be a creation of theory; perhaps the implied author is just an aspect of the real author (see David Herman in Herman et al., 50). We all take on different roles and different voices in different situations, but we count all these as belonging to the same person; perhaps the implied author is just one of these roles, specific to the task of telling a story. When I write a letter, for example, I take on a role—say the role of friend, or the role of citizen, or the role of employee—and none of these roles represents the whole of me as a flesh-and-blood person; but we would not ordinarily talk about the implied author of a letter, as if the flesh-and-blood author were not responsible for it. Nor, I think, do we talk about the implied author of an autobiography, even though the autobiographer is certainly not identical to the autobiographee. Nor do we talk about the implied composer of a piece of music. Mozart could write symphonies and operas and string quartets, and we just say that they were written by Mozart, without calling on any additional entity.

Collaborations, on the other hand, may seem to create an implied author that cannot simply be identified with the real authors. The science-fiction writers Cyril Kornbluth and Judith Merril wrote two novels in collaboration (*Gunner Cade* and *Outpost Mars*), published under the name Cyril Judd; in a sense this name represents the implied author created by the collaboration. But when two people join in a task such as cooking dinner, we don't feel the need to suppose that there is an implied chef different from the two cooks. Perhaps we should, in order to distinguish a planned collaborative meal from a potluck.

If I am telling you in person about something that happened to me, the real author and the implied author are identical—or as close to identical as can be. The implied author comes into existence when the narrative situation is abstracted and elaborated. I can tell a tall tale ("One time when I was driving cattle in Wyoming, it snowed so much . . .") in which I take on a persona rather different from my own, and the pronoun "I" does not mean me. I can write an autobiographical account of my wild youth, in which I may stand at a distance from the person I used to be. I can invent a character who tells his own story, or I can tell a story in a voice that seems to come from nowhere and to belong to no one.

The theorizing of an implied author accounts for the reader's response to an ethically unreliable narrator and acknowledges the various kinds of distance between the storyteller and the story. We all know that the author of a story should not be identified with the characters; what a character asserts is not asserted by the author. But in addition, the implied author may be quite different from the real author—in age, in sex, in race, in religion. The implied author may not share the opinions of the flesh-and-blood author—indeed, it may be impossible to know the opinions of an author, and even if we do know them, they may be irrelevant to the story. So whose opinions does the story convey? The opinions of the implied author. Those theorists who claim that we can't know the intentions of the author may find the implied author a convenient substitute. Other theorists, however, argue that the implied author is an unnecessary theoretical contrivance—there are simply authors, who take on different roles when writing, just as we all do all the time. I will sometimes find it useful to talk about the implied author, but without any ontological commitments.

If we move to the other side of the diagram, we find a curious symmetry: the real author, the implied author, and the narrator correspond to the real reader, the implied reader, and the narratee. But this symmetry will prove delusive.

The real reader, like the real author, is a flesh-and-blood person, but whereas the real author is most often singular—Jane Austen, say, or Charles Dickens—real readers can be countless, and these countless readers may read in countless different ways. Critics sometimes seem to assume that all readers will read the same way, which is usually the way this particular critic reads—"the reader will feel such and such" often means "I feel such and such, and so should you"—but there is no universal reader response. Critics often disagree with each other, so how can we imagine that all readers will agree? The critic should not shrink from interpretation, but all interpretation is provisional.

The great task of the author, of course, is to manage the responses of the various readers so that enough of them will respond more or less the same way, or at least in a way that keeps them reading. These efforts by the author and responses of the readers are at the heart of the literary experience. The reader as managed by the author can be called the implied reader. This implied reader seems to solve the problem of the affective fallacy: no matter how the multitude of readers may happen to respond, the implied reader will respond just this way. The implied reader is the ideal reader—or one of several kinds of ideal readers. Has the problem been solved?

The narratee is perhaps more straightforward. In the *Odyssey,* for instance, Odysseus, as a narrator inside the story, tells the story of his wanderings to the Phaiakians, who constitute a kind of group narratee. A narrative may have one general narratee or several as the story goes along. In Chatman's paradigm, however, the narratee is optional; in many stories there is no internal audience that hears the story.

Of these positions in the narrative situation, the one which has received the most discussion is the narrator. In what has become a standard account of point of view, narrators are categorized by grammatical person: first-person narrators, third-person narrators, and the occasional second-person narrator. Gérard Genette (1980 and 1982) has distinguished *homodiegetic* narrators (narrators inside the story) from *heterodiegetic* narrators (narrators outside the story); by and large, homodiegetic narrators are first-person, while heterodiegetic narrators are third-person—but with important qualifications, as we will see. Franz Stanzel proposed three narrative positions: the *first-person narrative situation,* the *authorial narrative situation,* and the *figural narrative situation.* In the first-person narrative situation, the narrator is a character in the fictional world "just as the other characters are"; in the authorial narrative situation, "the narrator is outside the world of the characters"; in the figural narrative situation, "the mediating narrator is replaced by a reflector: a character in the novel who thinks, feels, and perceives, but does not speak to the reader like a narrator" (Stanzel 1986, 4–5). Stanzel's examples of the reflector include Virginia Woolf's *Mrs. Dalloway,* but if he means that Clarissa Dalloway is the reflector, then he is simplifying a complex narrative situation, in which several characters act as reflectors.

The idea of point of view has to some extent been extended or replaced by Gérard Genette's theory of focalization (see Genette 1980, 189–98). In Genette's system, narration by an external omniscient narrator is *nonfocalized* or has *zero focalization.* A nonfocalized narrator can range freely through the story world, without being restricted to the knowledge or perception of any particular character; the narrator of the *Odyssey,* for example, moves from Olympus to Ithaca to the island of Calypso to the land of the Phaiakians and back to Ithaca, following at various times Athena, Telemachus, Penelope, Odysseus, and Nausikaa. If, however, the narrator follows the knowledge or perceptions of a particular character, the text is focalized, as, for instance, James's *What Maisie Knew* is focalized through Maisie. Focalization can be external, if the narrative is restricted to the actions of the characters, or internal, if the narrative includes thoughts and feelings. Focalization can be fixed, if it adopts the perspective of a single character, or variable, if it moves from one character to another.

The narration of consciousness has a particular importance, and not only in modern fiction. Dorrit Cohn distinguishes three basic techniques: "1. psycho-narration: the narrator's discourse about a character's consciousness; 2. quoted monologue: a character's mental discourse; 3. narrated monologue, a character's mental discourse in the guise of the narrator's discourse" (Cohn 1978, 14). (All of these are third-person forms, but Cohn also extends her analysis to first-person narrators.) Cohn gives these examples of the basic forms:

Psycho-narration: "He wondered if he was late."

Quoted monologue: "(He thought:) Am I late?"

Narrated monologue: "Was he late?" (105)

Psycho-narration in its simplest form is much like what a traditional grammarian would call indirect discourse: a narrator uses an introductory verb of saying, thinking, feeling or perceiving in the third-person followed by a subordinate construction. In quoted monologue (often called interior monologue) a character is represented as speaking or thinking to herself. Narrated monologue is also known as the free indirect style or free indirect speech (in French, *style indirect libre;* in German *erlebte Rede*): "Like psycho-narration it maintains the third-person reference and the tense of narration, but like quoted monologue it reproduces verbatim the character's own mental language" (14). Real narrative situations display many subtle variations of these basic forms.

Norman Friedman (1967, 119–31) proposed a set of eight narrative situations: (1) Editorial Omniscience (an external narrator is allowed to speak in the first person); (2) Neutral Omniscience (the narrator does not intrude); (3) "I" as Witness (the narrator is a minor character inside the story); (4) "I" as Protagonist (the narrator is the major character of the story); (5) Multiple Selective Omniscience (the story is told through the experience of various characters); (6) Selective Omniscience (the story is told through the experience of one character); (7) the Dramatic Mode (the reader is told only what the characters do and say); and (8) the Camera (the story is told as if there were no selection or arrangement of material).

It may well be possible to make further distinctions—for example, there may be narrative situations in between Editorial Omniscience and Neutral Omniscience, depending on what counts as an intrusion by the narrator and just how much the narrator speaks. Moreover, authors frequently mix narrative modes within a single text. Austen's *Pride and Prejudice,* for instance, begins with two famous sentences of some kind of Omniscience—perhaps Neutral, since the narrator does not use an intrusive first-person pronoun, or perhaps Editorial, since the narrator has a decided tone of voice:

> It is a truth universally acknowledged, that a single man in possession of a good fortune, must be in want of a wife.
> However little known the feelings or views of such a man may be on his first entering a neighbourhood, this truth is so well fixed in the minds of the surrounding families, that he is considered as the rightful property of some one or other of their daughters. (2001, 3)

After this omniscient introduction, there is a transition to what quickly becomes the Dramatic Mode: dialogue between Mr. Bennet and his wife, with only a very few brief comments by the narrator. Even these comments disappear, leaving just a couple of inquit formulas: "replied his wife" and "replied he." This Dramatic Mode continues for a couple of pages, and then the Omniscient Narrator comes back to end the chapter: "Mr Bennet was so odd a mixture of quick parts, sarcastic humour, reserve, and caprice that the experience of three and twenty years had been insufficient to make his wife understand his character. *Her* mind was less difficult to develope. She was a woman of mean understanding, little information, and uncertain temper. When she was discontented she fancied herself nervous. The business of her life was to get her daughters married; its solace was visiting and news" (4). This chapter follows a pattern typical of Austen: a passage almost completely in dialogue is framed by the narrator's commentary. Chapter 2 of *Pride and Prejudice* is similar, though with a little more commentary in the middle section of dialogue; chapter 4 has a longer commentary after the dialogue; chapter 5 begins with a long commentary but has a short commentary after the dialogue; and so on. Such mixed forms of narrative are common, as we will see throughout this chapter.

Each narrative, indeed, may have its own particular way of getting told. It's handy to have some categories, but what really matters is the experience of reading the story at hand. Indeed, novelists often seem to enjoy exploring the complexities of the narrative situation. The subtlety of art far outstrips any practical terminology, and the exceptions are usually more interesting than the rules. Many narratives use mixed forms of narration; it is clear that readers accept these mixed forms, and mixed forms are essential to certain aesthetic effects.

Narration Degree Zero

Every story has an author of some sort (though not all authors are individual flesh-and-blood people), but some stories seem to lack a narrator. Most plays are presented without a narrator. A script may include stage directions; these are supplied by the author or the implied author, rather than by a narrator. A director may use or ignore and will certainly supplement these directions.

The theoretical distinction between narrating and acting goes back to Plato, who recognized *diegesis,* in which a narrator tells everything, *mimesis,* in which actors speak and act for an audience, and a mixture of diegesis and mimesis, as we see in Homeric epic (*Republic* 3.393a–402a). Plato as a practical artist was very interested in various modes of presentation; some of his dialogues are narrated by Socrates himself, some are narrated by people who were present at the conversations represented, some are narrated by people who weren't present at the conversation but who have heard about what was said, and some are presented as little dramatic scripts, with no narrator at all. The *Euthyphro* is a good example of this last type; here is the beginning of the dialogue:

> EUTHYPHRO: What strange new thing has happened, Socrates, that you have left your hang-out in the Lyceum and now you're hanging out around the Stoa of the King Archon? For I don't suppose you have a suit before the King, as I do?
>
> SOCRATES: The Athenians don't call this a suit, Euthyphro, but an indictment.
>
> EUTHYPHRO: What are you saying? I suppose that someone has brought an indictment against you? For I don't believe that you have indicted someone else.

SOCRATES: Certainly not.

EUTHYPHRO: Then someone else has indicted you?

SOCRATES: Yes. (*Euthyphro* 1:2; my translation)

This is all mimesis with no diegesis, all drama with no narration.

Most modern novels, like the Homeric epics, are mixtures of diegesis and mimesis, but some are presented primarily as dialogue, like the *Euthyphro;* examples include *Jacques the Fatalist,* by Denis Diderot; *Kiss of the Spider Woman,* by Manuel Puig; *J R,* by William Gaddis; and *Pastors and Masters,* by Ivy Compton-Burnett.

Epistolary novels and diary novels also lack narrators; they are overheard (or overread) rather than narrated. Some novels are mixtures of letters and diary entries and other non-narrated forms, such as newspaper stories. Daniel Keyes's *Flowers for Algernon* (also called *Charlie* after the name of the movie based on it) takes advantage of the diary form to show the gradual change in the first-person protagonist. Andrew Weir's *The Martian* also uses the diary format to good effect, as it gives a day-by-day account of the hero's efforts to save himself when he is stranded on Mars. In these stories the omniscience of a third-person narrator or even the retrospective knowledge of a first-person narrator would weaken the effect of the gradual unfolding of events.

William Faulkner's *As I Lay Dying* consists of a series of fifty-nine short sections; each of these sections is titled with the name of one of the characters and each represents in some way that character's speech or thoughts, though it can't be said that any character is the narrator in the ordinary sense. One of the sections is given to Addie, who is dead. Because there are so many sections, and because the sections are generally short, no narrative perspective is established—as in a piece of music which modulates so much that there is no tonic. Faulkner carefully individualizes the language of each character, but he also breaks that characterization with language and thoughts that don't fit the character. Faulkner is clearly testing the limits of the narrative situation.

Another example of narration in fragments is *The Waves,* by Virginia Woolf. Most of the book consists of short sections, each ascribed to one of six characters: Bernard, Susan, Rhoda, Neville, Jinny, and Louis. The sections are not intended as literal transcriptions of speech, but rather some kind of account of mental activity. The story tracks the characters chronologically from early childhood into adulthood; the reader gets no information about the characters and the action aside from what can be inferred from these quasi-speech passages. Here is the first set:

> "I see a ring," said Bernard, "hanging above me. It quivers and hangs in a loop of light."
> "I see a slab of pale yellow," said Susan, "spreading away until it meets a purple stripe."
> "I hear a sound," said Rhoda, "cheep, chirp; cheep chirp; going up and down."
> "I see a globe," said Neville, "hanging down in a drop against the enormous flanks of some hill."
> "I see a crimson tassel," said Jinny, "twisted with gold threads."
> "I hear something stamping," said Louis. "A great beast's foot is chained. It stamps, and stamps, and stamps." (1977, 6)

These are the shortest passages; as the story develops, the passages get longer, and the final section, in Bernard's voice, takes up forty pages.

Homodiegetic and Heterodiegetic Narrators

Huck Finn is the narrator of *Huckleberry Finn* and he is also its hero:

> You don't know about me, without you have read a book by the name of "The Adventures of Tom Sawyer," but that ain't no matter. That book was made by Mr. Mark Twain, and he told the truth, mainly. There was things which he stretched, but mainly he told the truth. That is nothing. I never seen anybody but lied, one time or another, without it was Aunt Polly, or the widow, or maybe Mary. Aunt Polly—Tom's Aunt Polly, she is—and Mary, and the Widow Douglas, is all told about in that book—which is mostly a true book; with some stretchers, as I said before. (1912, 3)

Twain, of course, is making jokes. His fictional narrator refers to the author —or perhaps the implied author—as if Huck and Twain exist on the same level of reality, and Huck can even make judgments about the veracity of a previous novel, as if it were a work of nonfiction inside Huck's world. Many authors make jokes about the boundary between the real and the fictional.

Like most homodiegetic characters, Huck is telling the story at some temporal remove from the events. Huck is both the narrator and a character who is narrated. Sometimes this distinction makes little difference, if the narrator and the narrated character who becomes the narrator are indistinguishable. In many adventure stories, the hero doesn't change because of what happens. In some series, the narrator remains pretty much the same over many stories, as, for example, Archie Goodwin, in Rex Stout's Nero Wolfe stories, is the same from first to last. Indeed, some of the pleasure in reading a series may be the recognition of the familiar narrator.

But some narrating characters are changed by the events of the story, and the difference between a character as narrator and as narrated can become a significant part of the story. Huck the character at the beginning of the story hasn't thought much about slavery, and the way Huck the narrator tells the beginning of the story gives no hint that his attitudes will change as the story unfolds. Is the Huck who apologizes to Jim in Chapter XV the same Huck who narrates the trick he and Tom play on Jim in Chapter II? (There is a deeper question, one of the central problems in the interpretation of the novel: is the Huck who apologies to Jim the same Huck who goes along with Tom's elaborate charade at Jim's expense at the end of the book?) Authors regularly create first-person narrators who change during the story but tell the beginning of the story as if no change had occurred.

At the beginning of Apuleius's *The Golden Ass,* the protagonist Lucius is a dissolute young man with an unhealthy interest in witchcraft; he is turned into a donkey and goes through a series of adventures; by the end of the story he has become a priest of Isis. It is hard to believe that the Lucius we see at the end of the story could be the narrator of the beginning. Of course the reader is not asked to believe this; the effect precisely depends on not asking. This narrative trick is certainly not a fault; *The Golden Ass* is a great novel, and it works only if the reader both accepts and discounts the metamorphosis of the homodiegetic narrator.

Narrators often have a distinctive voice; indeed, we expect a first-person narrator to have an individual style. Huck Finn's distinctive voice is an essential element of *Huckleberry Finn*—though he also has a somewhat implausible ability to mimic the dialects of other characters. The creation of the first-person narrator's voice is often an important aspect of characterization. Here is the beginning of Herman Melville's *Moby-Dick:*

Call me Ishmael. Some years ago—never mind how long precisely—having little or no money in my purse, and nothing in particular to interest me on shore, I thought I would sail about a little and see the watery part of the world. It is a way I have of driving off the spleen, and regulating the circulation. Whenever I find myself growing grim about the mouth; whenever it is a damp, drizzly November in my soul; whenever I find myself involuntarily pausing before coffin warehouses, and bringing up the rear of every funeral I meet; and especially whenever my hypos get such an upper hand of me, that it requires a strong moral principle to prevent me from deliberately stepping into the street, and methodically knocking people's hats off—then, I account it high time to get to sea as soon as I can. (1972, 93)

Moby-Dick is yet another example of the metamorphosis of the homodiegetic narrator; the character who has gone through the events of the story could hardly take on the narrative tone we hear at the beginning.

It is natural enough for a homodiegetic narrator to have a voice that goes with the personality of the character, but many heterodiegetic narrators also have personality and characteristic voice. Here is the beginning of Jane Austen's *Persuasion:*

Sir Walter Elliot, of Kellynch Hall, in Somersetshire, was a man who, for his own amusement, never took up any book but the Baronetage; there he found occupation for an idle hour, and consolation in a distressed one; there his faculties were roused into admiration and respect by contemplating the limited remnant of the earliest patents; there any unwelcome sensations arising from domestic affairs changed naturally into pity and contempt as he turned over the almost endless creations of the last century; and there, if every other leaf were powerless, he could read his own history with an interest which never failed. (2003, 3)

Austen's narrator, following Flaubert's principle, is "like God in the universe, present everywhere and visible nowhere" (Letter to Louise Colet, December 9, 1852); but her presence is revealed through style. This opening sentence is long and complex, but always clear and controlled. The initial clause, which could have been an independent sentence, is followed by four subordinate clauses; these are all partly parallel but also all different; and within these clauses we have additional parallelism ("occupation for an idle hour" and "consolation in a distressed one") and doublets ("admiration and respect" and "pity and contempt"). And of course we hear Austen's ironic tone—or the ironic tone of her implied author. The grammar and the tone give the invisible narrator a definite personality.

The heterodiegetic narrator of Chinua Achebe's *Things Fall Apart* has a very different voice:

> Okonkwo was well known throughout the nine villages and even beyond. His fame rested on solid personal achievements. As a young man of eighteen he had brought honor to his village by throwing Amalinze the Cat. Amalinze was the great wrestler who for seven years was unbeaten, from Umuofia to Mbaino. He was called the Cat because his back would never touch the earth. It was this man that Okonkwo threw in a fight which the old men agreed was one of the fiercest since the founder of the town engaged a spirit of the wild for seven days and seven nights. (2009, 3)

The beginning of *Things Fall Apart,* like the beginning of *Persuasion,* introduces a character and places that character in a social position. Sir Walter Elliot will be a secondary character in *Persuasion,* and it is his daughter Anne who will be the heroine; Okonkwo will dominate *Things Fall Apart* from beginning to ending; even in this short passage the narrator treats him with respect. The narrators of both passages are heterodiegetic; neither is a character who appears in the world of the story. But both narrators are strongly characterized, and it is hard to imagine either story told by the narrator of the other.

Achebe's narrator speaks simply and directly, in a manner that avoids the complex syntax and the ironic judgment found in *Persuasion.* A fact is stated, and this fact leads naturally to the next statement of a fact. Okonkwo is famous. His fame is based on achievements. One such achievement is detailed: when he was young he defeated Amalinze. Who was Amalinze? He was a great wrestler. Okonkwo defeated him in a great fight which equaled a great fight from legend. The world consists of facts; each fact stands as a singular item in its own sentence, but there is also a natural connection from one sentence to the next, from one fact to the next. If for some reason a detail needs to be elaborated, the narrative digresses without fuss and then returns to the main line of the story. The simplicity of the narration is carefully constructed.

This style of narration continues throughout the novel. In chapter 3, for instance, we learn about Okonkwo's background: "Okonkwo did not have the start in life which many young men usually had. He did not inherit a barn from his father. There was no barn to inherit. The story was told in Umogia, of how his father, Unoka, had gone to consult the oracle of the Hills and the Caves to find out why he always had a miserable harvest" (16). Now the narrator needs to explain something about the oracle: "The oracle was called Agbala, and people came from far and near to consult it. They came when misfortune dogged their steps or when they had a dispute with their neighbors. They came to discover what the future held for them or to consult the spirits of their departed fathers" (16). The following two paragraphs give more detail about the operation of the oracle, and then the main narrative is resumed by means of a small ring: "Many years ago when Okonkwo was still a boy his father, Unoka, had gone to consult Agbala" (17).

The digression about the oracle is designed to assist a reader who does not belong to the world of the story. Anyone in the story or indeed a reader living in the world represented by the story would know about the oracle without being told. By contrast, in *Persuasion* Austen does not explain what the Baronetage is; she assumes that her reader will know. A modern reader may be able to guess at the reference, but this kind of detail at some point will require an editorial note.

A first-person narrator can be the central figure in the story, as in Daniel Defoe's *Robinson Crusoe* or *Moll Flanders,* Dickens's *David Copperfield* or *Great Expectations,* or countless others. A first-person narrator can also be a minor character, a witness to the deeds of the hero or heroine; examples include Nellie in Willa Cather's *My Mortal Enemy* and Ephraim Mackellar in Robert Louis Stevenson's *The Master of Ballantrae.* In Friedman's terms, Huck Finn is "I as Protagonist," while Nellie in *My Mortal Enemy* is "I as Witness." But there is a sliding scale between a witness and a protagonist. A witness character can become important, a kind of secondary hero: Nick Carraway in F. Scott Fitzgerald's *The Great Gatsby* or Chief Broom in Ken Kesey's *One Flew Over the Cuckoo's Nest.*[1]

In principle, first-person homodiegetic narrators can look into their own hearts, but they can't see into the hearts of other characters or tell anything they don't witness personally or haven't heard about from another character, but in practice these limitations can be disregarded. In Chapter VIII of *The Great Gatsby,* as James Phelan notes, Nick Carraway rather implausibly tells "in considerable detail how George Wilson spent the night after his wife Myrtle's death" but "most readers either don't notice or don't mind the break in the probability code."[2]

The heterodiegetic, third-person narrator stands outside the story—though we will find that a heterodiegetic narrator can use the first-person pronoun and can even step into and out of the story. Jane Austen's narrators are heterodiegetic, as we see, for example, at the beginning of *Sense and Sensibility:*

> The family of Dashwood had been long settled in Sussex. Their estate was large, and their residence was at Norland Park, in the centre of their property, where for many generations they had lived in so respectable a manner as to engage the general good opinion of their surrounding acquaintances. The late owner of this estate was a single man, who lived to a very advanced age, and who for many years of his life had a constant companion and housekeeper in his sister. But her death, which happened ten years before his own, produced a great alteration in his home; for to supply her loss, he invited and received into his house the family of his nephew, Mr. Henry Dashwood, the legal inheritor of the Norland estate, and the person to whom he intended to bequeath it. In the society of his nephew and niece, and their children, the old gentleman's days were comfortably spent. His attachment to them all increased. The constant attention of Mr. and Mrs. Henry Dashwood to his wishes, which proceeded not merely from interest, but from goodness of heart, gave him every degree of solid comfort which his age could receive; and the cheerfulness of the children added a relish to his existence. (2001, 3)

This narrator is in full command of all the facts, and also in full command of the feelings and motives of the characters, which are also presented as objective truth. We are told, and we believe, that old Mr. Dashwood feels affection for his nephew and niece and their children; we are told, and we believe, that their attentions to him are motivated by goodness of heart.

When I was young and first thinking about stories and how they are told, I imagined this style as the style of God's newspaper, either the newspaper written by God or the newspaper read by God at breakfast every morning; presumably these two newspapers are identical, and God is the publisher, the reporter, and the reader—all three in one.

Indeed, the narrative manner of some parts of the Bible is in some ways like the narrative manner of this passage from *Sense and Sensibility*. The narrator of *Genesis* knows the facts of the creation of the world, the creation of the sun and the moon and the stars, the creation of the animals, and the creation of Adam and Eve, as confidently as Austen's narrator knows the history of the Dashwood family. This biblical narrator overhears God talking to himself; this narrator even knows God's motives: "And God saw that the wickedness of man was great in the earth, and that every imagination of the thoughts of his heart was only evil continually. And it repented the Lord that he had made man on earth, and it grieved him at his heart" (Gen. 6:5–6).

James Joyce had a somewhat different idea of the God of the novel: "The artist, like the God of creation, remains within or behind or above his handiwork, invisible, refined out of existence, indifferent, paring his fingernails" (Joyce 1964, 215). The author is God, but this God should leave no traces in the text.

In any case, the omniscience of an omniscient narrator is not God's omniscience. God's newspaper presumably would report everything that happens, but a novel tells just what it has to tell when it has to tell it. No one but God would want to read a newspaper or a novel that told the whole story with nothing left out. If the narrator of Austen's *Emma* is omniscient, she must know from the beginning that Frank Churchill and Jane Fairfax are engaged, but she doesn't pass this information on to the reader until the right moment.

God's newspaper would tell everything, and it would also be completely objective; it would simply give an account of reality as it really is. God's language would be transparent, with no distortions caused by the medium itself. The languages that human beings actually use are not transparent (as I argued in chapter 1). If language were directly connected to the world, then everyone would describe the world with the same words. Perhaps a scientist writing a lab report aims for this kind of objectivity, but novelists do not. A third-person heterodiegetic narrator will have a style, just because it is impossible to write without a style. The voice of the narrator is part of what draws the reader into the story, and it is an essential element of creating the reader's impression of the story.

The gender of a heterodiegetic narrator is usually left unspecified. Most readers, I suspect, assume that Jane Austen's narrators are female, but I don't know that there is really much evidence one way or another. I would guess that the narrator of George Eliot's *The Mill on the Floss* is male, but the narrator of *Middlemarch* is female. Some narrators are evidently ageless: the story told in Thomas Mann's *Buddenbrooks* takes place over forty-seven years, but the narrator doesn't seem to age with the characters. The more god-like the narrator the less likely it is to have age, gender, or race.

The heterodiegetic narrator is not necessarily omniscient, as we see in William Golding's *The Lord of the Flies*. "The boy with fair hair lowered himself down the last few feet of rock and began to pick his way toward the lagoon" (2011, 1). The boy is unnamed. Then another character is introduced: "He was shorter than the fair boy and very fat" (2). The fat boy asks the fair boy, "What's your name?" and the fair boy answers "Ralph" (3–4). "The fat boy waited to be asked his name in turn but this proffer of acquaintance was not made; the fair boy named Ralph smiled vaguely, stood up, and began to make his way once more toward the lagoon." The narrator can use Ralph's name once Ralph has used it, but the fat boy is still unnamed. Eventually the fat boy reveals that his nickname at school was "Piggy," and Piggy he is called from that moment throughout the novel. The narrator seems to have no knowledge of names or nicknames until they are enunciated by a character.

The omniscient heterodiegetic narrators of Jane Austen's novels don't refer to themselves or otherwise thrust themselves into the stories they tell; in Friedman's terms, their omniscience is Neutral. By contrast, the heterodiegetic narrator of George Eliot's *Adam Bede* feels free to intrude, using what Friedman calls Editorial Omniscience, as we see right at the beginning: "With a single drop of ink for a mirror, the Egyptian sorcerer undertakes to reveal to any chance comer far-reaching visions of the past. This is what I undertake to do for you, reader. With this drop of ink at the end of my pen I will show you the roomy workshop of Mr Jonathan Burge, carpenter and builder in the village of Hayslope, as it appeared on the eighteenth of June, in the year of our Lord 1799" (1985, 7). The narrator then describes Adam Bede and his brother Seth in the workshop. The narrator continues to comment throughout the story. In chapter 3, for instance, Seth Bede declares his love for Dinah Morris and she rejects him:

> Dinah pressed his hand with rather a sad look in her loving eyes and then passed through the gate, while Seth turned away to walk lingeringly home. But instead of taking the direct road, he chose to turn back along the fields through which he and Dinah had already passed, and I think his blue linen handkerchief was very wet with tears long before he had made up his mind that it was time for him to set his face steadily homewards. He was but three-and-twenty, and had only just learned what it is to love—to love with that adoration which a young man gives to a woman whom he feels to be greater and better than himself. Love of this sort is hardly distinguishable from religious feeling. (38–39)

And so on for several paragraphs. The narrator comments on the characters and the action and writes a sort of essay. There are many such commentaries throughout the novel. One of the most interesting of these comes in chapter 17, at the very beginning of Part the Second. At the end of chapter 16, the end of Part the First, Arthur Donnithorn, the rich young man who will inherit the Donnithorn estate, has just been on the brink of telling the rector, Adolphus Irwine, about his affair with the farm-girl Hetty Sorrel, but the moment passes and the rector does not press the point. Chapter 17 begins:

> "This Rector of Broxton is little better than a pagan!" I hear one of my lady readers exclaim. "How much more edifying it would have been if you had made him give Arthur some truly spiritual advice. You might have put into his mouth the most beautiful things—quite as good as reading a sermon.
>
> Certainly I could, my fair critic, if I were a clever novelist, not obliged to creep servilely after nature and fact, but able to represent things as they never have been and never will be. Then, of course, my characters would be entirely of my own choosing, and I could select the most unexceptionable type of clergyman, and put my own admirable opinions into his mouth on all occasions. But you must have perceived long ago that I have no such lofty vocation, and that I aspire to give no

more than a faithful account of men and things as they have mirrored themselves in my mind. The mirror is doubtless defective, the outlines will sometimes be disturbed; the reflection faint or confused; but I feel as much bound to tell you, as precisely as I can, what that reflection is, as if I were in the witness-box narrating my experience on oath. (177)

This narrator is not a part of the story, but he is part of the reader's experience of the novel.

Many critics (and some authors speaking as critics) have disliked such intrusions by the author, or by the narrator—critics have not always clearly distinguished the two. These intrusions, it was argued, defeat the kind of readerly involvement that is part of the project of novelistic realism. Wayne Booth, in *The Rhetoric of Fiction,* has cataloged and critiqued critical objections to authorial intrusions. These objections were characteristic of a period, the period of high modernism in the early twentieth century, but they are not heard so much today. Intrusions can be done well or badly, of course. Sermonizing easily becomes dated, but there can be real aesthetic interest in playing with the boundaries of the narrative situation.

Even before Booth was making his critique of the critics, novelists were exploring the aesthetics of this kind of boundary crossing, which has now become a staple of postmodernism—and which was never really absent. There are many ways to cross the boundaries. Memoirs can have a strong novelistic flavor, and some narratives straddle the line between autobiography and fiction—one might mention Kenneth Rexroth's memoir, *An Autobiographical Novel,* or the novels of Henry Miller. Some novelists insert themselves or their surrogates into their novels—Philip Roth is a character in the novel *The Plot against America,* written by Philip Roth, and Philip K. Dick is a character in the novel *Valis,* written by Philip K. Dick. Dante is a character in Dante's *Divine Comedy.* Vladimir Nabokov sometimes gives a narrator some of his own traits just along the way—as in *Bend Sinister* and *Pnin.* All of these techniques can call into question the difference between the world inside and the world outside the story.

The narrator of Anthony Trollope's *The Warden* initially seems to be an intrusive omniscient narrator. This narrator (usually) has full knowledge of whatever any character does or feels; this narrator also freely and frequently introduces his own judgments about the characters and events of the story. Here are the first sentences: "The Rev. Septimus Harding was, a few years since, a beneficed clergyman residing in the cathedral town of—; let us call it Barchester. Were we to name Wells or Salisbury, Exeter, Hereford, or Gloucester, it might be presumed that something personal was intended, and as this tale will refer mainly to the cathedral dignitaries of the town in question, we are anxious that no personality may be suspected" (Trollope 1984, 1). The powers of this particularized narrator vary; at times he is clearly able to see inside rooms and inside hearts. In chapter 2 the narrator reports on a conversation between the archdeacon and his wife while they are in bed; and often the narrator confidently notes the unspoken thoughts and feelings of the characters. But sometimes the narrator's knowledge is limited: "Scandal at Barchester affirmed that had it not been for the beauty of his daughter, Mr Harding would have remained a minor canon; but here probably Scandal lied" (1984, 1). In the following passage he makes a general statement about the limited powers of a narrator: "What had passed between Eleanor Harding and Mary Bold need not be told. It is indeed a matter of thankfulness that neither the historian nor the novelist hears all that is said by their heroes or heroines, or how would three volumes or twenty suffice. In the present case so little of this sort have I overheard, that I live in hopes of finishing my work within 300 pages, and of completing that pleasant task—a novel in one volume; but something had passed between them" (54).

The narrator brings himself close to the world of the story by using the present tense where the narrative past tense would be expected: "Mr Harding is a small man, now verging on sixty years, but bearing few of the signs of age; his hair is rather grizzled, though not grey ..." (5); "There is living at Barchester a young man, a surgeon, named John Bold, and both Mr Harding and Dr Grantly are well aware that to him is owing the pestilent rebellious feeling which has shown itself in the hospital" (9). And at one point the narrator enters the world of the story quite directly:

> And yet I have never found the rectory a pleasant house. . . . In spite of these attractions, I generally found the rectory somewhat dull. After breakfast the deacon would retire, of course, to his clerical pursuits. Mrs. Grantly, I presume, inspected her kitchen, though she had a first-rate housekeeper, with sixty pounds a year; and attended to the lessons of Florinda and Grizel, though she had an excellent gov-

erness with thirty pounds a year; but at any rate she disappeared; and I never could make companions of the boys. . . .

On the whole, therefore, I found the rectory a dull house, though it must be admitted that everything there was of the very best. (68)

If the narrator is actually a guest in the rectory, it is hard to imagine that his two adult hosts would simply disappear and leave him to deal with the three boys. I suppose that Trollope is not seriously trying to make sense; he simply wants to make his point and have his joke without caring much about plausibility. His point and his joke depend on a flexible narrator—at times omniscient, at times with only limited knowledge, mostly outside the story, but sometimes inside. If he does step into the story, however, he has no effect on it.

The narrator of Vladimir Nabokov's *Pnin* seems at first to be heterodiegetic and omniscient. Here is the first sentence: "The elderly passenger sitting on the north-window side of that inexorably moving railway coach, next to an empty seat and facing two empty ones, was none other than Professor Timofey Pnin" (1985, 7). There follows a physical description of the hero, including details not evident to external observation: "Prior to the nineteen-forties, during the staid European era of his life, he had always worn long underwear, its terminals tucked into the tops of neat silk socks, which were clocked, soberly colored, and held up on his cotton-clad calves by garters. In those days, to reveal a glimpse of that white underwear by pulling up a trouser leg too high would have seemed to Pnin as indecent as showing himself to ladies minus collar and tie" (8). The narrator is aware of himself as a narrator and aware of his own omniscience: "Now a secret must be imparted. Professor Pnin was on the wrong train. He was unaware of it, and so was the conductor, already threading his way through the train to Pnin's coach" (8). Evidently the narrator can see into the minds of even minor characters.

This little passage does more than establish the omniscience of the narrator. Writing is a continual process of making choices among ways of making meaning. Here the narrator could have said more or he could have said less. He could have omitted the first sentence and gone straight to the factual point: "Professor Pnin was on the wrong train." Or he could have explicitly indicated himself and the reader: "And now, dear reader, I must impart a secret to you." Instead he chose to hide himself behind a passive transformation and deletion of the agent phrase and he chose to hide the reader inside the implied indirect object of the verb—but they are both there as absent presences, as the faint aroma of the rhetorical transaction between the two remains in the air.

The reader soon learns more about Professor Pnin. He is a teacher of Russian at Waindell College; he has only a few students, and there is no Russian department, so his courses are held in the German Department, whose chair, Dr. Hagen, protects the rather eccentric and ineffectual Professor Pnin (10–11). He is on his way to give a lecture to the Cremona Women's Club; he has brought a copy of his lecture, as well as another lecture he is scheduled to give the following Monday, and a paper by a graduate student, and he is very worried that he will bring the wrong set of papers to the Women's Club. (Toward the end of the chapter we learn that he solves his problem by bringing all three papers to the lecture.)

This omniscient narrator soon puts himself in the story. Just a few pages into the first chapter, the narrator remarks that Pnin carries in his wallet "two ten dollar bills, a newspaper clipping of a letter he had written, with my help, to the New York Times in 1945, anent the Yalta Conference, and his certificate of naturalization" (16). The narrator then takes himself out of the story for the rest of chapter 1; in chapter 2 he returns in a parenthesis: "the kind Russian lady (a relative of mine)" (47); then twice in chapter 5: "This was the first time Pnin was coming to The Pines but I had been there before" (117); and "I confess to have been myself, at one time, under the spell of angelic Konstatin Ivanich" (125); and twice again in chapter 6: "Pnin and I had long since accepted the disturbing but seldom discussed fact . . ." (148) and "My friend and compatriot soon realized that he could never be sure" (149).

These self-references are immediately apparent; others reveal themselves on second reading. In chapter 6 the reader learns that Dr. Hagen, Pnin's protector at Waindell College, is leaving for a better position. His likely successor, Dr. Falternfels, dislikes Pnin and will not keep him on staff; the chair of English "considered Pnin a joke, and was in fact, unofficially but hopefully haggling for the services of a prominent Anglo-Russian writer" (140). Toward the end of chapter 6 Hagen tells Pnin that he is leaving; that there will be no place for him in the German Department; and that the French Department has no room for him. "On the other hand," Hagen says, "you'll be glad to know that the English Department is inviting one of your most brilliant compatriots, a really fascinating lecturer—I have heard him once. I think he's an old friend of yours" (169). But when Pnin learns who this old friend is, he says, "Yes, I know him thirty years or more. We are friends, but there is one thing perfectly certain. I will never work under him" (170).

In chapter 7 the narrator brings himself fully into the story. "My first recollection of Timofey Pnin," he tells us, "is connected with a speck of coal dust that entered my left eye on a spring Sunday in 1911" (174). One could easily imagine this sentence at the beginning of the novel, but here it is delayed to the beginning of the final chapter. The narrator's mother takes him to see an ophthalmologist, Dr. Pavel Pnin, the father of our hero. Dr. Pnin's office is in his home, and during the medical visit he introduces his patient to his son and boasts that the young Pnin has just earned an A+ on an algebra test. The narrator and Pnin next meet five years later during a summer vacation in the country; and then again in the 1920s in Paris, where they are both in exile, at a reading by the narrator. During that time the narrator had an affair with a young medical student and aspiring poet Liza Bogolepov: "In the result of emotions and in the course of events, the narration of which would be of no public interest whatsoever, Liza swallowed a handful of sleeping pills. As she tumbled into unconsciousness she knocked over an open bottle of the deep-red ink which she used to write down her verses, and that bright trickle coming from under her door was noticed by Chris and Lew just in time to have her saved" (182). Two weeks later Liza, as the narrator is about to leave Paris, tells him that she has received an offer of marriage: "I shall wait till midnight. If I don't hear from you, I shall accept it" (182), and she encloses the letter that offers marriage, but with the signature torn off. The narrator learns some years later that Liza has married Timofey Pnin. At a social gathering of exiles the narrator sees them: "Taking advantage of Pnin's being engaged in a political discussion with Kerensky at the other end of the table, Liza informed me—with her usual crude candor—that she had 'told Timofey everything'; that he was 'a saint' and had 'pardoned me'" (184). There is more to be said, particularly about Liza—who leaves Pnin for another man, Eric Wind, then comes back to Pnin only in order to make it easier for her to get to the United States as World War II begins, leaves him again for Eric Wind, has a child whom we meet in chapter 3, and then leaves Eric Wind for another man—but for my purposes here it is enough to note that the narrator, far from being outside the story, actually has been in the story all along. And at this point—or on second reading—a number of earlier passages now become clear. In chapter 2: "Pnin wrote her [Liza] a tremendous love letter—now safe in a private collection—and she read it with tears of self pity while recovering from a pharmacological attempt at suicide because of a rather silly affair with a littérateur who is now——But no matter" (45). This littérateur is the narrator of the story; he is the man who caused Liza to try to kill herself, and he is also the brilliant compatriot who is coming to replace Pnin at Waindell. In addition there are a couple of references that link the narrator to the flesh-and-blood author: in chapter 5 (117) the narrator refers to a number of émigré writers, including Sirin, which was the flesh-and-blood Nabokov's pseudonym. Again in chapter 5, there is a reference to Vladimir Vladimirovich and his interest in entomology (128). It would be a misunderstanding of the joke, however, to think that Nabokov is intending to insert himself into the story.

"When I decided," the narrator says, "to accept a professorship at Waindell, I stipulated that I could invite whomever I wanted for teaching in the special Russian Division I planned to inaugurate" (186). When he writes to offer Pnin a position, Pnin replies curtly that he "was through with teaching and would not even bother to wait till the end of spring term"; he "would be leaving Waindell two or three days before the public lecture that I was to give there on Tuesday, February the fifteenth" (186). The reader has learned in chapter 3 that February the fifteenth is Pnin's birthday.

The narrator spends his first night at Waindell at the home of Jack Cockerell, one of Pnin's enemies, who has developed over the years a repertoire of imitations of Pnin and now performs them for the narrator. "He went on for at least two hours, showing me everything—Pnin teaching, Pnin eating, Pnin ogling a coed, Pnin narrating the epic of the electric fan which he had imprudently set going on a glass shelf right above the bathtub . . ." and so on (187). "Finally the whole thing grew to be such a bore that I fell wondering if by some poetical vengeance this Pnin business had not become with Cockerell the kind of fatal obsession which substitutes its own victim for that of the initial ridicule" (189).

The next morning the narrator takes a walk before breakfast and sees Pnin driving out of town; he tries to attract his attention, but Pnin drives away evidently without seeing him. The narrator returns to have breakfast; Cockerell greets him and says, "And now . . . I am going to tell you the story of Pnin rising to address the Cremona Women's Club and discovering that he had brought the wrong lecture" (191). This final sentence of the novel makes a satisfying ring with the first chapter. This whole chapter and Cockerell's final comment leave us with some narratological problems. How is it that Cockerell knew the story of Pnin's misadventure from chapter 1? Is it significant that he seems to have got the crucial details wrong?—since we learned in chapter 1 that Pnin had taken all three papers to the Women's Club. Or is his version of the story correct? How is it that the narrator knows so much that could be known only by an omniscient and heterodiegetic narrator? Could it be that the narrator is just as wrong as Jack Cockerell? I am not sure that there are good answers to these questions, and it may be that the aesthetic effect partly depends on an unresolved and unresolvable uncertainty.

Focalization

Ken Follett's thriller *The Eye of the Needle* begins with a passage in zero focalization, with a neutral omniscient narrator: "It was the coldest winter for forty-five years. Villages in the English countryside were cut off by the snow and the Thames froze over" (3). This narrative manner continues for two paragraphs, but then there is a change: "The city did not look much like the capital of a nation at war. There were signs of course; and Henry Faber, cycling from Waterloo Station toward Highgate, noted them: piles of sandbags outside important public buildings, Anderson shelters in suburban gardens, propaganda posters about evacuation and Air Raid Precautions. Faber watched such things—he was considerably more observant than the average railway clerk" (3). We see what Henry Faber sees; the text is focalized through Faber. This account of Faber's observations continues for a long paragraph; the word "signs" links from the beginning of this paragraph to the beginning of the next: "There were signs, yes; but there was something jokey about it all. . . . It was at once larger-than-life and trivial, like a moving picture show" (4). The short fifth paragraph then develops a hint dropped in the third: "Faber had a different point of view—but then, he was a different kind of person" (4). The reader is left for the moment to guess what kind of person he is.

Faber goes to his boardinghouse, owned by a widow, Mrs. Garden. He has dinner with her and the other boarders and then he goes up to his room. The initial sentences of the paragraphs at the end of this section make a subtle transition in point of view: "Faber spread margarine"; "Faber hurried through his tea"; "Mrs. Garden turned on the radio"; "Faber had heard the show" (5–6). The reader is prepared when the following section is focalized through Mrs. Garden.

After the radio show ends, Faber goes up to his room, the other boarders go their various ways, and Mrs. Garden is left alone, "thinking about Mr. Faber. She wished he wouldn't spend so much time in his room. She needed company, and he was the company she needed" (6). The narrator continues to report what Mrs. Garden thinks about Faber:

> Mr. Faber was a quiet one—that was the trouble. . . . She suspected he was quite clever, despite his humble job. . . . It was the same with his appearance. . . . And yet at first sight he was not the kind of man a woman would look at twice. The trousers of his old worn suit were never pressed—she would have done that for him, and gladly, but he never asked. . . . He needed a woman, there was no doubt of that. . . . Yet he never made a move. Sometimes she could scream with frustration. (6–7)

This passage is largely what Cohn calls narrated monologue, or what other theorists call free indirect discourse: we are reading the thoughts of the character in the language of the narrator. When the narrator says "The trousers of his old worn suit were never pressed—she would have done that for him," we are to understand that Mrs. Garden has thought "I would have done that for him."

Mrs. Garden decides to take the initiative. She goes upstairs, knocks on Faber's door, and then opens the door with her own key: "Without speaking, he came slowly toward her. . . . She took a step forward, and then his arms went around her and she closed her eyes and turned up her face, and he kissed her, and she moved slightly in his arms, and then there was a terrible, awful, unbearable sharp pain in her back and she opened her mouth to scream" (10). The focalization then immediately switches back to Faber: "He had heard her stumble on the stairs. If she'd waited another minute he would have had the radio transmitter back in its case and the code books in the drawer and there would have been no need for her to die" (10). And the rest of the chapter stays focalized on Faber. The effect of this episode depends on the author's control of the focalization. True omniscience would not work here; the perspective has to be limited and mutable: focalizing first through Faber, then through Mrs. Garden, and then again through Faber. Readers evidently have no difficulty with this kind of fast cutting back and forth. The narrator can go inside the minds of Faber and Mrs. Garden, but he has to control the reader's knowledge; the murder has to be a shock, and it would have been a mistake to present Faber's thoughts too soon. A typical mystery story, of course, would stay entirely outside the mind of the murderer, or else there would be no mystery. But many crime novels and thrillers want to present and explore the psychology of the criminal, and for that purpose focalization is often the best tool.

The following chapter begins with another change of focalization: "Henry II was a remarkable king. In an age when the term 'flying visit' had not yet been coined, he flitted between England and France with such rapidity that he was credited with magical power" (15). The paragraph then presents a puzzle in the record of the king's travels: in 1173 he evidently made a short visit to England, but the purpose of the visit remains a mystery. "This was the problem that taxed Percival Godliman in the summer of 1940" (15). What initially seems to be an objective and nonfocalized account of King Henry II is retrospectively focalized through Godliman: "Professor Godliman knew more about the Middle Ages than any man alive. His book on the Black Death upended every convention of medievalism; it had also been a best-seller and published as a Penguin Book. With that behind him he had turned to a slightly earlier and even more intractable period" (15). The next paragraph gives us a brief outside view of Godliman: "At 12:30 on a splendid June day in London, a secretary found Godliman hunched over an illuminated manuscript. . . . Godliman stood at a lectern, perched on one leg like a bird, his face lit bleakly by a spotlight above—he might have been the ghost of the monk who wrote the book. . . . He looked up, and when he saw her he smiled, and then he did not look like a ghost" (16). This passage shows us Godliman through the eyes of the secretary. The focalization then moves back to Godliman himself for the rest of the chapter and tells how he is recruited to work for the British Military Intelligence.

Focalization continues to shift throughout the novel. The third chapter introduces two new characters, Lucy and David, just getting married before he goes off to fly in the Royal Air Force; but on the night of his wedding, David is injured in an accident and his legs have to be amputated. This chapter is focalized through Lucy, who becomes a central character, especially at the very end of the story. Most of the novel is focalized through Faber, Godliman, Bloggs (who also works for British Intelligence), and Lucy, but there are passages given to the narrator, and some short sections focalized through other characters, including the German Field Marshal Erwin Rommel (251–55), Field Marshal Gerd von Rundstet (301–5), and Hitler himself (364–65). All in all, there are perhaps a dozen focalizers, though most of these are brief. This kind of multiple selective omniscience, as Norman Friedman would call it, works well in a certain kind of thriller, where there is no need to go deeply and continuously into the thoughts of any one character, but it can also be used to create a world of differing perspectives, as in Porter's *Ship of Fools*.

Dorothy B. Hughes's crime novel *In a Lonely Place* is ostensibly in third person, but from the beginning to the end of the story the narrator keeps the reader inside the mind of the main character, Dix Steele. Here is the beginning of the novel:

> It was good standing there on the promontory overlooking the evening sea, the fog lifting itself like gauzy veils to touch his face. There was something in it akin to flying; the sense of being lifted high above crawling earth, of being a part of the wildness of air. Something too of being closed within an unknown and strange world of mist and cloud and wind. He'd liked flying at night; he'd missed it after the war had crashed to a finish and dribbled to an end. It wasn't the same thing flying a private crate. He'd tried it; it was like returning to the stone ax after precision tools. He had found nothing yet to take the place of flying wild. (2017, 5)

All of this is somehow a representation of the mind of Dix Steele, the as-yet-unnamed protagonist of the story. He is the one who feels that it was good standing and looking at the sea; he is the one who feels that it is something like flying, and so on. I am not sure, however, that we are to imagine that Dix actually articulates these feelings. When the narrator says, "He'd liked flying at night," we can translate this into a direct thought, "I liked flying at night," and so it may be free indirect speech or narrated monologue; it may not represent something Dix actually says to himself, but it is at least part of his thought, if not at the surface.

Dix's contemplative mood is broken: "He did not like it when on the street behind him a sudden bus spattered his peace with its ugly sound and smell and light. He was sharply angry at the intrusion." This passage, I think, is simply the narrator's report of Dix's feelings, probably in narrated monologue; we don't hear Dix's interior monologue—he doesn't at any level say or think "I am angry"—but we are still inside his mind. Dix then sees a young woman (or a girl, as the narrator says in the idiom of the nineteen-forties):

> She was small, dark haired, with a round face. She was more than pretty, she was nice looking, a nice girl. Sketched in brown, the brown hair, brown suit, brown pumps and bag, even a small brown felt hat....
> He didn't follow her at once. Actually he didn't intend to follow her. It was entirely without volition that he found himself moving down the slant, winding walk. He didn't walk hard, as she did, nor did he walk fast. Yet she heard him coming behind her. He knew she heard him for her heel struck an extra beat, as if she had half stumbled. (6)

This passage is narrated in the voice of the narrator, but partly focalized through Dix's perceptions: "He could have caught up with her with ease, but he didn't. It was too soon. Better to hold back until he had passed the humped midsection of the walk, then to close in. She'd give a little scream, perhaps only a gasp, when he came up beside her. And he would say softly, 'Hello.' Only 'Hello,' but she would be more afraid" (7). This passage can be translated into Dix's thoughts and his imagination of what could happen: "I could catch up with her easily, but I won't. It's too soon. It's better to hold back until I've passed the humped midsection of the walk, and then close in. She'll give a little scream, perhaps only a gasp, when I come up beside her. And I'll say softly, 'Hello.' Only 'Hello,' but she will be more afraid." Again, we don't have to suppose that he actually articulated these sentences to himself; they represent what he feels; the narrator turns what Dix feels into a linguistic representation. But the narrator does not give us any view of the mind of the young woman—just Dix's fantasy about her.

Then a car turns; its headlights illuminate the street, and other cars pass, and the young woman is able to get away. "The girl was safe; he could feel the relaxation in her footsteps. Anger beat him like a drum" (7). Dix certainly does not say, "Anger beats me like a drum." We are back in the narrator's narrated monologue, still in Dix's mind. ("Anger," by the way, becomes one of the keywords in the text, along with "fog" and "luck" and "tremble.")

Later that night, after a visit with his old army buddy Brub Nicolai and Brub's wife Sylvia, Dix again takes a walk. Once again he is bothered by traffic: "The hideous noise of an oil truck, ignoring the stop sign, thundered past. A second one speeded after the first, and then a third, blasting the quietness with thumping wheels, clanging chains. Spewing greasy smoke into the fog. He stood there trembling in anger until they passed. He was still trembling when he reached the huddle of houses, and when he saw there what he saw his anger mounted" (17). He sees that he is on the street where the brown girl had disappeared, but there is no way to tell which house she entered. Dix gets on a bus, but then he sees another girl: "At Camden Drive he saw her. A girl, an unknown girl, standing alone, waiting alone there, by the bench which meant a crosstown bus would eventually come along. At night buses didn't run often. Dix pulled the buzzer cord but he was too late for Camden. He got off at the next stop, two blocks away. He didn't mind much. He crossed the boulevard and he was smiling with his lips as he started back. His stride was long, his steps were quiet" (19). At this point there is a break in the text, at the end of section two of the chapter; section three begins: "The phone was a jangle tearing sleep from a man's face. It was the scream of bus brakes, the clanging chain of an ugly oil truck on a beach road, the whine of a spiraling bomb. Dix opened his cramped eyes" (19). It is the next morning, and whatever happened the night before is left in the break between the sections. The reader no doubt has a suspicion, and this is confirmed indirectly by clues in the text. Dix gets up to look at the morning paper: "There was nothing unusual on the front page. . . . Nothing he was expecting on the second page. That meant there'd be nothing" (20). That's all the narrator says, but it's enough. We see the paper not as something with an independent existence, but only through Dix's perceptions and expectations. We know that Dix has killed the girl, but the narrator elides the murder and gives us no view of the mind of the victim.

Throughout the story the narrator keeps the reader inside Dix's mind. In the following passage, as the novel is moving toward a climax, Dix is waiting for Laurel, a woman with whom he is having an affair: "There was no reason to believe that she wouldn't come. Something she couldn't foresee had happened last night. Maybe a job out of town. He hadn't returned to the apartment until almost seven. She must have called him all afternoon, then had to leave without getting word to him. There was no way that she could leave a message. No possible way." This passage is classic free indirect speech, as the thoughts of the character take over the voice of the narrator; pronouns have been changed as necessary, and tenses as well, but the characteristic phrasing, including sentence fragments, is retained. A competent reader makes this translation automatically.

Here is another passage in free indirect discourse, after the second murder, as Dix tries to fabricate an alibi: "For Christ's sake, for whom was he plotting this minute alibi? He wasn't going to be questioned. He was nuts to think he had to account for his time as if he were a reform-school kid on parole or a henpecked husband. He didn't have to do a damn thing but climb into bed, take a couple of pills and get the dreamless sleep he needed. Who cared what he'd done all night and today? Who in hell cared why he'd done it?" (156). And here is its translation into direct discourse: "For Christ's sake, who am I plotting this minute alibi for? I'm not going to be questioned. I'm nuts to think I have to account for my time as if I were a reform-school kid on parole or a henpecked husband. I don't have to do a damn thing but climb into bed, take a couple of pills and get the dreamless sleep I need. Who cares what I did all night and today? Who in hell cares why I did it?" The following passages, all built on the same thought, can be translated out of free indirect discourse into direct discourse:

His laugh shot from his throat. He was lucky too; he was more than lucky, he was smart. (22)

You didn't ever have to give yourself away. Not if you were smart. (51)

But he knew how to get away from trouble, from grief and from fear. He knew better than to indwell with it. He was smart. (131)

She could wait. He was too foggy now to knock her awake and demand explanation. Even if foggy, he was smart. (146)

He wished the police were here to look him over. But he didn't go into the lighted building. He liked a chance but he was too smart for a risk. (150)

Translated into direct discourse, all of these say, "I am smart"—as he tells himself over and over that he is smart. But of course Dix is not smart; he leaves abundant clues, and he is caught.

Narrative Norms

Every narrative establishes, explicitly or implicitly, the physical, social, and moral norms of the world it represents. These norms are established by the narrator, or perhaps by the implied author, which (as I noted in the first section of this chapter) can be seen as "a set of implicit norms rather than as a speaker or a voice" (Rimmon-Kenan 1983, 88). Norms can be established not only by what is said, but also by what is not said. Norms may also be established by "the choice of focalizing characters—the decision to represent the consciousness of certain characters and not others, and hence to show the stance of certain personae, and not others, toward the narrative events" (Lanser 1981, 242).

When the norms of the implied author are different from those of the narrator, the narrator is unreliable. Unreliability can concern matters of fact or, more importantly, matters of morality. Usually the reader trusts the narrator to tell the truth about facts—that is, about the facts of fiction. If Archie Goodwin tells us that Nero Wolfe's house and office was a brownstone on the south side of West 35th Street in New York City, the reader simply accepts his word as truth—that is, truth within the story—even if different books in the series give different street addresses, and even if most of the addresses given would put the house in the Hudson River. Archie is telling the truth within the story, even if that doesn't match up with truth outside the story. Some narrators, however, can't be trusted to tell the truth, that is, the truth within the story.

Unreliability about facts is likely an index of a deeper unreliability. Unreliability about matters of morality occurs when the narrator takes a moral position that the author can safely assume no one among his readers—or among his preferred readers—will share. Moral unreliability is often used by writers interested in exploring pathological states of mind. Examples easily come to mind: Charles Kinbote in Vladimir Nabokov's

Pale Fire; the nameless narrator of Flann O'Brien's *The Third Policeman;* Frank Chambers in James M. Cain's *The Postman Always Rings Twice.*

Jack Isidore, who narrates parts of Philip K. Dick's *Confessions of a Crap Artist,* is unreliable about both facts and morality. Here he is talking with his friend Hermann Hauck on December 7, 1941, the day of the attack on Pearl Harbor:

> "This means Germany and Italy'll get right in," I told Hauck. "This means war with the Axis, not just the Japs. Of course we'll have to lick the Japs first, then turn our attention to Europe."
>
> "I'm sure glad to see our chance to clobber those Japs," Hauck said. We both agreed with that. "I'm itching to get in," he said. We both paced around my room, smoking and keeping our ears on the radio. "Those crummy little yellow-bellies," Herman said. "You know, they have no culture of their own. Their whole civilization, they stole it from the Chinese. You know, they're actually descended more from apes; they're not actually human beings. It's not like fighting real human beings."
>
> "That's true," I said.
>
> Of course, this was back in 1941, and an unscientific statement like that didn't get questioned. Today we know that the Chinese don't have any culture either. (1992, 4–5)

The penultimate sentence here looks like a correction in the direction of reliability, but then the final sentence only puts Isidore in a deeper hole. In the following paragraph Isidore describes the Japanese in his town, Seville, California:

> One ran a flower nursery, another had a grocery store—the usual small time businesses that they run, cutting pennies here and there, getting their ten kids to do all the work, and generally living on a bowl of rice a day. No white person can compete with them because they're willing to work for nothing. Anyhow, now they had to get out, whether they liked it or not. In my estimation it was for their own good anyhow, because a lot of us were stirred up about Japs sabotaging and spying. At Seville High a bunch of us chased a Jap kid and kicked him around a little, to show how we felt. His father was a dentist, as I recall. (6)

All of this is carefully constructed to show Isidore unconsciously giving evidence against his own judgments. Isidore also believes a lot of crack-pot science: "When the Oz books were first written, back around 1900, everybody took them to be completely fiction, as they did with Verne's books and H. G. Wells'. But now we're beginning to see that although the particular characters, such as Ozma and the Wizard and Dorothy, were all creations of Baum's mind, the notion of a civilization inside the world is not such a fantastic one" (6). But even with all his crazy ideas Isidore turns out to be a better person than the sane people in the story.

The norms of a narrative may be stated more or less explicitly. If an author expects the readers to share the norms of a narrative, then she may not bother to state them. Jane Austen, for example, doesn't bother to justify the economic structure of the societies she depicts. Sometimes the author may not even be aware of the norms; science-fiction stories from the 1930s through the 1950s, for instance, usually assume that the gender relations of the time of writing will continue in the future. Kurt Vonne-gut's first novel, *Player Piano,* published in 1952, takes place in the near future, in a society dominated by engineers and executives, more or less what we might call a meritocracy—all men. The few women in the story are secretaries or the wives of the engineers and executives. I doubt that Vonnegut was making a prediction; he simply took the gender relations of his time and replicated them in his story.

Often the norms of a story are simply the background within which it takes place; but some stories call the norms into question. The *Iliad,* for instance, begins by assuming a set of norms that critics have come to call the Heroic Code: human life is short, especially compared with the im-mortality of the gods; the compensation for short life is honor, which is ultimately achieved by facing death on the battlefield. Honor is measured by its external manifestations, such as the prizes heroes are awarded for bravery, and the apportioning of prizes is a fundamental sign of the esteem in which a warrior is held. At the beginning of the story, Achil-les adheres to this code, and therefore when Agamemnon threatens his honor by taking away his war-prize, Briseis, Achilles withdraws from the fighting. Over the course of the story, however, Achilles calls this code into question. As early as book 9 he says, "Fate is the same for the man who holds back, the same if he fights hard. We are all held in a single honor, the brave with the weakling" (*Iliad* 9.318–19). His doubts increase after the death of Patroklos. He is now consumed by violence; he no longer thinks of honor and the only community he recognizes is the community of the slayer and the slain. After he kills Hektor he mistreats the body in a way that shocks even the gods; as Apollo says, "Achilles has destroyed pity" (*Iliad* 24.44). His rage finally comes to an end when he faces Priam, Hektor's father, who has come to ransom his son's body. The two antagonists look on each other with a kind of respect (*Iliad* 24.628–32). The resolution of the challenge to the norms of the narrative comes not within his own community, but in deeper confrontation with his enemy, in which a kind of humanity transcends the Heroic Code of honor.

The norms of a narrative are established by the implied narrator, but they are accepted—or rejected—by the implied reader, and so we will return to them in the next chapter.

3

Readers

The Narratee

I now shift to the right side of Chatman's narrative diagram: the narratee, the implied reader, and the real reader. Real readers (like the real authors) stand outside of the narrative transaction, and therefore they are not directly the concern of Chatman's narrative model. Aristotle would have had a different view. An essential part of his rhetorical theory is the division of a rhetorical transaction—a speech—into three aspects: ethos, logos, and pathos. Logos is the argument itself; ethos is the character of the orator as he makes himself persuasive to an audience; and pathos is the experience of the audience. In order to persuade, the flesh-and-blood orator has to understand his flesh-and-blood audience—and Aristotle puts some effort into the description of various kinds of audiences and the reactions they are likely to have. As literature pulls away from the practice of oratory and immediate persuasion, as it pulls the flesh-and-blood orator away from the flesh-and-blood audience, the identification of the audience becomes more difficult but perhaps less essential. Even an obscure writer may find a few choice readers, and perhaps that's all the writer wants. The writer of best-sellers, of course, may have a very sharp sense of the mass audience and how to attract it.

The narratee is the story-listener. In Chatman's model, the narratee is optional, though perhaps in principle there is always an implied narratee. The implied narratee would be different from the implied reader, to be discussed below. A narratee may be internal—a character within the events of the story—or external—a character outside the events of the story.

An internal narratee is a character inside the story who listens to a story told by a narrator within the story. Thus in books 9 to 12 of the *Odyssey* Odysseus tells the story of his travels to the Phaiakians, who are an

64

internal group narratee. Odysseus is internal to the *Odyssey* as a whole; he is an internal narrator as he tells his story to the Phaiakians, in which he is himself a character; the Phaiakians are characters inside the *Odyssey*, but outside the story told by Odysseus. In addition, Odysseus tells brief stories, the so-called Cretan lies, to Athena (in book 13), to Eumaeus the swineherd (in book 17) and to Penelope (in book 18). In book 4, Menelaos tells the story of his own travels to Telemachos. Whenever a character in a story tells a story to another character in the story, the one is an internal narrator and the other an internal narratee, if only for a moment. In book 9 of the *Iliad*, Phoinix tells Achilles the story of Meleager; Achilles is an internal narratee; he is internal to the *Iliad* as a whole, but external to the story he hears within the *Iliad*.

Just as a narrator may narrate the whole of a novel, a narratee can be the audience of the whole novel. The ancient Greek novel *Leucippe and Clitophon*, written by Achilles Tatius perhaps in the late second century AD, begins with an elaborate set-up: the narrator (the first narrator, that is) recounts (to the reader) his visit to Sidon; there he sees a painting of Europa and the Bull, who are being led away by Eros. As he looks at the painting he exclaims, "To think that a child [Eros, that is] can have such power over heaven and earth and sea" (177).[1] A young man standing near him replies, "How well I know it—for all the indignities Love has made *me* suffer" (177). And the young man—who will turn out to be Clitophon— proceeds to tell his story, which is the novel itself. Clitophon takes over as narrator, and the nameless first narrator becomes Clitophon's narratee; this narratee disappears from the story, however, never to return, and Clitophon might as well simply to be talking directly to us, the readers. As readers, however, we exist outside the story; our existence may be implied but it is never stated.

Daphnis and Chloe is another of the Greek novels, written by Longus probably also in the second century AD; its narrative situation is in some ways like that of *Leucippe and Clitophon*. The story begins: "When I was hunting in Lesbos, I saw the most beautiful sight I have ever seen, in a grove that was sacred to the Nymphs: a painting that told a story of love." The narrator then describes the painting: "women giving birth, animals suckling them, shepherds adopting them, young people pledging love, a pirates' raid, an enemy attack—and more, much more, all of it romantic." The narrator searches out someone who can interpret this painting and he turns what the interpreter says into the novel. The narrator is thus able to tell the story because it has been told to him, because he has been the narratee.

Daphnis is an orphan, abandoned at birth and adopted by a goatherd; two years later the infant Chloe is found and adopted by a neighboring shepherd. The two children grow up together as slaves on a great estate near Mytilene. They have various adventures, as depicted in the painting, and they grow to love each other. At the end of the story it is revealed that they are really the children of rich families in Mytilene; they marry and live happily ever after. Just as in *Leucippe and Clitophon,* the narrator does not make an appearance at the end.

The novel *Paul and Virginia,* published in 1788 by the French writer Jacques-Henri Bernardin de Saint-Pierre, takes place on the island of Mauritius (called the Ile de France in the novel). The novel begins: "On the eastern slope of the mountain that rises behind the town of Port Louis on the Ile de France may be seen, on a piece of ground once under cultivation, the remains of two small cabins" (1989, 39). After an elaborate description of the landscape a first-person narrator speaks: "I loved to visit this place where I could enjoy at once a boundless view and the deepest solitude. One day, while I was seated beside the cabins and contemplating their ruined conditions, a man well advanced in years passed by" (40). The unnamed narrator asks this old man about the cabins, and the novel is the story told by the old man. Once again the initial narrator becomes the narratee. The story concerns two young people, Paul and Virginia, who grow up together in a pastoral setting and fall in love. The story ends tragically, however, unlike the Greek novels. The story is in some ways very like *Daphnis and Chloe,* which is obviously an important model, but it is also very different; the question of the relationship of the two novels would take us far out of our way, but very briefly I will say that *Paul and Virginia* is infused with the influence of Rousseau in a way that would have been incomprehensible to an ancient Greek audience. At the very end Bernardin de Sainte-Pierre rounds off the story with the reappearance of the first narrator—"As he spoke these words the good old man went away shedding tears, and my own had fallen more than once in the course of his melancholy narration" (136–37)—and with this return of the first narrator he repairs what some might see as an oversight in both *Daphnis and Chloe* and in *Leucippe and Clitophon.*

Albert Camus's *The Fall* (*La Chute*) is entirely a narration directed by an internal narrator to an internal narratee; the reader is in effect somehow overhearing the story. Here is the beginning:

> May I, *monsieur*, offer my services without running the risk of intruding? I fear you may not be able to make yourself understood by the worthy ape who presides over the fate of this establishment. In fact, he speaks nothing but Dutch. Unless you authorize me to plead your case, he will not guess that you want gin. There, I dare hope he understood me; that nod must mean that he yields to my arguments. He is taking steps; indeed, he is making haste with prudent deliberation. You are lucky; he didn't grunt. When he refuses to serve someone, he merely grunts. No one insists. Being master of one's moods is the privilege of the larger animals. Now I shall withdraw, *monsieur*, happy to have been of help to you. Thank you, I'd accept if I were sure of not being a nuisance. You are too kind. Then I shall bring my glass over beside yours. (1991, 3)

The whole novel is written in the words of this one character, Jean-Baptiste Clamence, as he talks—on several occasions, over several days—to an unnamed interlocutor who never speaks. We do, however, get an idea of what the silent interlocutor says from what Clamence says. Toward the end of this passage, for instance, Clamence makes a move toward stopping the conversation: "No I shall withdraw, monsieur," but we can tell that the interlocutor has asked him to stay and talk: "Thank you, I'd accept if I were sure of not being a nuisance." The interlocutor evidently insists, and Clamence says, "You are too kind."

Most of the story consists of the confessions of Clamence, as he recounts in vivid and searching detail his life of hypocrisy. One of the crucial episodes describes a night when Clamence failed to react when a young woman threw herself into the Seine. Toward the end, however, he inverts his confession: "The more I accuse myself, the more I have a right to judge you. Even better, I provoke you into judging yourself. . . . I shall listen, you may be sure, to your own confession with a great feeling of fraternity" (140).

One might argue that Clamence is the first-person narrator of the story, and in a sense that's true: he is the narrator within the story, and he has an audience inside the story, a narratee; but we as readers are only overhearing this conversation, which is not narrated to us. The narratee, the unnamed interlocutor, is probably a stand-in for the reader, but at a distance, and this distance allows Camus to make his accusation of the reader indirect. At the very end the narratee fades into the narrator, or into no one, or into everyone:

> Are we not all alike, constantly talking and to no one, forever up against the same questions although we know the answers in advance? Then please tell me what happened to you one night on the quays of the Seine and how you managed never to risk your life. You yourself utter the words that for years have never ceased echoing through my nights and that I shall at last say through your mouth: "O young woman, throw yourself into the water again so that I may a second time have the chance of saving both of us!" A second time, eh, what a risky suggestion! Just suppose, *cher maître,* that we should be taken literally? We'd have to go through with it. Brr...! The water's so cold! But let's not worry. It's too late now. It will always be too late. Fortunately! (147)

The inversion of judgment operates through this blank and speechless figure, the story-listener within the story.

In a sense every narrated story implies a narratee; a storyteller has to be telling the story to someone, someone outside the story. Most often, of course, this external narrator is never mentioned; but a narrator, third-person or first-person, can address an external narratee, an invented figure who is not a character in the events of the story but who functions as a stand-in for the real reader. Such an external narratee sits on the boundary between the real world and the world of the story, sometimes leaning in toward the story, sometimes out toward the real world. In the opening of *Adam Bede* (quoted in the previous chapter), the narrator speaks to the reader—"With a single drop of ink for a mirror, the Egyptian sorcerer undertakes to reveal to any chance comer far-reaching visions of the past. This is what I undertake to do for you, reader." In chapter 17 of *Adam Bede,* Eliot's narrator reports the complaint made by a reader, and answers. The joke then continues, as the narrator excuses herself because she is not, after all, a novelist, but just a mirror to reality (177).

There is a somewhat similar effect at the beginning of Charlotte Brönte's *Shirley:*

> Of late years an abundant shower of curates has fallen upon the north of England; they lie very thick on the hills; every parish has one or more of them; they are young enough to be very active, and ought to be doing a great deal of good. But not of late years are we about to speak; we are going back to the beginning of this century: late years—present years are dusty, sunburnt, hot, arid; we will evade the noon, forget it in siesta, pass the midday in slumber, and dream of dawn.
>
> If you think, from this prelude, that anything like a romance is preparing for you, reader, you never were more mistaken. Do you expect passion, and stimulus, and melodrama? Calm your expectations; reduce them to a lowly standard. Something real, cool, and solid lies before you; something unromantic as Monday morning, when all who have work wake with the consciousness that they must rise and betake themselves thereto. (2009, 3)

This narrator outside the story seems to be addressing a reader also outside the story, an external narratee. As the story continues there are further such addresses; in chapter 2: "Malone waxed very exultant over the supper. He laughed aloud at trifles, made bad jokes and applauded them himself, and, in short, grew increasingly noisy. His host, on the contrary, remained quiet as before. It is time, reader, that you should have some idea of the appearance of this same host. I must endeavour to sketch him as he sits at table" (20). In chapter 3:

> I am aware, reader, and you need not remind me, that it is a dreadful thing for a parson to be warlike; I am aware that he should be a man of peace. I have some faint outline of the idea of what a clergyman's mission is amongst mankind, and I remember distinctly whose servant he is, whose message he delivers, whose example he should follow; yet, with all this, if you are a parson-hater, you need not expect me to go along with you every step of your dismal, downward-tending, unchristian road; you need not expect me to join in your anathemas, at once so narrow and so sweeping, in your poisonous rancour, so intense and so absurd, against 'the cloth.' (27)

The second person here is pretty clearly not intended to address the real reader, but a sort of strawman reader invented by Brontë or Brontë's narrator for the purpose.

The narrator continues to address the reader throughout,[2] and the story closes with a final address: "The story is told. I think I now see the judicious reader putting on his spectacles to look for the moral. It would be an insult to his sagacity to offer directions. I only say, God speed him in his quest!" (482). Although Brontë's narrator addresses the narratee as "reader," this "reader" is not, I think, the flesh-and-blood reader, who sits outside the story; this "reader" has been brought inside the narrative by the narrator's direct address.

A first-person narrator also can bring an external narratee into the story; we have already seen Huckleberry Finn address his readers; but perhaps the most famous example is Laurence Sterne's *Tristram Shandy*. Not only does the narrator address the reader, but the reader talks back to the narrator. At the very beginning, Tristram explains how he knows that he was conceived on the night between the first Sunday and the first Monday of March 1718; the reader asks, "But pray, Sir, What was your father doing all December, January and February?" And Tristram replies, "Why, Madam,—he was all that time afflicted with a Sciatica" (7). Addresses to the reader continue throughout, and now and again we find a short dialogue, as at the beginning of Chapter XX:

> —How could you, Madam, be so inattentive in reading the last chapter? I told you in it, *That my mother was not a papist.*—Papist! You told me no such thing, Sir. Madam, I beg leave to repeat it over and over again, that I told you as plain, at least, as words, by direct inference, could tell you such a thing.—Then, Sir, I must have miss'd a page.— No Madam, you have not miss'd a word. Then I was asleep, Sir.—My pride, Madam, cannot allow you such a refuge.—Then I declare, I know nothing at all about the matter. (1964, 62)

Tristram then orders the lady, as he calls her, to go back and reread the previous chapter, as he explains to what must be another reader: "I have imposed this penance upon the lady, neither out of wantonness nor cruelty; but from the best of motives; and therefore shall make her no apology for it when she returns back" (63). I think it is clear in all of these examples that the external narratee is not the real reader, even if the narrator pretends to be addressing the real reader. The external narratee is not part of the story but it is part of the fiction.

The Implied Reader

An author constructs a story, and in a sense a story constructs an audience. If we follow Chatman's schema, this constructed audience is the implied reader: "not the flesh-and-bones you or I sitting in our living rooms reading the book, but the audience presupposed by the narrative itself" (Chatman 1978, 149–50). Gerald Prince, in his *Dictionary of Narratology,* follows this definition closely but then expands it: the implied reader is "the audience presupposed by the text"; this presupposed audience is "a real reader's second self," which is "shaped in accordance with the implied author's values and cultural norms" (Prince 1987, 43). In this section I want to investigate some of the ways a text can shape its audience.

James Phelan (following Peter Rabinowitz) divides the implied audience in two: he distinguishes "the authorial audience, the hypothetical group for whom the author writes—the group that shares the knowledge, values, prejudices, fears, and experiences that the author expected in his or her readers"—from the "the narrative audience, an observer position within the storyworld" (Phelan 2017, 7). The narrative audience in effect reads the story as if it were nonfiction, while the authorial audience knows that the story is fiction. Thus, for example, the authorial audience of a fantasy novel does not believe in witches and wizards, but the narrative audience does. If the actual audience enters the narrative audience, it enters the world of the story, but only as an observer, not as a participant.

Audiences, however, are complex, and an author may write for more than one group of readers, more than one authorial audience. Some readers may miss allusions that other readers will get: James M. Cain's *The Postman Always Rings Twice,* for instance, alludes to Aeschylus's *Agamemnon,* and the allusion adds to the meaning of the story, but it's perfectly possible to enjoy the novel without catching the allusion. Some readers may share the values, etcetera, of the story right away, but others will have to be convinced. Some readers may never share all the values of the story, but will go along for the sake of the reading experience. As Mikhail Bakhtin notes, novels typically involve a dialogue of values that can't be reduced to a single authorial position.

An interesting example of the narrative audience can be found near the beginning of Charlotte Brontë's *Shirley;* in passages I have quoted above, the narrator opens the novel with general comments on curates, both in her time and at the time of the story, 1811 or 1812, and also with a direct address to the narratee. Then in the fourth paragraph, she introduces three curates who will be characters in the story:

> Yet even in those days of scarcity there were curates; the precious plant was rare, but it might be found. A certain favoured district in the West Riding of Yorkshire could boast three rods of Aaron blossoming within a circuit of twenty miles. You shall see them, reader. Step into the neat garden-house on the skirts of Whinbury, walk forward into the little parlour. There they are at dinner. Allow me to introduce them to you: Mr Donne, curate of Whinbury; Mr Malone, curate of Briarfield; Mr Sweeting, curate of Nunnely. These are Mr Donne's lodgings, being the habitation of one John Gale, a small clothier. Mr Donne has kindly invited his brethren to regale with him. You and I will join the party, see what is to be seen, and hear what is to be heard. At present, however, they are only eating, and while they eat we will talk aside. (4)

The narrative audience addressed in this passage I take to be an external narratee, pulled further into the story than usual. If this narrative audience really could step into the story, it would not be necessary for the narrator to narrate. This narrative audience is a fiction within the fiction.

I am not convinced, however, that any part of the flesh-and-blood reader actually joins this narrative audience, nor that it's a good thing to try. Perhaps the narrative audience is postulated to explain the kind of credence readers give to fictions and fantasies, and also the kind of engagement that readers feel when they lose themselves in a book.

The authorial audience and the narrative audience may be ways of describing what an actual flesh-and-blood reader might do: that is, an actual reader may or may not accept the values (etc.) of the author or the implied author, and an actual reader may or may not in some sense believe that the events of the story are true, if only with the truth of fiction. If so, it may be possible to skip the authorial audience and the narrative audience and the implied reader, and just talk about readers and how they read. At times

Phelan's terminology can be a useful shorthand, but there may be better and more parsimonious accounts of these experiences. First, healthy readers never really believe in the fictions they read. Second, getting lost in a book has nothing to do with believing in it, but rather with a psychological experience in which other kinds of stimuli temporarily fade out of attention—though these other stimuli can come into attention again at any moment, say, when the phone rings.

Any given text will appeal to some readers and won't appeal to others, for all sorts of reasons. In this sense a text—or an author—presupposes or selects certain readers—or certain readers select certain texts. The author expects these readers to share, as Phelan says, "the knowledge, values, prejudices, fears, and experiences" expressed in the text; those who don't probably won't read the book. But the relationship between a text and a reader, an actual reader, is both imperfect and dynamic.

The reader, even the authorial and narrative reader postulated by Phelan, doesn't have to share all the knowledge, values, and so on, that the author may expect or want. A reader comes to a book knowing some things, having certain values, with certain prejudices and fears, but the experience of reading may change all these. Indeed, this kind of change is often what we look for in reading a novel. Moreover, a narrative may express more than one set of values. The *Iliad,* as I have discussed above, expresses a set of values we can call the Heroic Code, but it also expresses a critique of that code.

The process of joining the authorial audience can be difficult if the knowledge, values, and so on, of the story world are very different from those of the actual reader. An author can't always assume that a reader will come to a story with the values assumed by the story; the reader then has to be persuaded to join the authorial audience, at least long enough to finish the book.

We can see this process of persuasion in Stephen Hunter's thriller *Point of Impact.* The hero of this story is Bob Lee Swagger, a loner, a disaffected Vietnam vet who lives with his dog in a trailer in the Ouachita Mountains of Arkansas. In Vietnam he was a sniper, with an official kill total of eighty-seven. Snipers, like archers in the Homeric epics, are ambiguous heroes: they kill at a distance, from hiding, and though they have skill they don't necessarily have courage. In Hunter's first book, *The Mas-*

ter Sniper, the sniper is the villain. In *Point of Impact,* however, the sniper is the hero and the moral center of the story. Hunter creates his hero partly by writing against expectation, in matters both large and small.

The plot of the book is clever and complex, with several interwoven stories; very briefly, Swagger is framed for an assassination attempt on the President, in which a Salvadoran archbishop is killed; Swagger is badly wounded but he manages to get away and eventually he turns the tables on those who framed him.

Early in the narrative we overhear an extensive report about Swagger by a psychiatrist, Dr. David Dobbler, who works for RamDyne Security, a front organization responsible for the plot that organizes the story. Dobbler tells his audience (and the author tells the reader) that Swagger has a typical double-barreled Southern name, but he prefers to be called just Bob (9). Bob graduated from high school in 1964; in school, Dobbler says, "he got—this is perhaps not as amazing as it seems—excellent grades" (1993, 10). Clearly the implied author thinks the reader will find this amazing. Bob is not only a sniper, he is also the victim of a sniper in Vietnam, who wounded Swagger and killed Swagger's friend and spotter, Donny Fenn (12). And as Dobbler says, "His heroism was of a sort that makes many Americans uneasy"—here the implied author is surely speaking to and about a possible reader. "He wasn't an inspiring leader, he didn't save lives, he didn't rise in the chain of command. He was simply and explicitly an extraordinary killer" (12). "Bob is, in many ways, a child of the embarrassing Second Amendment" (9); "he's the man we've been taught to hate. He's the solitary American gun nut" (13).

But this description is given by one of the bad guys; the implied author is using it as a sort of inoculation. Some readers of this thriller, no doubt, are themselves "children of the Second Amendment," but others (I among them) are not, and Hunter works hard to make Bob Lee Swagger an appealing hero even for those who don't much like guns. Crucially, Bob no longer kills—until he does. Much of the first chapter is taken up with an elaborate set-up episode, which looks until the very last moment as if Bob is hunting Old Tim, a grand old stag of the Ouachitas, on the day before hunting season begins. (This episode is written in a series of short sections, interwoven with Dobbler's description of Bob.) We see Bob take his position in the pine forest and wait for seventeen hours (1–3). We see Old Tim finally appear; we see Bob lift his rifle and aim (7–8); we see him shoot and we see the shot hit Old Tim (13–14). The description at this point becomes vivid, as the stag falls to the ground:

> The animal wheezed, its head beat against the ground. . . .
> The animal's tongue hung from its half-opened mouth as the deeper paralysis overcame all its systems. . . .
> Tim snorted piteously, thrashing again. . . .
> Bob touched the throat, then pulled out his knife, an old Randall Survivor, murderously sharp.
> Be over in a second, partner, he thought, bending toward Tim. (14–15)

At this point the reader—the first-time reader—will probably expect Bob to kill Old Tim by cutting his throat with the murderously sharp knife. But the narrative breaks off and returns to Dobbler's analysis of Bob, and this section ends as Dobbler says that Bob presents "one terrible, terrible problem. He has a deep flaw" (16). But we don't hear what that flaw is, as the narrative returns to Bob and Old Tim, and we see that Bob is cutting off Old Tim's antlers so that Old Tim won't be an attractive target for the hunters who will appear the next day. Now Dobbler completes his report:

> "His flaw," said the doctor, "is that he will not kill anymore. He still hunts. He goes to great lengths and puts himself through extraordinary ordeals to fire at trophy animals. But he hits them with his own extremely light bullets machined of Delrin plastic at a hundred yards range. If he hits the creatures right and he always does—he aims for the shoulder above the spine—he can literally stun them off their feet for five or six minutes. . . . Then he saws their antlers off. So that no hunter will shoot them for a trophy. He hates trophy hunting. After all, he's *been* a trophy." (17–18)

These interwoven episodes are designed to arouse a set of expectations, to tease the first-time reader and then make the reader reconsider the values of the story. Bob Swagger—not Bob Lee but just Bob—is the good old boy who got good grades, the sniper who has been shot, the hunter who will not hunt.

The implied author's creation of the authorial audience, and his creation of Bob as the moral center, continues throughout the story. The implied author makes sure to tell the authorial audience that Bob, a good-old-boy, the son of a Southern sheriff, is not a racist, nor was his father (see 45, 65, 128, etc.)—though the reader may notice that there are no important characters of color in the story. (Dr. Dobbler, a bad guy who switches sides, is Jewish.) The implied author includes a defense of the morality of hunting (68) and also a denunciation of city hunters who just slaughter their prey (2). The implied author tells us that Bob was a good writer who knows the rules of grammar and has "a small quiet gift for expressing himself clearly" (130)—though he usually speaks a nonstandard dialect. We find out that Bob has read Henry David Thoreau (252), Siegfried Sassoon, Wilfred Owen, and Robert Graves (245). The implied author also refers to *King Lear* and *Catch-22* (194); William Butler Yeats's "The Second Coming" (196: "mere anarchy is loosed around the podium"); the *Iliad* (214); *Othello* (364); *Crime and Punishment, Portnoy's Complaint,* and *The Great War and Modern Memory* (384). The implied author is constructing Bob and also constructing the authorial reader: he wants the reader to know that someone who loves guns can also love literature, and conversely, someone who loves literature should be able to love guns. But the implied author also expresses a kind of anti-intellectualism. Thus, for example, one of the gun collectors Bob deals with reads the *New York Review of Books,* but only to make fun of "New York intellectuals" (357–58); and Bob talks about "smart boys" who "have all the answers, always telling you what's wrong and why what you done, you should be ashamed of " (236).

Running through the book from beginning to end is a defense of gun culture and a critique of gun control advocates. The implied author writes clever parodies of editorials written just after the assassination attempt; his version of the *Washington Post* looks forward to "the day when only policemen and soldiers and a few forest rangers have guns" and his version of the Baltimore *Evening Sun* writes about "demented men who kill animals for pleasure" (181–83). The narrator ironically describes what Swagger represents: "the Dixie gun nut . . . the sullen white trash, yankee-hatin' shooter, a character out of Faulkner, a Flem Snopes with a rifle" (183). Bob himself complains that the country as a whole "thinks anybody that fought in Vietnam is some kind of crazy sniper who shoots at the president and any man who owns a gun is a crazy man" (485).

Bob himself is the primary argument against this stereotype. The whole of the plot is constructed to show Bob's intelligence, his morality, and his heroism. He states his code laconically: "I was just taught to hurt no man except the man who hurt me and mine" (253). Shooting itself is depicted, at its best, as almost a kind of Zen meditation. At the very beginning of the story we see him get into position to shoot and save Old Tim:

> He sat in perfect silence and perfect stillness. . . . This was Bob's first gift: the gift of stillness. He acquired it naturally, without instruction, from some inner pool where stress never reached. . . . Now and then his hip throbbed from a wound from long ago. He instructed his brain to ignore the phantom ache. He was in some other place. . . . Bob was in his seventeenth hour of sitting. He had sat all night in the cold; and when, about four, sleet had started, he still sat. He was so cold and wet he was hardly alive. . . . Bob just sat there, next to his tree. (1–3)

It is perhaps too much to think of Bob's tree as the Buddha's Bo tree. But anyone who has read Eugen Herrigel's *Zen and the Art of Archery* should not be too quick to dismiss the mystical potential in Bob's way of shooting—at least at this point in the story. At a later point, when Bob has started to hunt and kill people again, we see him enter a kind of berserker state of mind: "he was into the zone, the rifle so a part of him that it felt organic; he could not remember, ever, not having the rifle, not having a world of targets. He slipped into craziness, the sniper's twisted identification with an angry God" (433). Shooting is not just a game of accuracy; guns were invented to kill people, and even the moral sniper can fall into the dark side.

As a flesh-and-blood reader I can't say that I have joined Hunter's authorial audience. I admire Hunter's skill as a writer; he does what he does about as well as it can be done. But as hard as he has worked to make the values of the book attractive, at no point in my reading did I find myself persuaded. The ideology of the book is fundamentally confused, and it makes its point only by hiding its contradictions. At the beginning of the story the thrill of watching Bob shoot Old Tim is masked by the moral satisfaction of finding out that Bob is saving him; this sleight-of-hand is the master figure of the whole narrative.

The reader of Chinua Achebe's *Things Fall Apart* likely needs a lot of direction. The overall story falls into three parts: the first part occurs in an Ibo village, Umuofia, in what we now call Nigeria, at a time when there was relatively little influence of European culture; the second part tells about the coming of Europeans; and the third part completes the tragedy of the story.

In the first part the narrator carefully constructs an authorial reader who can sympathize at least in part with the indigenous culture. For instance, chapter 7 tells about an invasion of locusts, which is welcomed by the people of Umuofia because the locusts are good to eat. Most likely the reader of this story has never eaten locusts, and would not be eager to do so, but the reader has no trouble accepting this custom. The implied author is constructing an authorial reader who can accept unfamiliar ways of life. But the story also vividly represents actions which challenge the reader's sympathy. It is not easy to know exactly how to join the authorial audience.

The precontact Ibo culture is not homogeneous. Even before Europeans arrive, the people in the story are very aware of cultural differences among the various villages in the area. Most of chapter 8 is taken up with marriage negotiations between two families. It is clear that the young man and young woman involved don't know each other and have very little to say about the marriage. Representatives of the two families meet—all men; the bride's family makes an offer by presenting the groom's family a bundle of thirty broomsticks. The groom's family in turn gives them back a bundle of fifteen sticks. The bride's family returns a bundle of twenty-five sticks, and so on until they agree on twenty sticks, which stand for a bride price of twenty bags of cowrie shells.

Afterward the men sit and talk:

> As the men ate and drank palm-wine they talked about the customs of their neighbors.
>
> "It was only this morning," said Obierika, "that Okonkwo and I were talking about Abame and Aninta, where titled men climb trees and pound foo-foo for their wives."
>
> "All their customs are upside-down. They do not decide bride-price as we do, with sticks. They haggle and bargain as if they were buying a goat or a cow on the market."
>
> "That is very bad," said Obierika's eldest brother. "But what is good in one place is bad in another place. In Umunso they do not bar-

gain at all, not even with broomsticks. The suitor just goes on bringing bags of cowries until his in-laws tell him to stop. It is a bad custom because it always leads to a quarrel."

"The world is large," said Okonkwo. "I have even heard that in some tribes a man's children belong to his wife and her family."

"That cannot be," said Machi. "You might as well say that the woman lies on top of the man when they are making the children."

"It is like the story of white men who, they say, are white like this piece of chalk." (2009, 73–74)

This, by the way, is the first mention of white men in the novel. Clearly none of these villagers has seen a white man, but white men will play an important role in the second part of the novel.

The hero of the story, Okonkwo, is energetic, wealthy, and respected in his community. His father, Unoka, was a lazy man who died in debt. "Fortunately, among these people a man was judged according to his worth and not according to the worth of his father" (8). Okonkwo, however, is ashamed of his father, and makes great efforts to become respected: "Unlike his father he could stand the sight of blood. In Umuofia's latest war he was the first to bring home a human head. That was his fifth head; and he was not an old man yet. On great occasions such as the funeral of a village celebrity he drank his palm-wine from his first human head" (10). Many readers will understand bravery in war; probably most are not comfortable with the thought of drinking from a human skull. The actual reader does not have to approve of this custom; some may find the idea so repulsive that they have to put the story down, but an authorial reader who can accept it as the norm of a different society can continue to read the story. The narrator's commentary teaches us how to read the story, and there is much more the reader will have to learn and accept.

Okonkwo's energy and bravery are in fact responses to the shame he feels about his father: "his whole life was dominated by fear, the fear of failure and of weakness. . . . It was not external, but lay deep within himself. It was the fear of himself, lest he should be found to resemble his father" (13).

The episode that dominates the first part of the story concerns the captive boy Ikemefuna. His name is first mentioned almost in passing at the very end of chapter 1, and then again in chapter 2, which explains how Ikemefuna came to the village. A woman of the Umuofia, the wife of Ogbuefi Udo, has been killed in the market at Mbaino. The village assembly selects Okonkwo, as a leading figure of the village, to go to the Mbaino with an ultimatum, "asking them to choose between war on the one hand, and on the other the offer of a young man and a virgin as compensation" (11). The Mbaino understand that Umuofia is in the right, and Okonkwo returns with the virgin and the young boy: "The lad's name was Ikemefuma, whose sad story is still told in Umuofia to this day" (12).

The virgin was given to Udo, and the clan gave Ikemefuma to Okonkwo to look after until his fate should be decided: "The elders of the clan had decided that Ikemefuna should be in Okonkwo's care for a while. But no one thought it would be as long as three years. They seemed to forget all about him as soon as they had taken the decision" (27).

Ikemefuna gradually became accustomed to living in Umuofia with Okonkwo's family, and he became very popular, especially with Nwoye, Okonkwo's son, and even Okonkwo grew fond of him (28); "Ikemefuna had begun to feel like a member of Okonkwo's family" (34).

The story of Ikemefuna comes to a climax in chapter 7, which begins: "For three years Ikemefuna lived in Okonkwo's household, and the elders of Umuofia seemed to have forgotten about him. He grew rapidly like a yam tendril in the rainy season, and was full of the sap of life. He had become wholly absorbed into his new family" (52). But after three years the oracle announces that Ikemefuna must be sacrificed. The news is brought to Okonkwo by Ogbuefi Ezeudu, one of the elders, who tells him: "That boy calls you father. Do not bear a hand in his death." Okonkwo was surprised, and was about to say something when the old man continued: "Yes, Umuofia has decided to kill him. The Oracle of the Hills and the Caves has pronounced it. They will take him outside Umuofia as is the custom, and kill him there. But I want you to have nothing to do with it. He calls you his father" (57).

The official story is that Ikemefuna is going to go home; everyone knows what is really going to happen, except for Ikemefuna. The following day, a group of elders come to take Ikemefuna away, and Okonkwo goes with them. The narrative at this point enters Ikemefuna's thoughts at some length as he thinks he is being taken home; clearly the narrator is increasing our sympathy for the boy:

One of the men behind him cleared his throat. Ikemefuna looked back, and the man growled at him to go on and not stand looking back. The way he said it sent cold fear down Ikemefuna's back. . . .

As the man who had cleared his throat drew up and raised his machete, Okonkwo looked away. He heard the blow. . . . He heard Ikemefuna cry, "My father, they have killed me!" as he ran towards him. Dazed with fear, Okonkwo drew his machete and cut him down. He was afraid of being thought weak. (60–61)

Immediately after this incident we learn that among the Ibo twin children are exposed to die (61–62). The judgements here are complex. On the one hand, we judge Ibo society: Why should innocent children be sacrificed? We judge Ibo society, but on the other hand, we judge Okonkwo as an individual: his fear of appearing weak has led him to participate in this killing. Okonkwo's friend Obierika tells him that he should not have done so (67).

Another crisis in Okonkwo's life comes when his gun accidentally explodes and kills a young man of the village. Even though the death was accidental, Okonkwo has to flee the village with his family and live in another village for seven years: "As soon as the day broke, a large crowd of men from Ezeudu's quarter stormed Okonkwo's compound, dressed in garbs of war. They set fire to his houses, demolished his red walls, killed his animals and destroyed his barn. It was the justice of the earth goddess, and they were merely her messengers. They had no hatred in their hearts against Okonkwo. His greatest friend, Obierika, was among them. They were merely cleansing the land which Okonkwo had polluted with the blood of a kinsman" (124–25). Even though Obierika participated in this action, he is troubled and ponders within himself about the justice of the punishment:

Why should a man suffer so grievously for an offense he had committed inadvertently? But although he thought for a long time he found no answer. He was merely led into greater complexities. He remembered his wife's twin children, whom he had thrown away. What crime had they committed? The Earth had decreed that they were an offense on the land and must be destroyed. And if the clan did not exact punishment for an offense against the great goddess, her wrath was loosed on all the land and not just on the offender. As the elders said, if one finger brought oil it soiled the others. (125)

This passage ends Part I of the novel; the placement of this passage suggests that this moment of evaluation is the point toward which the story so far has been aiming—in Greek this would be called a "telos," which means not just an end, but an accomplishment, completion, or fulfillment. Now the story enters its second phase, which will have its own telos.

Part II begins as Okonkwo and his family move to his mother's natal village, Mbanta. He is well received there, but he falls into a depression because his ambition to become the leading man in Umuofia has been blocked. Very quickly, however, the story moves in another direction. News is brought that another village, Abame, has been wiped out. A white man had come to the village, riding an iron horse (a bicycle). The Oracle warned against him, so the villagers killed him and tied his iron horse to a tree. Sometime later, three white men came and saw the iron horse; they went away, but eventually returned and killed almost everyone in the village (139).

Some two years later, Okonkwo's friend Obierika paid a visit to Okonkwo and told him that Christian missionaries had come to Umuofia; they built a church and won a number of converts; among them was Okonkwo's oldest son, Nwoye. Okonkwo did not want to talk about Nwoye, but Obierika learned what had happened from Nwoye's mother. Missionaries had come to Mbanta, led by a white man, who spoke to them through an Ibo interpreter. He told them that their gods were false. Most of the villagers just laughed at this message:

> But there was a young lad who had been captivated. His name was Nwoye, Okonkwo's first son. It was not the mad logic of the Trinity that captivated him. He did not understand it. It was the poetry of the new religion, something felt in the marrow. The hymn about brothers who sat in darkness and in fear seemed to answer a vague and persistent question that haunted his young soul—the question of the twins crying in the bush and the question of Ikemefuna, who was killed. He felt a relief within as the hymn poured into his parched soul. The words of the hymn were like drops of frozen rain melting on the dry palate of the panting earth. Nwoye's callow mind was greatly puzzled. (147)

Thus Nwoye's conversion is directly linked to the questions posed by Obierika at the end of Part I.

The people of Mbanta disagree about how they should deal with the rise of Christian influence. Okonkwo prefers an aggressive response, but the assembly decides simply to ostracize the Christian converts.

In Part III Okonkwo and his family return to Umuofia; there they find that the new church has attracted many converts, and the white men have established a government:

> They had built a court where the District Commissioner judged cases in ignorance. He had court messengers who brought men to him for trial. . . . These court messengers were greatly hated in Umuofia because they were foreigners and also arrogant and high-handed. They were called *kotma,* and because of their ash-colored shorts they earned the additional name of Ashy-Buttocks. They guarded the prison, which was full of men who had offended against the white man's law. Some of these prisoners had thrown away their twins and some had molested the Christians. They were beaten in the prison and made to work every morning clearing the government compound and fetching wood for the white Commissioner and the court messengers. Some of these prisoners were men of title who should be above such mean occupations. (174–75)

This passage raises complex and shifting judgments; at times the text asks the reader to sympathize with the villagers—the Commissioner judges in ignorance, and the prisoners are beaten by the *kotma*—but then it reminds us that the villagers kill twin babies.

Okonkwo and his friend Obierika find the new situation hard to bear. As Obierika says, the white man has been very clever; at first the villagers were amused by his foolishness, but now the white man "has put a knife on the things that held us together and we have fallen apart" (176). But others in the village accept the white men, the market and schools that they build, and even the new religion. The first missionary, Mr. Brown, treats the villagers with respect, but he is replaced by a much harsher missionary, Mr. Smith, who was "a different kind of man": "He condemned openly Mr. Brown's policy of compromise and accommodation. He saw things as black and white. And black was evil. He saw the world as a battle field in which the children of light were locked in mortal conflict with the sons of darkness" (184). Eventually the conflict becomes violent: the leading men of the village (acting in masquerade as figures of their gods) burn down the church; they are arrested, whipped, and kept without food or water for several days; and the villagers are told that they must pay a large fine or the leading men will be taken away to be tried and perhaps hanged. The whole life of the village is thrown into confusion: "Umuofia was like a startled animal with ears erect, sniffing the silent, ominous air and not knowing which way to run" (196). The fine is paid and the men are set free.

A great assembly is held to decide what the village should do about the white men. As the discussion is beginning, messengers from the white men's court come and declare that the meeting must stop. Okonkwo draws his machete and kills the head messenger, but the villagers allow the other messengers to escape, and Okonkwo knows that the village will not go to war to protect their traditions.

In the short final chapter, there is a significant change in focalization: "When the District Commissioner arrived at Okonkwo's compound at the head of an armed band of soldiers and court messengers he found a small crowd of men sitting wearily in the *obi*" (206; the *obi* is the main room of Okonkwo's dwelling). From now on what matters is the perspective of the white men. The Commissioner asks for Okonkwo, and the men take him to the bush behind the compound, where they find that Okonkwo has hanged himself. "The District Commissioner changed instantaneously. The resolute administrator in him gave way to the student of primitive customs" (207). Before we have seen the customs of the village from the inside, but now the focalization comes from the outside.

The Commissioner orders the messenger to take down the body; a Commissioner should never perform such an action himself:

> Such attention would give the natives a poor opinion of him. In the book which he planned to write he would stress that point. As he walked back to the court he thought about that book. Every day brought him some new material. The story of this man who had killed a messenger and hanged himself would make interesting reading. One could almost write a whole chapter on him. Perhaps not a whole chapter but a reasonable paragraph, at any rate. There was so much else to include, and one must be firm in cutting out details. He had already chosen the title of the book, after much thought: *The Pacification of the Primitive Tribes of the Lower Niger*. (208–9)

In this final paragraph, the novel that the reader has just completed is re-duced to a single paragraph, but the experience of reading the whole novel is an implicit critique of this reduction, and this critique, and the experi-ence it is based on, is really one of the primary themes of the story. Achebe does not present the society of the Ibo as perfect; even people within that society question its values. Nor does he present the white society as all bad; the new religion clearly speaks to deficiencies perceived by members of the Ibo society. The reader has to negotiate a complex set of interwoven judgments, perhaps without a final resolution.

4

The Use and Meaning of Rhetorical Schemes

Rhetorical figures are often divided into two groups: tropes, such as metaphor or irony, which change the meaning of words, and schemes, such as alliteration or anaphora or palilogia, which do not change meanings. Many discussions of the figures take the tropes more seriously than the schemes, which are often seen as merely ornamental. I'm not sure what's wrong with ornament. Some styles are ornamented, others are not, and anyone is free to have preferences, but if we want to have a broad understanding of narrative art, an understanding that goes beyond fashion, then we have to have an account of the ornamental styles as well as the plain styles. A rejection of ornamental styles is a rejection of many great writers—Dickens and Joyce and Faulkner, among others.

Moreover, many of the schemes create meaning, which is therefore not the province of the tropes alone.[1] It is not always easy to state these meanings, since many of them do not translate well into simple thematic propositions. In this chapter I will examine a number of schemes, to see if we can understand something about their function and meaning in specific contexts. Different figures have different meanings and different effects; some are more emotional and some are more intellectual. Sometimes the figures add life to the language, somewhat the way vibrato adds life to a musical tone. The specific effect of each instance needs to be interpreted on its own, but some generalizations may be possible.

Epitheton: I begin with one of the simpler schemes, epitheton. Lanham defines epitheton as follows: "Qualifying the subject with an appropriate adjective; an adjective that frequently or habitually accompanies a noun." This definition seems to cover two different figures: the general use of adjectives and the specific use of epithets. Some writers use a lot of vivid adjectives, but others are more sparing. In *Absalom, Absalom,* Faulkner piles up his adjectives: "the long still hot weary dead September afternoon," "a dim hot airless room," "dead old dried paint," "a dry vivid dusty sound," "that grim haggard amazed voice"—all these from the very first page. On the second page we find "outraged recapitulation evoked, quiet, inattentive and harmless," "the biding and dreamy and victorious dust," "dim coffin-smelling gloom sweet and oversweet," "the safe quiet September sun impacted distilled and hyperdistilled," "the loud cloudy flutter of the sparrows," and so on. Many of these adjectives are more or less metaphorical: "weary" modifying "afternoon," "dusty" modifying "sound," "dreamy" modifying "dust," "cloudy" modifying "flutter."

In *Ship of Fools,* Katherine Anne Porter occasionally uses a pile of adjectives for specific effect. The following passage comes after one of the passengers on the ship, Herr Freytag, has been removed from the Captain's dinner table because it has been discovered that his wife—who is not on the ship—is Jewish. Freytag says to another passenger, Mrs. Treadwell:

> "It is not just this one thing—no no, it is a lifetime of it, it is a world of it—it's not being able ever to hope for an end to it—It is seeing the one you love best in the world treated like dirt by people not fit to breathe the same air with her! If you could see her, you would know what I am talking about. Mrs. Treadwell, she is a little golden thin nervous thing, most beautiful and gay in the morning, she is innocent, innocent, she makes life charming where she is, when she talks it is like a bird singing in a tree." (1984, 258)

There are a number of figures here, including epizeuxis, anaphora with variation, asyndeton, and a (somewhat banal) simile, as well as the pile of adjectives—"little golden thin nervous thing . . . beautiful . . . gay . . . innocent, innocent." But whereas Faulkner's use of epitheton is a general characteristic of the narrative style of *Absalom, Absalom,* epitheton here is in the voice of one of the characters, combined with other figures at a moment of high emotion.

In addition to this general use of adjectives, Lanham's definition of epitheton also includes "an adjective that frequently or habitually accompanies a noun." This definition probably referred originally to Homer's use of repeated epithets—"swift-footed Achilles" or "crafty Odysseus"—as a fundamental tool of oral-formulaic composition. But the use of epithets is by no means restricted to oral literature or to Homer. In *Little Dorrit,* for example, Flora's father, Mr. Casby, is regularly called "the Patriarch," and this epithet comes to replace Mr. Casby's proper name. A rhetorician might call this figure by the more specific term antonomasia, which I think we can safely consider as a subtype of epitheton.

Still in *Little Dorrit*—when Mrs. Merdle is introduced the narrator makes much of her bosom: "The lady was not young and fresh from the hand of Nature, but was young and fresh from the hand of her maid. She had large unfeeling handsome eyes, and dark unfeeling handsome hair, and a broad unfeeling handsome bosom, and was made the most of in every particular" (1980, 284). A few pages later there is another reference to Mrs. Merdle's bosom; she speaks to Fanny, "reviewing the breadth of bosom which seemed essential to her having room enough to be unfeeling in" (287). A few pages later we learn about Mr. Merdle's use of the bosom to attract admiration: "This great and fortunate man had provided that extensive bosom which required so much room to be unfeeling enough in, with a nest of crimson and gold some fifteen years before. It was not a bosom to repose on, but it was a capital bosom to hang jewels upon. . . . The bosom moving in Society with jewels displayed upon it, attracted general admiration" (293). Eventually the bosom comes to represent the whole person, in the figure called synecdoche, where the part stands for the whole; Mr. Merdle is giving a dinner party while Mrs. Merdle is traveling on the continent: "The Chief Butler, the Avenging Spirit of this great man's life, relaxed nothing of his severity. He looked on these dinners when the bosom was not there, as he looked on other dinners when the bosom was there. . . . If he missed the presiding bosom, it was as a part of his own state of which he was, from unavoidable circumstances, temporarily deprived."[2]

Even the "Little" in "Little Dorrit" is an epithet: Little Dorrit's name is Amy. The name "Pip" in *Great Expectations* is a sort of an epithet, a nick-name. In *Hard Times,* naming is something of an issue at the very beginning, when Sissy Jupe is first introduced:

"Girl number twenty," said Mr. Gradgrind, squarely pointing with his square forefinger, "I don't know that girl. Who is that girl?"

"Sissy Jupe, sir," explained number twenty, blushing, standing up, and curtseying.

"Sissy is not a name," said Mr. Gradgrind. "Don't call yourself Sissy. Call yourself Cecilia."

"It's father as calls me Sissy, sir," returned the young girl in a trembling voice, and with another curtsy.

"Then he has no business to do it," said Mr. Gradgrind. "Tell him he mustn't. Cecilia Jupe." (2008, 8)

She can be called Girl Number 20, but not Sissy. Mr. Gradgrind and the teacher Mr. McChoakumchild both have names that may as well be epithets.

Two of the (many) characters in Katherine Anne Porter's *Ship of Fools* are a young (unmarried) couple, David Scott and Jenny Brown, who have pet names for each other—Jenny calls David "David darling" and David calls Jenny "Jenny angel"—but they use these epithets only at times; here they are at the first dinner on the ship: "'Pig's knuckles, David darling,' said Jenny, restoring his private particular name to David Scott for the first time in three days. His own mood was not so easy—he reflected that she probably would not become Jenny angel to him for several days more—if ever. How much simple fraying of the nervous system can love survive? How many scenes?" (1984, 40–41). Jenny says "David darling" twice more on this page; on the next page the narrator ironically adopts Jenny's epithet for David: "'They should have been flattered,' said David darling, meanly." And then on the following page David finally uses his epithet for Jenny: "'Jenny angel,' he said. Instantly she felt her heart—she believed her heart could feel—melting just a little, timidly and distrustfully; she knew what David could and would do to her if she let herself be 'caught soft' as he described it. Yet she could not stop herself. She leaned forward and said, 'You old thing, you! Oh, let's try to be happy. Let's not spoil our first voyage together, it could be so gay. I'll try, really David darling, I promise—let's try. Don't you know I love you?'" (43). Then the narrator uses the epithets a little later: "'Let's be real tourists this once,' said Jenny angel to David darling, for so they were feeling towards each other for the moment" (52); and in the same conversation David calls her "Jenny angel" (56).

One of the other passengers, Frau Rittersdorf, overhears Jenny and David and misunderstands their epithets as real names; she writes in her diary: "'These young Americans have the affectation of addressing each other always by their full names, perhaps the only formality they maintain between themselves, and a very gauche sort of thing it is. . . . The names are musical, if somewhat sentimental: Jenny Angel—the real name, I suppose, Jane, Johanna Engel it would be, and much better, in the German—and David Darling. The latter is a common surname as well as a usual term of affection among Americans, I believe'" (84). But later Frau Rittersdorf discovers her mistake: "'It seems that those young Americans,'" wrote Frau Rittersdorf neatly, 'have quite commonplace names, after all. Scott and Brown. . . . Angel and Darling are their love-names for each other. In quite bad taste of course, and much exaggerated besides, as neither of them is in the slightest degree attractive'" (154). Jenny and David continue to use these epithets throughout the novel, and it is possible to use them to track the state of their relationship. Towards the end of the book the two almost go different ways, but at the very end they decide to continue traveling together. On the last-but-one page David asks, "'Are you cold, Jenny angel? Let me help you.' He took her coat off her arm and held it for her to put on" (496). On the last page, he says, "Let's think of something pleasant," and she answers, "You think of something, David darling." The epithets at the end indicate some kind of temporary accommodation, at least.

The first-person narrator of Anthony Burgess's *A Clockwork Orange*, Alex, regularly uses an epithet to refer to himself in his frequent asides to the reader—an internal narrator speaking to an external narratee: on page 69 (1986) he is "Your Humble Narrator"; on page 75 "your handsome young Narrator"; "your/Your Humble Narrator" on pages 91, 97, 101, and 108; on 114 he is "your Humble Narrator and Friend"; then, on page 138, when he is prison and in the middle of the brutal course of treatments to cure his violence, he becomes "Your Humble and Suffering Narrator," and on page 142 "your poor and suffering Friend and Narrator." On page 149—now that the treatments are over and he has been returned to civilian life—he is once again "Your Humble Narrator," as also on page 160 and 163. On page 164 he is "your friend and Humble Narrator"; on page 181 "Y.H.N."; then "Your Humble Narrator" on pages 191, 197, and 200; and finally, on page 201, simply "Your Humble." Clearly the epithets in the central part of the story track Alex's state of mind, his self-pity as he goes through the treatment. The epithets are not, I suppose, crucial to the interpretation of the story, and I have not noticed that critics generally mention them, but Burgess went to the trouble of using them, and using them very deliberately, and they do contribute, even if in a small way, to the gradual accumulation of meaning in the story, so there is some point in paying attention to how they work.

Congeries: A congeries is a heap of words. Exactly how big a heap should be is a matter of judgment; as a rule of thumb, it should be big enough to stand out, or to trip over. We find heaps of verbs and heaps of adjectives, but most congeries are heaps of nouns. A heap of things and a heap of actions are quite different kinds of heaps. A heap of nouns may represent a heap of material objects, but heaps of abstractions certainly occur.

A heap of objects can be a random jumble, as in the examples quoted earlier from Conrad's *The Secret Agent* and from Chandler's *The High Window,* or it can be a catalog of similar items. Most of book 2 of the *Iliad* is taken up with the Catalog of the Ships, which lists all the Greek contingents that have come to besiege Troy. In a later passage Zeus lists—to his wife Hera—his previous loves: the wife of Ixion (unnamed in the *Iliad,* but perhaps Dia), Danaë, Europa, Semele, Alkmene, Demeter, and Leto (14.315ff.). In the *Odyssey* (11.225ff.), when Odysseus is in the land of the dead, he sees another group of women famous in myth: Tyro, Antiope, Alkmene, Megara, Epikaste (more familiar as Jocasta), Chloris, Leda, Iphimedeia, Phaidra, Prokris, Ariadne, Maira, Klymene, and Eriphyle—and more whom Odysseus does not name. At *Iliad* 18.39ff. Homer names the daughters of Nereus, thirty some names all in an uninterrupted list; the trick is naming them all while retaining the meter. The impulse to record catalogs can be seen also in Hesiod's *Theogony* and in his *Catalog of Women,* which survives only in fragments. Later epic poets followed Homer's lead: see, for example, the great catalog of the heroes in Apollonius's *Argonautica* 1.23–333; the list of Amazon warriors in Quintus's *Posthomerica* 1.42ff., and the catalog of heathen gods in Milton's *Paradise Lost* 1.376–521. But catalogs may not count as congeries—they may include too much extra information in addition to the items listed—so perhaps they should be considered a different figure.

Don DeLillo's *White Noise* begins with a most impressive congeries. Here the narrator is describing the arrival of college students, driven to the campus by their parents, at the beginning of the school year:

The station wagons arrived at noon, a long shining line that coursed through the west campus. In single file they eased around the orange

I-beam sculpture and moved towards the dormitories. The roofs of the station wagons were loaded down with carefully secured suitcases full of light and heavy clothing; with boxes of blankets, boots and shoes, stationery and books, sheets, pillows, quilts; with rolled up rugs and sleeping bags; with bicycles, skis, rucksacks, English and Western saddles, inflated rafts. As cars slowed to a crawl and stopped, students sprang out and raced to the rear doors to begin removing the objects inside; the stereo sets, radios, personal computers; small refrigerators and table ranges; the cartons of phonograph records and cassettes; the hairdryers and styling irons; the tennis rackets, soccer balls, hockey and lacrosse sticks, bows and arrows; the controlled substances, the birth control pills and devices; the junk food still in shopping bags— onion-and-garlic chips, nacho thins, peanut crème patties, Waffelos and Kabooks, fruit chews and toffee popcorn; the Dum-Dum pops, the Mystic mints. (1985, 3–4)

Here some of the items form little groups: clothing, bedding, sports equipment, etc., ending with a list of junk food. Taken all together this congeries is a representation of the obsessive consumerism of modern American culture. The superabundance of reference is itself part of what is represented.

There is a similarly extensive congeries at the end of Vonnegut's *Player Piano*—one of five congeries in the book; the story takes place in a dystopian future in which almost all ordinary jobs have been eliminated by automation, leaving most people to live lives of unfulfilled emptiness. The climax of the book is a revolt of the masses in which the mechanisms of the automated society are destroyed, leaving a heap of detritus:

In the early light, the town seemed an enormous jewel box, lined with the black and gray velvet of fly-ash, and filled with millions of twinkling treasures: bits of air conditioners, amplidynes, analyzers, arc welders, batteries, belts, billers, bookkeeping machines, bottlers, canners, capacitors, circuit-breakers, clocks, coin boxes, calorimeters, colorimeters, computers, condensers, conduits, controls, converters, conveyers, cryostats, counters, cutouts, densitometers, detectors, dust precipitators, dishwashers, dispensers, dynamometers, dynamotors, electrodes, electronic tubes, exciters, fans, filers, filters, frequency

changers, furnaces, fuses, gages, garbage disposers, gears, generators, heat exchangers, insulators, lamps, loudspeakers, magnets,
mass spectrometers, motor generators, motors, noisemeters, oscillo-
graphs, panelboards, personnel machines, photoelectric cells, poten-
tiometers, pushbuttons, radios, radiation detectors, reactors, recorders, rectifiers, reducers, regulators, relays, remote controls, resistors,
rheostats, selsyns, servos, solenoids, sorters, spectrophotometers,
spectroscopes, springs, starters, straingages, switchboards, switches,
tape recorders, tachometers, telemeters, television sets, television
cameras, testers, thermocouples, thermostats, timers, toasters,
torquemeters, traffic controls, transistors, transducers, transformers,
turbines, vacuum cleaners, vacuum gages, vacuum tubes, venders, vi-
bration meters, viscosimeters, water heaters, wheels, X-ray spectro-
goniometers, zymometers. . . . (1980, 335–36; ellipsis in original)

The alphabetical arrangement I think serves to point out the lack of order
in the debris.

The very first pages of Porter's *Ship of Fools,* before the story even begins, are taken up with a kind of congeries: a long list of the characters,
some fifty or so—truly a random jumble of people, all thrown together on
the ship. In a sense, the shape of the book is just the shape of this figure.

Porter includes a half dozen or so congeries of various sorts throughout the story. When the ship is about to leave, the passengers watch as it
is loaded: "In straying groups, mute, unrelated, they [the passengers]
returned to the docks and stood about idly watching the longshore-
men hauling on the ropes of the loading cranes. Shapeless bundles and
bales, badly packed bedsprings and mattresses, cheap-looking sofas and
kitchen stoves, lightly crated pianos and old leather trunks were being
swung into the hold, along with a carload of Pueblo tile and a few thou-
sand bars of silver for England; a ton of raw chicle, bundles of hemp, and
sugar for Europe" (18–19).

The next passage is a sort of a heap, but the wit (such as it is) lies in
the isocolon rather than in the congeries: "The Huttens remembered a
Mexican saying that the Germans in Mexico were never tired of repeat-
ing: Mexicans loathe the Americans, despise the Jews, hate the Spanish,
distrust the English, admire the French and love the Germans" (79–80).
On the same page we find a somewhat similar construction of repeated

parallel verb phrases: "Now and again, standing at the window of his classroom in the big solid Mexican-French house which the German colony had bought and remodelled in the seemly German style, Professor Hutten watched the children walking sedately yet vigorously in small groups, their faces and their simple clothing so immaculate; observed the meek looks and good manners of the German young, heard them speak their mother tongue with good accent and pure diction, and fancied that he might almost imagine himself to be in Germany" (80). The length of the clauses, however, reduces the effect.

The following passage concerns La Condesa, who is a sort of high-class prisoner on the ship, deported from Cuba for rather vague political reasons; she is also a drug addict, but the ship's doctor, Dr. Schumann, feels a strange romantic attraction to her. Just before this passage she has smashed a couple of bottles of wine sent to her by the Captain. Dr. Schumann wonders, in a congeries of verbs, "Who was La Condesa smashing, he wondered—himself, or the Captain, or both? Or another man, or other men in the past who had resisted her, restrained her, baffled her, denied her, and finally evaded her?" (237).

A number of characters in the story rehearse at some length the troubles of their lives (often in free indirect discourse)—the abundance is an abundance of complaint. In this passage Frau Hutten is pondering her life with her husband, Herr Professor Hutten, an impractical academic bore:

> He was boring them to death again, she could feel it like vinegar in her veins. All in one vast drowning movement she remembered those many years when she had interposed herself, literally, bodily, between her husband and the seamy, grimy, mean, sordid, tiresome side of life that he simply could not endure. All those stupid details, all those endless errands, all that long war with the trickeries and the cheats and the slackness of the dishonest, the unscrupulous, the lazy and the indolent, the ignorant, the wayward, the greedy people of whom the entire workingclass from top to bottom seemed to consist; she had dealt with them all, with that endless parade of them through the days of her life, without once disturbing her husband or asking for his help. (291)

In the following passage, Denny, one of the most unpleasant of this mostly unpleasant group, is regretting his trip and longing to go home: "Denny began to feel tired in the head. He began to look forward to the end of his stay in Germany, and to getting back to Brownsville once again, where a man knew who was who and what was what, and niggers, crazy Swedes, Jews, greasers, bone-headed nicks, polacks, wops, Guineas and damn Yankees knew their place and stayed in it" (333–34). The ship's bulletin board provides an opportunity for a good congeries:

> The bulletin board once again bristled with seagoing information: ship departures and arrivals, maritime strikes and other disturbances in world ports; troubles in Cuba, troubles in Spain, troubles in Germany, knots, latitudes, longitudes, sun risings and settings, phases of the moon, today's prophecies of weather for tomorrow; besides the games and horse races and moving pictures and the ship's pool; and an announcement by the zarzuela company that the long-awaited gala evening in homage to the honored Captain of the *Vera* would take place this very evening, with a dinner, music, and dancing, a brilliant performance of comedy by the members of the zarzuela company, hosts of the evening; and a final drawing of numbers for the splendid prizes offered to the fortunate holders of tickets for the raffle. (403)

This congeries begins with a list of mostly unrelated items of no particular importance for the characters, but it ends with the announcement of the gala, the event that forms the climax to the whole story. (See also 376, 384, and 459.)

The meaning of a congeries depends on the context. A congeries can be a meaningless jumble of things, but it can also create a feeling of exhaustion of possibilities. In all cases, I think, the meaning comes from some kind of abundance, but exactly what that abundance means depends on the particularities of each passage. Some writers are interested in abundance or even excess; it is no surprise to find that Dickens is fond of congeries. But some writers are not inclined to use the figure. In Austen's *Pride and Prejudice,* Mrs. Bennet gives her husband a catalog of Mr. Bingley's dancing partners at the ball: "Mr. Bingley thought [Jane] quite beautiful, and danced with her twice. Only think of that my dear; he actually danced with her twice; and she was the only creature in the room that he asked a second time. First of all, he asked Miss Lucas . . . and he seemed quite struck with Jane . . . and asked her for the two next. Then, the two third he danced with Miss King, and the two fourth with Maria Lucas, and the two fifth with Jane again, and the two sixth with Lizzy." Mr. Bennet's comment perhaps shows Austen's opinion of the figure: "If he had had any compassion for me . . ., he would not have danced half so much! For God's sake, say no more of his partners. Oh! That he had sprained his ankle in the first dance!" (2001, 9–10).[3]

Polysyndeton and Asyndeton: Ordinarily a list of items ends with a conjunction between the last two items (eggs, butter, milk, and cheese); polysyndeton occurs if there is a conjunction between each pair of items (eggs and butter and milk and cheese); and asyndeton occurs if there is no conjunction at all (eggs, butter, milk, cheese). Polysyndeton is a figure of repetition, whereas asyndeton is a figure of omission. Both are common, and they sometimes occur close together. Here are a few examples—from *Little Dorrit* and from *Ship of Fools,* but many texts would provide examples.

This first example occurs when the Dorrit family, restored to wealth, are traveling in Europe. They have stayed overnight at the convent of the Great Saint Bernard; the next morning they are at breakfast, where they are joined by Mrs. General, who has been hired as a sort of chaperone for Fanny and Amy; and then they prepare to leave: "The entrance of the lady whom he announced, to take her place at the breakfast table, terminated the discussion. Shortly afterwards, the courier announced that the valet, and the footman, and the two maids, and the four guides, and the fourteen mules, were in readiness; so the breakfast party went out to the convent door to join the cavalcade" (1980, 508). This passage combines polysyndeton and congeries. Much of the effect here, I think, comes from the rhythm, as each new item is added to the list, each making its appearance as if in a kind of magic trick: "Shortly afterwards, the courier announced that the valet . . . AND the footman . . . AND the two maids . . . AND the four guides . . . AND the fourteen mules, were in readiness." How long, the reader asks, will this parade go on?

A somewhat different effect is created in the following passage, again a congeries with polysyndeton. Here one of the members of the Barnacle family, who works at the Circumlocution Office, is describing what Mr. Dorrit did before he got into debt: "He was a partner in a house in some large way—spirits, or buttons, or wine, or blacking, or oatmeal, or woollen, or pork, or hooks and eyes, or iron, or treacle, or shoes, or something or other that was wanted for troops, or seamen, or somebody" (620). Here the polysyndeton reinforces the randomness of the list; clearly Barnacle doesn't care what business Mr. Dorrit was in.[4]

In the following passage, from *Ship of Fools*, I think the polysyndeton gives the feeling that every possible reaction has been considered: "Jenny turned upon him a severe, censorious face, not angry, nor wounded, nor intimidated, nor resentful—just a regard of critical disapproval" (1984, 397). Likewise in this passage: "She wondered again at David's appetite that never failed no matter what, like a particularly voracious bird rearing up its gaping beak with blind punctuality to swallow whatever was dangled before it. At least, he had fairly good manners; he did not wolf or gulp or gobble or crunch or talk with his mouth full" (399–400).[5]

Here is an example of asyndeton from *Little Dorrit*. Arthur has run into Mr. Meagles and Daniel Doyce at the Circumlocution office; Mr. Meagles thinks that Doyce has been treated there as if he were a criminal: "He is a public offender. What has he been guilty of? Murder, manslaughter, arson, forgery, swindling, housebreaking, highway robbery, larceny, conspiracy, fraud? What would you say now?" (1980, 160). The asyndeton here, I think, gives the feeling that the list could be extended indefinitely, and thus a conjunction at the end would end the series prematurely.

The effect of the following passage, from *Ship of Fools*, I think is somewhat different. The ship has just set sail, and most of the passengers are seasick: "All had taken to a diet of black coffee, lukewarm beer, bottled synthetic lemonade, damp salted biscuits in tin boxes, coconut milk drunk directly from the shell" (1984, 11). It is instructive to see the effect of the unmarked form of the series, with just a single conjunction at the end—"black coffee, lukewarm beer, bottled synthetic lemonade, damp salted biscuits in tin boxes, and coconut milk drunk directly from the shell"—which gives a sense that this is a precise menu which each passenger eats, rather than a list from which they choose whatever is palatable; and of the series in polysyndeton—"black coffee and lukewarm beer and bottled synthetic lemonade and damp salted biscuits in tin boxes and coconut milk drunk directly from the shell"—which sounds almost like force-feeding.

Polysyndeton and asyndeton can occur together, as in this passage, part of a long soliloquy in interior monologue in which Mrs. Treadwell laments the circumstances of her life: "She had fallen in love with the wrong man, how wrong her parents never knew, for they never saw him, and she never went home afterwards—and the long nightmare had set in. Ten years of a kind of marriage, and ten years of divorce, shady, shabby, lonely, transient, sitting in cafés and hotel and boats and trains and theatres and strange houses with others as transient as herself, for half her life, half her life, and none of it had really happened" (210).[6]

The effects of polysyndeton and asyndeton are subtle, but they are real. I suspect most writers don't worry about the precise analysis of each instance; the decision to use one or the other of these figures is perhaps a matter of rhythm and feeling, but they are not used randomly and it is worthwhile trying to understand what each one does in its own context.

Chiasmus: This figure—ABBA—is one of the most commonly used schemes. Here is an example from *Little Dorrit:* "The Barnacles were a very high family, and a very large family. They were dispersed all over the public offices, and held all sorts of public places. Either the nation was under a load of obligation to the Barnacles, or the Barnacles were under a load of obligation to the nation. It was not quite unanimously settled which; the Barnacles having their opinion, the nation theirs" (148). The point of this kind of chiasmus is a reversal in superordination and subordination: there is one relation in the AB section, and the reverse in the BA section. The reversal in form expresses a conceptual reversal. We can see a reversal also in this next passage: Arthur Clennam is pondering on the effects of his overly strict religious upbringing:

> He was a dreamer in such wise, because he was a man who had deep-rooted in his nature, a belief in all the gentle and good things his life had been without. Bred in meanness and hard-dealing, this had rescued him to be a man of honourable and open hand. Bred in coldness and severity, this had rescued him to have a warm and sympathetic heart. Bred in a creed too darkly audacious to pursue, through its process of reserving the making of man in the image of his Creator to the making of his Creator in the image of an erring man, this had rescued him to judge not, and in humility to be merciful, and have love and charity. (206–7)

We can note, along the way, the three sentences with anaphora and overall parallel structure—but the point here is the chiasmus: "the making of man in the image of his Creator" and "the making of his Creator in the image of an erring man." Mrs. Clennam's religion has reversed the proper relation of man and God.

A reversal in power can be seen in the following passage from *Ship of Fools;* David refuses to see equality in his relationship with Jenny, and in particular his desire to look at her private papers: "He detested Jenny's obstinate insistence that there was any comparable connection between his ways with hers and her ways with him. She fought with him bitterly about his habit of opening her letters—he had no such right, she said. 'I don't open your letters,' she argued" (340). The power relationships in such instances of chiasmus are easy to see, but there are times when the figure seems less fraught. Here Dr. Schumann is thinking about whether or not he will watch the Spanish dance troupe perform: "He knew well that the next time that gang of hoodlums chose to put on their dancing dress and bring out their instruments to sing and dance and clatter and strum in their enchanting way, he would drift into their rhythms without a thought or care for what they were in truth, for in truth what were they?" (349). It would have been just as correct to write "without a thought or care for what they were in truth, for what were they in truth?"—as correct, but hardly as elegant. In the following passage, La Condesa is talking (to herself?) about her children, who have become political fugitives: "Hunted like beasts, my children, my children, my lovely ones, and they ran away to sleep in the woods . . . and I could only wait and suffer, suffer and wait—I could not lift a hand for them—." I don't see any great addition of meaning here, but there is a reminder that the language is not a neutral reflector of reality, but an instrument to be played.

Epizeuxis, Diacope, and Extended Epizeuxis: Epizeuxis is the repetition of a word with no words between; diacope is the repetition of a word with one or a few words between. In practice, epizeuxis can repeat more than one word, as in these examples from *Little Dorrit:* "But, why not, but why not?" (796); "for the good of the country, for the good of the country" (612). Very often an epizeuxis will either stand on its own as an exclamation or sit at the end of the sentence, though any word in a sentence can be repeated for emphasis.

We will start with a couple of straightforward examples. In this passage from *Ship of Fools,* Frau Rittersdorf is writing in her diary about the two unruly children of the Spanish Dance troupe, Ric and Rac: "'The effective practice of severity—I learned this with those beastly English children—lies in ceaseless, relentless, utter persistence, never an instant's letdown, but vigilance, vigilance, all the way, or they will be upon you like a pack of hyenas'" (274). And a few lines later she repeats the words, by themselves: "Vigilance, vigilance." Here the repeated repetition reinforces Frau Rittersdorf's point about persistence.

Sometimes the words in epizeuxis are exclamations, without grammatical construction: "Never, never!" (*Little Dorrit:* 144); "No, no—never again, never again" (*Ship of Fools:* 385). But sometimes they sit in the grammar of a sentence, and usually the grammar of the repeated word is the same as the grammar of the first use of the word: "you are such a preposterous good moral dull ridiculous man, but charming, charming!" (*Ship of Fools:* 121); here the epizeuxis is one final addition to a string of epithets, all modifying the noun "man."

Diacope can be considered a variation of epizeuxis, an interrupted epizeuxis: where epizeuxis is "X X," diacope is "X Y X." In this diacope from *Ship of Fools* David is feeling anxious about growing older: "Years might pass before it happened once for all, but there would come a day, an unspeakable day, when he would be bald, as his father and his grandfather and his great-grandfathers were before him" (129). The day of his baldness will be not just a day, but an unspeakable day. A similar emphasis is found in the following example from Anthony Trollope's *Dr Thorne;* the hero of the story has just been told by the woman he loves that "it would be wise that they should not see each other any more": "Dr Thorne, so counselled, at such a moment—so informed then, when he most required comfort from his love, at once swore loudly and said to himself that the world was bad, all bad" (30).

Epizeuxis is often used to show heightened emotion; in *Ship of Fools,* there are many instances, either in the direct speech of a character or in the narrator's report of a character's interior monologue: "Frau Rittersdorf gathered up her things and walked away in a chill of horror as if a bony hand reached out of the past clutching her coldly and drawing her again into the awful wallow of ignorance and poverty and brutish living she had escaped oh barely—barely!" (383). Here Mrs. Treadwell is reflecting on growing older: "Forty-six is the second awkward age. Which would turn out worse, to be fourteen, not child, not woman; or as she was now, not young, not old? What is expected of me now, I wonder, she asked herself as she had done at fourteen, almost in the same bewilderment. I still dance as well as I did, still ride, still swim, still like doing most of the young things I did like—still, still—what a terrible word" (413). This epizeuxis picks up the preceding anaphora: two figures of repetition with the same word.

In a variation of the figure, the second word of an epizeuxis can be further extended or qualified; in this variation, the epizeuxis does not sit at the end of the sentence. To my knowledge this variation has never been named, but it should be noted as a figure in its own right; I will simply call it an extended epizeuxis. Here is an example from *Ship of Fools,* a description of the Captain: "In still immaculate white with bits of gold braid and lettering disposed hieratically upon his chest, collar and shoulders, he bore himself rigidly, and his face was that of a pompous minor god: a god who had grown somewhat petulant and more than a little mean in his efforts to maintain his authority" (94–95). In many of the previous examples, epizeuxis is used for emotional effect—"never, never," "barely, barely." Extended epizeuxis, however, is not usually emotional, though it can create emphasis. Often the repeated word serves as a peg for some kind of comment or explanation.

Henry James uses this kind of extended epizeuxis often. The following example (introduced with a chiasmus) comes from the beginning of *Wings of the Dove.* Kate Croy is visiting her father, who has written to say that he wants to see her because he is ill: "She tried to be sad, so as not to be angry; but it made her angry that she couldn't be sad. And yet, where was misery, misery too beaten for blame and chalk-marked by fate like a 'lot' at a common auction, if not in these merciless signs of mere mean, stale feelings" (1964, 10).[7] Here the word "misery" has the same grammatical construction both times; it would be awkward, however, to leave out the repetition—"And yet, where was misery, too beaten for blame"; the extension works better if it is attached to the second "misery." On the following page James constructs a figure which is both interrupted in diacope and extended by an explanatory infinitive phrase: "He had written her that he was ill, too ill to leave his room" (11). This would work without the repetition—"He had written her that he was too ill to leave his room"—but the repetition certainly adds emphasis. James is very fond of extended epizeuxis or similar constructions, which allow him to make a statement and then expand on it in some way. In the following passage, the narrator of *The Wings of the Dove* is commenting on Kate Croy's mysterious ability to attract the eye of those around her:

> She was handsome, but the degree of it was not sustained by items and aids; a circumstance moreover playing its part at almost any time in the impression produced. The impression was one that remained, but as the sources of it no sum in addition would have made up the total. She had stature without height, grace without motion, presence without mass. Slender and simple, frequently soundless, she was somehow always in the line of the eye—she counted singularly for its pleasure. More "dressed," often, with fewer accessories, than other women, or less dressed, should occasion require, with more, she probably could not have given the key to these felicities. They were mysteries of which her friends were conscious—those friends whose general explanation was to say that she was clever, whether or no it were taken by the world as the cause or the effect of her charm. (10–11)

The passage includes a number of figures; we can note, for example, the phrases in isocolon in the sentence, "She had stature without height, grace without motion, presence without mass," and the antitheses in "More 'dressed,' often, with fewer accessories, than other women, or less dressed, should occasion require, with more." But the point at hand is the repetition of "friends," with an extension that tells what those friends would say about Kate. Earlier in the passage we can note the repetition of "impression"—in different sentences; this repetition I think does not count as either epizeuxis or diacope, nor precisely as anadiplosis; elsewhere I have called this kind of repetition a link. James uses a great many links; he characteristically uses links not just to connect but to add a new comment, as he also uses extended epizeuxis to make a further comment; examples are easy to find.

In the following extended epizeuxis from *Ship of Fools* the repetition is again not grammatically necessary, but it is effective: "At the top of the stairs they were almost overwhelmed from the back by the troupe of Spanish dancers, who simply went through, over and around them like a wave, a wave with elbows" (39). In these examples, the reader is asked to look at the situation twice and the second time to see more of it. This form can be extended even further; at the very beginning of *Dr. Thorne,* Trollope is describing the area where the story is to take place: "It is purely agricultural: agricultural in its produce, agricultural in its poor, agricultural in its pleasures" (5). Because of the strong punctuation, one might be tempted to think of this as anadiplosis, but because the members of the following tricolon are fragments, I would still call it epizeuxis. But terminology is not the essence of the exercise: the goal is an increased appreciation for what the figures can do.

In the following passage, from the gala party at the end of *Ship of Fools,* Herr Rieber is getting more than a little drunk:

> Taking a fresh grip on Lizzi's waist and hand, he pressed his hard little stomach against her and burst wordlessly into high tenor song. "La dedada, la dedada, la, de, da de daa!" sang Herr Rieber, frisking like a faun, turning lightly on his toes gazing up in ecstasy at Lizzi, who answered at once "La dedada," like Echo herself. He felt he was a faun, a fleet prancing faun deep in the forest glade, stamping a pattern of cleft flowers into the leaf mold under his sharp little polished hoofs; with the winds moaning like violins in the treetops, the sweet voices of birds calling la de da to each other among the branches where the harp strings were sighing, and the nymph waiting for the young goat-boy, half god, light on his hoofs and ready to leap the likely, long-legged creature in the green gown who loved a good caper! Ah, ladedada, de da, sang the young faun at the top of his voice in a panic rapture as he spun wildly on the very tiptoe of his sharp hoofs, while the nymph, leaning backward from the waist, whirled steadily her lace skirts rose and spread out slowly upward at the back like an opening fan. (1984, 447)

In this interrupted and extended epizeuxis—"a faun, a fleet prancing faun deep in the forest glade"—the repeated word takes on a life of its own and develops into a lush fantasy of sexual conquest.

Doublets, Antitheses, and Tricola: Doublets, antitheses, and tricola are common, though not found in every style. These figures often achieve their effects through a combination of sense and rhythm, each of which reinforces the other. The figure can create an impression not only of fitness but even of inevitability, and it can also create increasing emphasis. I begin with a few examples from *The Decline and Fall of the Roman Empire*, by the eighteenth-century historian Edward Gibbon. I haven't generally included passages from nonfiction, but Gibbon is too great an influence to omit. Here is the very beginning of the book: "In the second century of the Christian era, the Empire of Rome comprehended the fairest part of the earth, and the most civilized portion of mankind. The frontiers of that extensive monarchy were guarded by ancient renown and disciplined valour. The gentle but powerful influence of laws and manners had gradually cemented the union of the provinces. Their peaceful inhabitants enjoyed and abused the advantages of wealth and luxury" (1993, 3). Here are the doublets: "the fairest part of the earth"/"the most civilized portion of mankind"; "ancient renown"/"disciplined valour"; "gentle"/"powerful"; "laws"/"manners"; "enjoyed"/"abused"; and "wealth"/"luxury." In three sentences we find five doublets of various sorts and lengths. These doublets variously add one idea to another ("ancient renown"/"disciplined valour"), combine near synonyms ("wealth"/"luxury"), or state some kind of contrast, though perhaps not a strong antithesis ("gentle"/"powerful"; "enjoyed"/"abused"). No idea is allowed into the world without some kind of companion idea.

The second paragraph of the first chapter begins with a tricolon, in which the elements of the tricolon seem to exhaust the possibilities: "The principal conquests of the Romans were achieved under the republic; and the emperors, for the most part, were satisfied with preserving those dominions which had been acquired by the policy of the senate, the active emulation of the consuls, and the martial enthusiasm of the people" (3). The Roman state could be understood to consist precisely of the senate, the consuls, and the people, and the tricolon specifies the role of each element in the management of the state. As often happens, the rhythm of the tricolon is reinforced by isocolon and parallel structure. It is easy to find examples of doublets, antitheses, and tricola in Gibbon's text; here are a few: "Happily for the repose of mankind, the moderate system recommended by the wisdom of Augustus, was adopted by the fears and vices of his immediate successors" (5). Here the doublet of "fear and vices" follows "wisdom"; the figure as a whole is thus a kind of disguised tricolon. Here is the very next sentence: "Engaged in the pursuit of pleasure, or in the exercise of tyranny, the first Caesars seldom showed themselves to the armies, or to the provinces; nor were they disposed to suffer, that those triumphs which *their* indolence neglected should be usurped by the conduct and valour of their lieutenants" (5). This passage includes an instance of hendiadys, in which a noun and qualifier are stated as two nouns: "valourous conduct" becomes "conduct and valour."

The following paragraph explains that the conquest of part of Britain was an exception to the rule: "In this single instance the successors of Caesar and Augustus were persuaded to follow the example of the former rather than the precept of the latter. . . . After a war of about forty years, undertaken by the most stupid, maintained by the most dissolute, and terminated by the most timid of all the emperors, the far greater part of the island submitted to the Roman yoke" (5–6). The doublet in the first sentence is followed by a tricolon in the second; this tricolon consists of two sets of three elements: "undertaken/"maintained"/"terminated" and "most stupid"/"most dissolute"/"most timid."

It would be easy to collect further examples; there must be hundreds. I will stop with just one more, one of the most famous in all of Gibbon: "The policy of the emperors and the senate, as far as it concerned religion, was happily seconded by the reflections of the enlightened, and by the habits of the superstitious, part of their subjects. The various modes of worship, which prevailed in the Roman world, were all considered by the people, as equally true; by the philosopher, as equally false; and by the magistrate, as equally useful" (34). One might have expected that the antithesis of "true" and "false" might be exhaustive, but Gibbon points out, somewhat cynically, that there is a third possibility, "useful," which trumps the true and the false.

Jane Austen was very fond of doublets and tricola, often in combination; they contribute to her characteristic wit and irony. In earlier work (Clark and Phelan 2020) I discussed tricolon in *Emma;* here I will give some examples from *Persuasion.* In Chapter I we read that Lady Elliot, while she was alive, moderated the folly of her husband, Sir Walter Elliot: "She had humoured, or softened, or concealed his failings, and promoted his real respectability for seventeen years, and though not the very happiest being in the world herself, had found enough in her duties, her friends, and her children, to attach her to life, and make it no matter of indifference to her when she was obliged to quit them" (2003, 6). The sentence begins with a tricolon with polysyndeton ("humoured, or softened, or concealed his failings"); the rest of the sentence is an antithesis ("and though . . . had found enough") which itself contains another tricolon ("her duties, her friends, and her children") and a doublet ("to attach . . . and make it no matter of indifference").

When Anne Elliot is introduced, we read that she has "an elegance of mind and sweetness of character" and that Lady Russell regarded her as "a most dear and highly valued god-daughter, favourite, and friend" (7): a doublet and a tricolon. A little later we are told that while Lady Elliot was alive the family was managed with "method, moderation, and economy" (10). After Lady Elliot's death, the family's finances suffer through Sir Walter's folly, and Lady Russell has to intervene: "She was of strict integrity herself, with a delicate sense of honour; but she was as desirous of saving Sir Walter's feelings, as solicitous for the credit of the family, as aristocratic in her ideas of what was due to them, as anybody of sense and honesty could well be. She was a benevolent, charitable, good woman, and capable of strong attachments; most correct in her conduct, strict in her notions of decorum, and with manners that were held a standard of good breeding" (12). The first sentence begins with a doublet ("of strict integrity herself, with a delicate sense of honour") and continues with a tricolon ("as desirous . . . as solicitous . . . as aristocratic"), and a doublet ("sense and honesty"). The second sentence begins with a tricolon ("she was a benevolent, charitable, good woman") that itself becomes the first part of a doublet ("She was . . . and capable of strong attachments"), and the sentence ends with another tricolon ("Most correct . . . strict . . . and with manners").

There are abundant instances of these figures throughout the novel; a complete collection would be impressive, even overwhelming, but a few examples with some general comments will be sufficient. First, many of Austen's doublets are antithetical: "Every emendation of Anne's had been on the side of honesty against importance" (13); "she should yet have been a happier woman in maintaining the engagement, than she had been in the sacrifice of it" (29); "She had been forced into prudence in her youth, she learned romance as she grew older—the natural sequel of an unnatural beginning" (29).[8]

Second, the elements of the tricolon can be short or long. Some consist of three single words: "god-daughter, favourite, and friend" (7); "method, moderation, and economy" (10); "a benevolent, charitable, good woman" (12); "birth, beauty, and mind" (26); "wondered, grieved, and feared" (33); "conversation, opinion, and idea" (40); "talking, laughing, and singing" (44); and so on. Others consist of phrases: in Chapter II the Elliots are forced to leave their home and look for something more economical: "A small house in their own neighbourhood, where they might still have Lady Russell's society, still be near Mary, and still have the pleasure of sometimes seeing the lawns and groves of Kellynch, was the object of her ambition" (14); we note the anaphora of "still ... still ... still," and the crescendo, as the final element is the longest of the series.

Third, constructions are not always exactly parallel. When the Elliots have to find someone to rent their house, Sir Walter refuses something so vulgar as an advertisement: "Sir Walter spurned the idea of its being offered in any manner; forbad the slightest hint being dropped of his having such an intention; and it was only on the supposition of his being spontaneously solicited by some most unexceptionable applicant, on his own terms, and as a great favor, that he would let it at all" (16). The first two elements here begin with parallel verb forms, "spurned" and "forbad"; but the third, which is the longest, takes a completely different construction, perhaps because the end of the sentence turns a different direction, from No and No to Well, maybe. Here is another irregular tricolon, which expresses three moments in a process: "Captain Wentworth was already on his way thither. Before Mrs. Croft had written, he was arrived; and the very next time Anne walked out, she saw him" (164).

Fourth, a common effect of either a doublet or a tricolon is the impression that all relevant aspects of a situation have been considered. "There was no wound, no blood, no visible bruise; but her eyes were closed, she breathed not, her face was like death" (102).

Fifth, the tricolon may fall in different parts of the sentence, with different effect. A tricolon at the end of a sentence can be either epigrammatic or emphatic: "Anne had not wanted this visit to Uppercross, to learn that a removal from one set of people to another, though at a distance of only three miles, will often include a total change of conversation, opinion, and idea" (40); "Captain Harville, though not equalling Captain Wentworth in manners, was a perfect gentleman, unaffected, warm, and obliging" (91). But the epigrammatic effect may be reduced if the tricolon sits in the middle of a sentence: "Her manners were open, easy, and decided, like one who had no distrust of herself, and no doubts of what to do; without any approach to coarseness, however, or any want of good humour" (46); here the tricolon ("open, easy, and decided") is buried in the accumulation of description. A tricolon can be just one element of a complex sentence: "The theatre or the rooms, where he was most likely to be, were not fashionable enough for the Elliots, whose evening amusements were solely in the elegant stupidity of private parties, in which they were getting more and more engaged: and Anne, wearied of such a state of stagnation, sick of knowing nothing, and fancying herself stronger because her strength was not tried, was quite quite impatient for the concert evening" (169).

Sixth, a tricolon may be extended with a fourth point. This fourth point may be an addition: "Still, however, she had enough to feel! It was agitation, pain, pleasure, a something between delight and misery" (165); "she had feelings for the tender, spirits for the gay, attention for the scientific, and patience for the wearisome" (176)—or it may be a qualification: "Mr. Elliot was rational, discreet, polished—but he was not open" (151). I believe that there is no name in traditional rhetoric for structures of four elements; they certainly occur, and though they are not as frequent as doublets, antitheses, and tricola, they are not rare, and they deserve notice as well.

Examples of these figures from other authors can show some of the variety of effects the figures can create. Here are a few from Henry James's *The Wings of the Dove:* "She had stature without height, grace without motion, presence without mass" (1964, 22); "The inconvenience—as always happens in such cases—was not that you minded what was false, but that you missed what was true" (23); "Her haunting harassing father, her menacing uncompromising aunt, her portionless little nephews and nieces, were figures that caused the chord of natural piety superabundantly to vibrate" (38); "the more you gave yourself the less of you was left" (39); "her freedom, her fortune and her fancy were her law" (114); "She made up for failures of gravity by failures of mirth" (128).[9]

And a few from Ford Madox Ford's *The Good Soldier:* "I was aware of something treacherous, something frightful, something evil in the day" (1997, 42); "She looked me straight in the eye, and for a moment I had the feeling that those two blue discs were immense, were overwhelming, were like a wall of blue that shut me off from the rest of the world" (42); "We are all so afraid, we are all so alone, we all need from the outside the assurance of our own worthiness to exist" (97); "When the palpitating creature was at last asleep in his arms he discovered that he was madly, was passionately, was overwhelmingly in love with her" (129). In these passages the figure is used as an emphatic expression of emotion.[10]

Anadiplosis and Gradatio or Climax: Anadiplosis occurs when the end of one structure is repeated at the beginning of the next: "(. . .) A || A (. . .)." Lanham does not give an example of anadiplosis: he jumps right to gradatio (AB, BC, CD, etc.), which is anadiplosis in series; I will discuss gradatio below. But examples of anadiplosis within and between sentences are not hard to find; here are two from *Ship of Fools:*

> All believed they were bound for a place for some reason more desirable than the place they were leaving, but it was necessary to make the change with the least possible delay and expense. Delay and expense had been their common portion. . . ." (10)

> But I was restless, a good living was not good enough for me. I must go and run a hotel somewhere else besides Switzerland. Switzerland, for me, was too peaceful. (1984, 101)

Anadiplosis can also occur from the end of one paragraph to the beginning of the next, to form a link between the paragraphs; here is a paragraph anadiplosis from Anthony Trollope's *Framley Parsonage:*

> And so Mrs Proudie on retiring to rest gave the necessary orders, to the great annoyance of her household.
> To the great annoyance, at least, of her servants! (2004, 101)

And here is a paragraph anadiplosis from Trollope's *Dr. Thorne;* Frank Gresham is distrusted by both Tories and Whigs and therefore loses an election:

> So between the two stools he fell to the ground, and, as a politician, he never again rose to his feet.
> He never again rose to his feet; but twice again he made violent efforts to do so. (2004, 9)

I think the following, also from *Dr. Thorne,* counts as paragraph anadiplosis, although the second A is Not-A; Frank Gresham's father is throwing a party for Frank's birthday, but he no longer has the money to do so in proper style:

> Mr Gresham was now an embarrassed man, and though the world did not know it, or, at any rate, did not know that he was deeply embarrassed, he had not the heart to throw open his mansion and park and receive the county with a free hand as though all things were going well with him.
>
> Nothing was going well with him. (12)

Anadiplosis can occur from the end of one chapter to the beginning of the next. In *Framley Parsonage,* chapter 9 ends "And now, how was he to tell his wife?" and chapter 10 begins "And now, how was he to tell his wife?" The figure here marks a strong emphasis.

Gradatio is anadiplosis in series: not just AB/B but AB/BC/CD. . . . In the first chapter of *Gargantua* (the first book of François Rabelais's *Gargantua and Pantagruel*) the narrator notes the sequence of world empires, leading from the ancient world to the French empire of his own time: "the amazing transferences of crowns and empires from the Assyrians to the Medes, from the Medes to the Persians, from the Persians to the Macedonians, from the Macedonians to the Romans, from the Romans to the Greeks, from the Greeks to the French."[11] Thus the gradatio is Assyrians > Medes | Medes > Persians | Persians > Macedonians | Macedonians > Romans | Romans > Greeks | Greeks > French. It would have been possible to write the series without the repetition, in the figure called incrementum: "the amazing transferences of crowns and empires from the Assyrians to the Medes, to the Persians, to the Macedonians, to the Romans, to the Greeks, to the French." The effect, I think, is very different. The incrementum creates just a succession, with no sense of connection from one item to the next, but the gradatio creates the feeling that each empire hands its power on to the next, as a runner in a relay race hands on the baton to the next runner.

The term *gradatio* means "staircase" in Latin, and *climax* means the same in Greek. But in most modern usage, the climax of a process or series is the end point, rather than all the steps, so the term gradatio for this figure is probably to be preferred. Gradatio is one of a set of related figures; others in the set are articulus, which is just a list; partitio or diaeresis, in which a whole is divided into parts; congeries, the heap, which we have already considered; and incrementum or auxesis, in which there is a clear order and progression from one item to the next. For our purposes here, the most important distinction falls between incrementum and gradatio; in the example above from *Gargantua,* Rabelais's version is a gradatio, my revision an incrementum.

Incrementum and gradatio are the rhetorical form of what Jeanne Fahnestock (1996) calls series reasoning. Both of these figures express (or create) a graded hierarchy, with an origin, an end, and steps that connect the extremes. The series must be organized according to some principle: smallest to greatest, earliest to latest, most primitive to most developed, and so on. According to Kenneth Burke (1962, 58), these figures "awaken an attitude of collaborative expectancy"—once we see the pattern, we desire its symmetrical completion. He quotes an example from the days of the 1948 Berlin crisis—"Who controls Berlin, controls Germany; who controls Germany, controls Europe; who controls Europe controls the world." Even if the reader has doubts about the truth of the proposition or of its morality, "by the time you arrive at the second of its three stages, you feel how it is destined to develop—and on the level of purely formal assent you would collaborate to round out its symmetry by spontaneously willing its completion and perfection as an utterance." Both incrementum and gradatio can be organized in a graded series, but gradatio in addition suggests that the items in the series—or perhaps the propositions containing the items—overlap. To take Burke's example, the second term of each proposition—"who controls X controls Y"—becomes the first term of the next proposition—"who controls Y controls Z."

Fahnestock (1996) describes in detail how these figures can function in scientific argument—with special attention to the figures in Darwinian theory, where gradation is essential. Indeed, one of my favorite examples of gradatio comes from a book of popular science; here Lawrence Krauss explains that if the energy of "empty" space—the "vacuum energy" or the cosmological constant—were significantly greater than it seems to be, then galaxies would not have formed. "But if galaxies hadn't formed, then stars wouldn't have formed. And if stars hadn't formed, planets wouldn't have formed. And if planets hadn't formed, then astronomers wouldn't have formed!" (Krauss 2012, 125). This gradatio creates a series that ranges from the size of galaxies to the size of a person.

Some literary examples also seem to have a kind of persuasive force. In this gradatio from Shakespeare's *As You Like It,* Rosalind is explaining to Oliver how X and Y fell in love: "'Your brother and my sister no sooner met but they **looked,** no sooner **looked** but they **loved,** no sooner **loved** but they **sighed,** no sooner **sighed** but they asked one another the **reason,** no sooner knew the **reason** but they sought the remedy; and in these degrees have they made a pair of stairs to marriage'" (V.2.31–36). The figure suggests a kind of inevitability. We can note that Shakespeare gives the name of the figure at the end: "a pair of stairs." This is just one of many indications that Shakespeare knew his figures by name; they were part of the standard high school curriculum of his day. Shakespeare was fond of gradatio; I have found other examples in *Richard II, Richard III, Henry IV Part One, Troilus and Cressida, The Comedy of Errors, The Rape of Lucrece, Love's Labor Lost,* and I am sure there are more.

The figure is also used by modern writers. Here is a fine example from Henry James's *The Wings of the Dove:* "He was acting for Kate, and not, by the deviation of an inch, for her friend. He was accordingly not interested, for had he been interested, he would have cared, and had he cared he would have wanted to know. Had he wanted to know he wouldn't have been purely passive, and it was his pure passivity that had to represent his honour. His honour, at the same time, let us add, fortunately fell short, to-night, of spoiling his little talk with Susan Shepherd" (359).

Nabokov uses the figure in *Bend Sinister:* "This night there was only a diffused glow where a Neptune of granite loomed upon his square rock which rock continued as a parapet which parapet was lost in the mist" (Nabokov 1974, 17). I have found two examples in *Ship of Fools.* Here the Spanish exile La Condesa is speaking to Dr. Schumann: "I could never endure to think that any secret or any pleasure was being kept from me. I surmised without help, everything, very early. From there to experience, it was only a step; from experience to habit a matter of moments" (1984, 199). In this next example, the old man Herr Graff, on the edge of death, is contemplating his end: "'O, God, darken the sun and the moon, put out Your planets and I would blow out candles. Drop from Your great nerveless hands darkness and silence, silence and stillness, stillness of dust buried under dust, the darkness and silence and stillness of the eyeless deeps of the sea'" (444). The gradatio—"darkness and silence, silence and stillness, stillness of dust"—is extended by repetitions of the three key terms. The following, from a popular thriller, *G-Man,* by Stephen Hunter, is a very effective account of a shootout between two characters, Johnny and Charles. The narrator notes that "Johnny was fast. Charles was faster. Mind to arm, arm to hand, hand to trigger, trigger to hammer, hammer to cartridge, cartridge to powder, powder to bullet, the need to act and the act itself were almost simultaneous" (Hunter 2017, 209–10). And finally, a lovely passage from a children's book, *Stuart Little,* by E. B. White (1973, 100); Stuart is traveling:

> In the loveliest town of all, where the houses were white and high and the elm trees were green and higher than the houses, where the front yards were wide and pleasant and the back yards were bushy and worth finding out about, where the streets sloped down to the stream and the stream flowed quietly under the bridge, where the lawns ended in orchards and the orchards ended in fields and the fields ended in pastures and the pastures climbed the hill and disappeared over the top toward the wonderful wide sky, in this loveliest of all towns Stuart stopped to get a drink of sarsaparilla.

This complex passage deserves a graphic analysis:

> In the loveliest town of all,
>   *where* the houses were [white and high] and
>   the elms trees were [green and higher than the houses],
>   *where* the front yards were [wide and pleasant] and
>   the back yards were [bushy and worth finding out about],
>   *where* the streets sloped down to the stream and
>   the stream flowed quietly under the bridge,
>   *where* the lawns ended in orchards and
>   the orchards ended in fields and
>   the fields ended in pastures and
>   the pastures climbed the hill and disappeared over the top
>   toward the wonderful wide sky,
> in this loveliest of all towns Stuart stopped to get a drink of sarsaparilla.

The sentence is a suspended period with a repeated locative and delayed main clause; it combines anaphora, parallel structures with crescendo, an anadiplosis, and then a full gradatio—and the structures reveal themselves in the physical experience of reading. The figures in this passage, and the rhythms they create, slow down the reading, to create a kind of idyllic leisure.

How then are we to read rhetorical figures like these and the others discussed in this chapter? How much attention should we give to them? Does attention to the figures get in the way of an appropriate emotional response to a story? Should the response remain an unanalyzed feeling, or should the reader take up the scholar's dissecting tools?

The answers to these questions are to some extent personal, and I have no desire to legislate reading practices. Many readers will prefer to read first without analysis, as a music lover may first enjoy listening to a performance without analyzing the form or the counterpoint or the modulations or the motivic development. But rereading, like relistening, can provide an opportunity to understand how the art does its job—for those who want to know.

5

Rhetorical Schemes in Dickens, Brontë, and Morrison

In chapter 1 I attempted to show that the language of novels is not usually transparent, despite the strictures of critics and theorists, and in chapter 4 I described the use and meaning of some schemes in specific contexts. Some novelists may try to give the impression of transparency, but a careful reading reveals the manipulation of language even in the most innocent narrative. And many novelists, perhaps most novelists, don't hide their devices. This chapter gives a partial account of the figures in Charles Dickens's *Little Dorrit,* Anne Brontë's *Agnes Grey,* and Toni Morrison's *Jazz.* We will see that all three of these authors deploy a variety of figures, but for very different rhetorical effects.

Rhetorical Figures in *Little Dorrit*

A complete catalog of figures in *Little Dorrit* (Dickens 1980) would be very long, but a summary will make the point. I can imagine that some readers will find even this summary too much—of course they can skip and skim—but part of the point is just how many examples can be found. A full appreciation of these passages would need more or less extensive contextualizing, but the figures should be evident even if the meaning is not entirely explicit.

I begin with a good congeries. Tip, Little Dorrit's brother, has tried a number of different occupations, without being able to settle on any one of them. He starts out working in the office of an attorney, but he leaves that job after a few months:

> "I am so tired of it," said Tip, "that I have cut it."
> Tip was tired of everything. . . . [Little Dorrit] got him into a warehouse, into a market garden, into the hop trade, into the law again,

into an auctioneer's, into a brewery, into a stockbroker's, into the law again, into a coach office, into a waggon office, into the law again, into a general dealer's, into a distillery, into the law again, into a wool house, into a dry goods house, into the Billingsgate trade, into the foreign fruit trade, and into the docks. But whatever Tip went into, he came out of tired, announcing that he had cut it. (115–16)

This congeries represents the randomness of the succession of jobs; the repetition of "into the law again" only reinforces the futility of Little Dorrit's attempts to find him a place; this congeries also creates the feeling that all possibilities have been exhausted. The passage also features anaphora, as all the phrases begin with "into"; as the passage continues, there are further repetitions, for instance of "tired" and "cut it." I've quoted enough to make the point.

The following passage is a congeries of verb phrases in parallel structure, organized geographically: "Next morning's sun saw Mr Dorrit's equipage upon the Dover road, where every red-jacketed postilion was the sign of a cruel house, established for the unmerciful plundering of travellers. The whole business of the human race, between London and Dover, being spoliation, Mr Dorrit was waylaid at Dartford, pillaged at Gravesend, rifled at Rochester, fleeced at Sittingbourne, and sacked at Canterbury." The effect here is to pile up various kinds of plundering; there is no particular reason that the verbs come in this particular order, but there is a sense that any addition would be just more of the same.[1]

Anaphora is very common in *Little Dorrit*. In the following passage, Monsieur Rigaud, one of the villains of the story, has got out of jail in Marseilles; now he is tramping through France and finding the tramp very hard: "'To the devil with this plain that has no end! To the devil with these stones that cut like knives! To the devil with this dismal darkness, wrapping itself about one with a chill!'" (166). "To the devil" is one of Rigaud's signature phrases. Here the phrase is emphasized by the alliteration with "dismal darkness." Then Rigaud reaches a small town: "There was the hotel with its gateway, and its savoury smell of cooking; there was the café with its bright windows, and its rattling of dominoes; there was the dyer's with its strips of red cloths on the doorposts; there was the silversmith's with its earrings, and its offerings for altars; there was the tobacco dealer's with its lively group of soldier customers coming out pipe in mouth; there were the bad odors of the town" (166). The full form of the phase in anaphora might be "There was the X with its Y," where the variables X and the Y are really the point. Probably two forms of anaphora should be distinguished: one in which the first word bears a lot of semantic weight— we will see examples shortly—and another, such as this, where the repeated word itself is weak and mostly serves to set up what follows, which is usually a set of words in the figure *variatio,* which just means variation: "hotel... café... dyer's... silversmith's... tobacco dealer's."

Rigaud finds an inn, the Break of Day, where he enters and orders a meal. The customers and the landlady of the inn are discussing the case of a notorious murderer from Marseilles—Rigaud, in fact, though they don't know that—and in the discussion the landlady gives her opinion of human nature:

> "I know what I have seen, and what I have looked in the face of this world here, where I find myself. And I tell you this, my friend, that there are people (men and women both, unfortunately) who have no good in them—none. That there are people whom it is necessary to detest without compromise. That there are people who must be dealt with as enemies of the human race. That there are people who have no human heart, and who must be crushed like savage beasts and cleared out of the way." (168–69)

Thus we find three rather striking instances of anaphora in just a few pages.

In the next passage, Arthur Clennam sees his old flame Flora for the first time since his return from China: "Flora, always tall, had grown to be very broad too, and short of breath; but that was not much. Flora, whom he had left a lily, had become a peony; but that was not much. Flora, who had seemed enchanting in all she said and thought, was diffuse and silly. That was much. Flora, who had been spoiled and artless long ago, was determined to be spoiled and artless now. That was a fatal blow" (191–92). Here the word in anaphora has semantic weight: "Flora... Flora... Flora ... Flora." We also see the similar endings, "but that was not much," "but that was not much," in the figure known as *epistrophe* (or *antistrope*), and then *variatio* the third and fourth time—"But that was much" and "That was a fatal blow"—in separate sentences for emphasis. The structure of the phrases is (1) Flora, (2) as she was then, (3) as she is now, (4) but that was not much/but that was much/that was a fatal blow: a combination of anaphora, epistrophe, and variatio.

Dickens uses epistrophe almost as often as he uses anaphora.[2] In the description of Rigaud's tramp, just a few pages before the passages quoted above, we find the following, with epistrophe in the three phrases at the end:

> With an old sheepskin knapsack at his back, and a rough, unbarked stick cut out of some wood in his hand, miry, footsore, his shoes and gaiters trodden out, his hair and beard untrimmed; the cloak he carried over his shoulder, and the clothes he wore, sodden with wet; limping along in pain and difficulty; he looked as if the clouds were hurrying from him, as if the wail of the wind and the shuddering of the grass were directed against him, as if the low mysterious plashing of the water murmured at him, as if the fitful autumn night were disturbed by him. (165–66)

Here again we see a combination of anaphora and epistrophe with variation: "as if . . . from him," "as if . . . against him," "as if . . . at him," "as if . . . by him." The variation in prepositional phrases is like the variation "of the people . . . by the people . . . for the people" in *The Gettysburg Address*. In the following passage Mrs Chivery, the wife of the turnkey at the prison, is speaking to Arthur Clennam about the Dorrit family: "'Sir,' said she in continuation, 'you are acquainted with the family, and have interested yourself in the family, and are influential with the family'" (303).

Several of the common rhetorical figures are figures of repetition— thus anaphora is initial repetition, epistrophe is terminal repetition, epizeuxis is the repetition of a word or phrase with no words in between, and diacope is repetition with one or a few words between. The usual effect of these figures is some degree of emphasis. The following passage has a mild epizeuxis toward the end. Here Mr. Dorrit's daughters, Fanny and Amy (Little Dorrit), have persuaded their father that Fanny should live with her uncle rather than in the debtors' prison; they are not telling him that Fanny will be working as a dancer: "'Well, Amy, well. I don't quite follow you, but it's natural I suppose that Fanny should prefer to be outside, and even that you often should, too. So, you and Fanny and your uncle, my dear, will have your own way. Good, good. I'll not meddle; don't mind me'" (115). A little more emphasis is conveyed by the epizeuxis in the next passage. Here Arthur has followed Little Dorrit to the debtors' prison, Marshalsea, where he meets her father, Mr. Dorrit, who has been a prisoner there for twenty-five years. Mr. Dorrit in effect begs some money from Arthur, and Little Dorrit makes an embarrassed gesture: "To see her hand upon his arm in mute entreaty, half-repressed, and her timid little shrinking figure turning away was to see a sad, sad sight" (123). There are many examples of such mild epizeuxis, but there are also a number that are more emphatic. This passage, as Little Dorrit awaits the death of her father, combines epizeuxis and anaphora (the Castle is the Castle in the Air which Mr. Dorrit has fancifully imagined): "Quietly, quietly, all the lines of the plan of the great Castle melted one after another. Quietly, quietly, the ruled and cross-ruled countenance on which they were traced, became fair and blank. Quietly, quietly, the reflected marks of the prison bars and of the zig-zag iron on the wall-top, faded away. Quietly, quietly, the face subsided into a far younger likeness of her own than she had ever seen under the grey hair, and sank to rest" (712). Epizeuxis is the characteristic speech pattern of Mr. Casby, Flora's father: "'Your respected mother was rather jealous of her son, maybe; when I say her son, I mean your worthy self, your worthy self. . . . Those times, however, pursued Mr Casby, 'are past and gone, past and gone. I do myself the pleasure of making a visit to your respected mother occasionally, and of admiring the fortitude and strength of mind with which she bears her trials, bears her trials'" (188). Toward the end of the story, Arthur himself has been imprisoned in Marshalsea for debt, and Little Dorrit comes to see him; at the end of her long speech she twice uses a triple epizeuxis: "'I can't think of you here where I have seen so much, and be as calm and comforting as I ought. My tears will make their way. I cannot keep them back. But pray, pray, pray, do not turn from your Little Dorrit, now, in your affliction! Pray, pray, pray, I beg you and implore you with all my grieving heart, my friend—dear!—take all I have, and make it a Blessing to me!'" (828). Epizeuxis is frequent throughout the novel, but toward the end the examples seem to be more emphatic.[3]

Dickens is very fond of palilogia, the frequent use of a word, either in a short space or throughout the whole text. A word repeated throughout a text is likely to be a keyword. The word "gentleman" is a keyword in

Little Dorrit, but it has two uses, one emphatic and one less so. In its less emphatic use, the word is simply a more or less neutral word for an adult male of a certain respectability; the emphatic use, which is more frequent, occurs in situations where its application is questionable; in this emphatic use, the word tends to appear in clumps. For instance, the word occurs at the beginning of the novel, when we first meet Rigaud, who is in prison for a tawdry murder but who insists on his respectability. He refers to himself as a gentleman once on page 46, six times on page 47, three times on page 48, and once more on page 49. The word is then used in its neutral sense on pages 61 and 62, but then it disappears until page 98, when it refers to Mr. Dorrit, as he enters the debtors' prison. It appears once each on pages 100, 101, 104, 121, 123, 124, 128, and 137; all of these refer directly to Mr. Dorrit or more generally to the debtors' prison. Those in the next clump all refer to civil servants in the Circumlocution Office: twice on page 146, seven times on page 147, once on page 149, twice on page 151, once on page 153, twice on page 154, five times on page 155, and twice on page 156. The next clump again refers to Rigaud, six times from pages 172 to 174. There are incidental and probably neutral uses on pages 180, 187, 205, 208, and 210; and then another clump of six on pages 245 to 253, all but one referring to Henry Gowan, Arthur Clennam's rival for the affections of Millie Meagles. And so on. Without belaboring the point, there is a strong tendency throughout the novel for the word to be used in reference to Rigaud, Mr. Dorrit, the civil servants in the Circumlocution Office, and Henry Gowan; in each case there is some irony at least in the application of the word.

Sometimes the repetition of a word occurs only within a short space; I call this local palilogia. The repetition may fall within one or two sentences, as "bottle-green" appears in the following passage, a description of Mr. Casby, Flora's father: "Upon this Mr Casby rose up in his list shoes, and with a slow heavy step (he was of an elephantine build), made for the door. He had a long wide-skirted bottle-green coat on, and a bottle-green pair of trousers, and a bottle green waistcoat. The Patriarchs were not dressed in bottle-green broadcloth, and yet his clothes looked patriarchal" (189). Repetitions concentrated within a paragraph or two are common: "There was a dinner giving in the Harley Street establishment, while Little Dorrit was stitching her father's new shirts by his side that night; and there were magnates from the court and magnates from the

City, magnates from the Common and magnates from the Lords, magnates from the bench and magnates from the bar, Bishop magnates, Treasury magnates, Horse Guard magnates, Admiralty magnates—all the magnates that keep us going, and sometimes trip us up" (294). The beginning of Book the Second has a very striking instance of local palilogia, with the word "grapes" repeated eight times in a single paragraph.

Sometimes the repetitions in palilogia may also occur with *polyptoton,* where a word appears in more than one form, as "cloud" and "clouds" and "cloudy" appear in the following: "Up here in the clouds everything was seen through a cloud, and seemed dissolving into cloud. The breath of the men was cloud, the breath of the mules was cloud, the lights were encircled by cloud, speakers close at hand were not seen for cloud, though their voices and all other sounds were surprisingly clear. Of the cloudy line of mules hastily tied to rings in the wall . . ." (484). And here is another instance of polyptoton, as the villain Rigaud is on the tramp:

"I, hungry, thirsty, weary. You, imbeciles, where the lights are yonder, eating and drinking, and warming yourselves at fires! I wish I had the sacking of your town; I would repay you, my children!"

But the teeth he set at the town, and the hand he shook at the town, brought the town no nearer; and the man was yet hungrier, and thirstier, and wearier, when his feet were on its jagged pavement, and he stood looking about him. (166)

This polyptoton involves the positive and comparative degrees of the adjectives: hungry/hungrier; thirsty/thirstier; weary/wearier. In addition, "hungry" matches "eating," "thirsty" matches "drinking," and "weary" (almost) matches "warming yourselves at fires." In the following example Dickens directly comments on the construction of the figure: "The doctor's friend was in the positive degree of hoarseness, puffiness, redfacedness, all fours, tobacco, dirt, and brandy; the doctor in the comparative—hoarser, puffier, more red-faced, more all-fourey, tobaccoer, dirtier, and brandier" (100). In this example and in the next Dickens invents words to make the polyptoton work; here Tip is taking over the position of doing small tasks for the inmates of the debtors' prison: "Then Mrs Bangham, long popular medium of communication with the outer world, began to be infirm, and to be found oftener than usual comatose on pavements, with her basket of purchases spilt, and the change of her clients ninepence short. [Mr. Dorrit's] son began to supersede Mrs Bangham, and to execute commissions in a knowing manner, and to be of the prison prisonous, of the streets streety" (105). Here Dickens is probably alluding to a famous biblical text, which refers to Adam and then to Christ: "The first man was of the earth earthly, and second man was the Lord from Heaven heavenly" (1 Corinthians 15.45).

Repetitions often create emphasis, but they can also create considerable emotion. Just before the following passage, Arthur Clennam has paid off the debt owed by Little Dorrit's brother Tip, so he can get out of prison. Arthur has tried to keep this act of generosity a secret from Little Dorrit, but of course she guesses, and she tells him what she would say to her benefactor if she knew his identity:

> "And what I was going to say, sir, is," said Little Dorrit, trembling more and more, "that if I knew him, and I might, I would tell him that he can never, never know how I feel his goodness, and how my good father would feel it. And what I was going to say, sir, is, that if I knew him, and I might—but I don't know him and I must not—I know that!— I would tell him that I shall never any more lie down to sleep without having prayed to Heaven to bless him and reward him. And if I knew him, and I might, I would go down on my knees to him, and take his hand and kiss it and ask him not to draw it away, but to leave it—O to leave it for a moment—and let my thankful tears fall on it; for I have no other thanks to give him!" (210–11)

I am not sure that there are precise technical terms for the various kinds of repetition we find here, but the effect is evident. We can also notice the stage direction included in the dialogue, as Little Dorrit does indeed take Clennam's hand and kiss it.

Dickens uses repetition as a mark of character traits. The villain Rigaud, for instance, is characterized by his physiognomy:

> When Monsieur Rigaud laughed, a change took place in his face that was more remarkable than prepossessing. His moustache went up under his nose, and his nose came down over his moustache, in a very sinister and cruel manner. (44)

As she placed the soup before the guest, who changed his attitude to a sitting one, he looked her full in the face, and his moustache went up under his nose, and his nose came down over his moustache. (169)

He laughed at Mistress Affery's start and cry; and as he laughed, his moustache went up under his nose, and his nose came down over his moustache. (393)

In the second and third passages, the name of the character has not been used, but the repeated description tells the reader who it is. Rigaud also has characteristic turns of phrase:

"I am sensitive and brave. I do not advance it as a merit to be sensitive and brave, but it is my character . . . and I too am a man whose character it is to govern. . . . Frankness is a part of my character." (49–50)

"You know that I am sensitive and brave, and that it is my character to govern." (174)

"Now, madame, frankly—frankness is part of my character—shall I open the door for you?" . . . "Let me make, then, a fair proposal. Fairness is a part of my character." (394)

This kind of repetition of traits and phrases is a fundamental feature of Dickens's depiction of characters. Traditional rhetoric does not have a name for this technique, but in more recent times critics have used the term *leitmotif.*

Anaphora and epizeuxis and palilogia are very frequent in *Little Dorrit,* but a number of other figures may be found as well. The following is a list of some of these less frequent figures.

Gradatio or climax: repetition in the form AB/BC/CD, and so on. Dickens doesn't use it much, but it does occur. Here is one instance: "The bell at the gate had scarcely sounded when Mr Meagles came out to receive them. Mr Meagles had scarcely come out, when Mrs Meagles came out. Mrs Meagles had scarcely come out, when Pet came out. Pet had scarcely come out, when Tattycoram came out. Never had visitors a more hospitable reception" (235). And another:

Jeremiah made all despatch and said, on his return, "She'll be glad to see you, sir; but, being conscious that her sick room has no attractions, wishes me to say that she won't hold you to your offer, if you should think better of it.

"To think better of it," returned the gallant Blandois, "would be to slight a lady; to slight a lady would be to be deficient in chivalry towards the sex; and chivalry towards the sex is a part of my character!" (401)

Chiasmus: repetition in the form AB:BA, as in "Either the nation was under a load of obligation to the Barnacles, or the Barnacles were under a load of obligation to the nation" (148, see also 206, 374).

Tricolon: the arrangement of words or clauses in sets of three. Tricolon can occur at different levels of structure, from words to phrases to clauses and even larger structures. Garret Stewart (2001, 67) notes Dickens's fondness for triplet adjectives, such as "It was a Sunday evening in London, gloomy, close, and stale." As this same passage continues, we find a triplet of antitheses: "Maddening church bells of all degrees of dissonance, sharp and flat, cracked and clear, fast and slow, made the brick-and-mortar echoes hideous." Then a little later in the same passage, a triplet of prepositional phrases and a triplet of participles: "In every thoroughfare, up almost every alley, and down almost every turning, some doleful bell was throbbing, jerking, tolling, as if the Plague were in the city and the dead-carts were going round." And then a few sentences later a doubled triplet in epizeuxis: "Nothing to see but streets, streets, streets. Nothing to breathe but streets, streets, streets" (67–68).

Very often the phrases in tricolon form parallel structure, more or less exact. The three phrases in the tricolon quoted above are almost the same length, but not quite; Dickens thus avoids isocolon, which is a common feature of emphatic tricolon. In another common form, called tricolon crescendo, the three clauses increase in length: "'I have met him twice. Both times near home. Both times at night, when I was going back. Both times I thought (though that may easily be my mistake), that he hardly looked as if he had met me by accident'" (213). When Miss Ward is convincing Tattycoram not to return to the Meagles to be Millie's companion, she uses a tricolon crescendo: "You can be, again, a foil to his pretty daughter, a slave to her pleasant wilfulness, and a toy in the house showing the goodness of the family" (377).

Dickens also sometimes makes use of erotesis, a general term for rhetorical questions. There are also more specific forms of questioning. Pysma is the asking of a series of questions: "'What does it matter whether I eat or starve? What does it matter whether such a blighted life as mine comes to an end, now, next week, or next year? What am I worth to any-one? A poor prisoner, fed on alms and broken victuals; a squalid, disgraced wretch!'" (272). Asking a question and giving the answer is hypophora:

"And yet I have some respect here. I have made some stand against it. I am not quite trodden down. Go out and ask who is the chief person in the place. They'll tell you it's your father. Go out and ask who is never trifled with, and who is always treated with some delicacy. They'll say, your father. Go out and ask what funeral here (it must be here, I know it can be nowhere else) will make more talk, and perhaps more grief, than any that has ever gone out at the gate. They'll say your father's. Well then. Amy! Amy! Is your father so universally despised? Is there nothing to redeem him? Will you have nothing to remember him by but his ruin and decay? Will you be able to have no affection for him when he is gone, poor castaway, gone?" (273)

Polysyndeton, the repetition of conjunctions, is also to be found in *Little Dorrit*: "There was the girls and their mothers a working at their sewing, or their shoe-binding, or their trimming, or their waistcoat mak-ing, day and night and night and day" (184; see also 518). The absence of a conjunction where it would be expected is called asyndeton: "Poor as you see us, master, we're always grinding, drudging, toiling, every minute we're awake" (202).

Little Dorrit also employs antithesis, the conjoining of oppositions. In a sense the whole of *the novel* is structured as an antithesis: Book the First is titled "Poverty," Book the Second is titled "Riches." The movement of the novel is actually more complex than this static antithesis might sug-gest. In Book the First, the Dorrits begin in poverty and then become rich; in Book the Second, they begin rich and end poor once again.

Small-scale antitheses also occur. Little Dorrit, for instance, is "a slen-der child in body, a strong heroine in soul" (433). In another passage John Chivery has got himself dressed up to make a declaration of affection to Little Dorrit: "There really was a genuineness in the poor fellow, and a contrast between the hardness of his hat and the softness of his heart (albeit, perhaps, of his head, too), that was moving" (262). The following passage contrasts the two brothers, William Dorrit (who is imprisoned for debt) and Frederick Dorrit (who makes a poor living as a musician): "Frederick the free, was so humbled, bowed, withered, and faded; William the bond, was so courtly, condescending, and benevolently conscious of a position; that in this regard only, if in no other, the brothers were a spectacle to wonder at" (264). And the antithesis is continued: "As the brothers paced the yard, William the bond looked about him to receive salutes, returned them by graciously lifting off his hat, and, with an engaging air, prevented Frederick the free from running against the company, or being jostled by the wall" (266). The antithesis contrasts the pride of the brother who is in debtor's prison and the abasement of the brother who is free, in a sense, though hardly more well off than his debtor brother.

Zeugma or syllepsis occurs when a verb takes two different kinds of objects; here Arthur Clennam and his business partner Daniel Doyce are going to visit the Meagles: "The senior partner took the coach, and the junior partner took his walking stick" (381; see also 270). To take a coach is to get into it, to take a walking stick is to pick it up. Garrett Stewart (2001) finds many instances of zeugma (which he calls syllepsis) in Dickens generally and in *Little Dorrit* specifically; in his view this figure is essential to Dickens's tendency to confound the human and material aspects of reality.

Aposiopesis occurs when a person falls silent in the middle of speaking. Aposiopesis is most effective when the silence is caused by embarrassment or some other strong emotion. Here Little Dorrit and her friend Maggy have come to visit Arthur on a cold night, and Arthur is worried about them: "'And I have no fire,' said Clennam. 'And you are—' He was going to say so lightly clad, but stopped himself in what would have been a reference to her poverty, saying instead, 'And it is so cold'" (209). Here Arthur and Daniel Doyce are talking about Minnie Meagles: Arthur is in love with her, as Daniel knows, but she is in love with Henry Gowan, though her parents disapprove. Daniel says:

> "The truth is, [her father] has twice taken his daughter abroad in the hope of separating her from Mr Gowan. He rather thinks she is disposed to like him, and he has painful doubts (I quite agree with him, as I dare say you do) of the hopefulness of such a marriage."

"There—" Clennam choked, and coughed, and stopped.

"Yes, you have taken cold," said Daniel Doyce. But without looking at him.

"—There is an engagement between them, of course," said Clennam airily. (253; see also183, 296, 355)

Epitheton can be simply the use of adjectives, as in this description of Plornish, the plasterer who is a friend of Mr. Dorrit from the prison: "A smooth-cheeked, fresh-coloured, sandy-whiskered man of thirty. Long in the legs, yielding in the knees, foolish in the face, flannel-jacketed, lime-whitened" (179). But epitheton can also occur when a descriptive term is used instead of a name; thus Flora's father, Mr. Casby, is regularly called "The Patriarch."

Periodic construction occurs when the grammar of a sentence is suspended by subordinate structures until it is finally brought to a close at the end. Periods are relatively easy to construct in Latin, but they can be somewhat awkward in English. Dickens does use a few. In the following passage Arthur is trying to argue himself out of falling in love with Minnie Meagles:

"Suppose that a man," so his thoughts ran, "who had been of age some twenty years or so; who was a diffident man, from the circumstances of his youth; who was rather a grave man, from the tenor of his life; who knew himself to be deficient in many little engaging qualities which he admired in others, from having been long in a distant region, with nothing softening near him; who had no kind sister to present to her; who had no congenial home to make her known in; who was a stranger in the land; who had not a fortune to compensate, in any measure, for these defects; who had nothing in his favour but his honest love and his general wish to do right—suppose such a man were to come in the house, and were to yield to the captivation of this charming girl, and were to persuade himself that he could hope to win her; what a weakness it would be!" (244; see also 145, 254, 444)

This brief account of the style of *Little Dorrit* has noted nearly thirty figures: congeries, anaphora, alliteration, epistrophe, epizeuxis (and diacope), palilogia, variatio, erotesis (and pysma and hypophora), tricolon and tricolon crescendo, polysyndeton and asyndeton, parallel structure, periodic structure, leitmotif, epanalepsis, rings, gradatio or climax, chiasmus, isocolon, antithesis, zeugma or syllepsis, aposiopesis, and epitheton.

This account is by no means complete; it leaves out, for example, the tropes—such as metaphor, simile, metonymy, and irony—and it does not attempt to relate the figures to the themes of the story. It does suggest, however, the extent of Dickens's use of the figures. Every page shows attention to the arts of language, and many passages are almost exercises in rhetorical technique. This style is not transparent: the language fairly jumps off the page and waves its arms for attention. The play of figures is essential to the experience of reading *Little Dorrit.* Each figure has a meaning where it occurs in the story, but there is also a cumulative effect. It is not easy to characterize this effect with precision; I would say that the constant figuration creates a kind of vivid emotion, heightened almost to the point of sensationalism.

Rhetorical Figures in *Agnes Grey*

Different rhetorical styles can have very different effects. Consider, for example, the first chapter of Anne Brontë's novel *Agnes Grey;* this is just as rhetorical as *Little Dorrit,* but the rhetoric here is in the service of a very different representation of reality. The more emotionally charged figures, such as epizeuxis or aposiopesis, are absent; instead figures such as antithesis and parallelism dominate, and they are used in the service of a kind of intellectual analysis. Here is the first paragraph, in the voice of Agnes, the first-person narrator:

> All true histories contain instruction; though, in some, the treasure may be hard to find, and when found, so trivial in quantity, that the dry, shrivelled kernel scarcely compensates for the trouble of cracking the nut. Whether this be the case with my history or not, I am hardly competent to judge. I sometimes think it might prove useful to some, and entertaining to others; but the world may judge for itself. Shielded by my own obscurity, and by the lapse of years, and a few fictitious names, I do not fear to venture; and will candidly lay before the public what I would not disclose to the most intimate friend. (2019, 5)

The first sentence is complex: it begins with a gnomic statement ("All true histories contain instruction"), which is then extended by a concessive clause ("though, in some, the treasure may be hard to find"), which narrows the scope from "all" to "some"; this clause in turn is extended by a conjoined qualifying phrase ("and when found, so trivial in quantity . . ."); and the sentence ends with a metaphor in a result clause ("that the dry shrivelled kernel scarcely compensates for the cracking of the nut"). The varied forms "to find" and "found" make a polyptoton, and "kernel" contrasts with "nut." It is truly a pleasure to read such a complex sentence so neatly turned. The author of such a sentence must be a careful artist and a clear thinker. Thus the reader can deduce something about the character of the narrator, Agnes. She has a command of complex grammatical constructions and the complex thoughts they express. Her impulse is to represent a world in order—balanced, parallel, organized. The figurative level of rhetoric contributes to the representation of character, and these lead to the presentation of a certain conception of reality.

This impression of the narrative voice is confirmed as the paragraph continues. The second and third sentences may be treated together, since the second introduces an idea ("I am hardly competent to judge") that is completed in antithesis at the end of the third ("the world may judge for itself"). Moreover, the beginning of the third sentence includes a careful parallel construction ("useful to some, and entertaining to others"). The fourth sentence ends with the antithesis "public" and "most intimate friend."

The carefully balanced constructions continue throughout the chapter. The second paragraph introduces Agnes's parents and their circumstances: her father was a clergyman of modest means, while her mother was the daughter of a prosperous squire, who disapproved of the match and threatened to disinherit his daughter: by her marriage she would lose her carriage and her maid: "A carriage and a lady's-maid were great conveniences; but, thank heaven, she had feet to carry her, and hands to minister to her own necessities." Here "carriage" is parallel to "feet to carry her," while "lady's-maid" is parallel to "hands to minister to her own necessities." The paragraph ends with an antithesis within an antithesis: "An elegant house and spacious grounds were not to be despised, but she would rather live in a cottage with Richard Grey than in a palace with any other man in the world." The structure is "A but (B rather than C)." Throughout this long paragraph—too long to quote conveniently—there is a consistent parallelism—on the one hand, Agnes's father, on the other, her mother.

At any rate, they did marry, and happily. Of six children, two survived, Mary and Agnes. Agnes was the younger by five or six years and was spoiled by her parents and sister:

> not by foolish indulgence
>> to render me fractious and ungovernable,
> but by ceaseless kindness,
>> to make me too helpless and dependent. (6)

Mary and Agnes were educated at home, but Agnes developed a desire to see more of the world. Meanwhile, Agnes's father worried about money and contrived schemes to increase his little fortune. He did not go into debt, but he spent what he had: "he liked to see his house comfortable, and his wife and daughters well clothed, and well attended; and besides, he was charitably disposed, and liked to give to the poor, according to his means: or, as some might think, beyond them." Eventually he invested with a friendly merchant; but despite his "bright hopes and sanguine expectations," the merchant was shipwrecked, and their investment was lost. The phrases "bright hopes" and "sanguine expectations" are more or less synonymous. Synonymous doublets are common from the Renaissance through the neoclassical period; by Brontë's time they were dropping out of fashion, but this chapter shows several examples.

Agnes soon recovered from the shock of their loss: "Though riches had charms, poverty had no terrors . . . there was something exhilarating in the idea of being driven to straits, and thrown upon our own resources." Again an antithesis ("riches . . . charms" and "poverty . . . terror") and a synonymous doublet ("driven to straits" and "thrown on our own resources"). Anges wished that

> instead of lamenting past calamities
> we might all cheerfully set to work to remedy them
>> and the greater the difficulties,
>> the harder our present privations,
>> the greater should be our cheerfulness to endure the latter,
>>> and our vigour to contend against the former. (8)

Mary sank into a depression, which Agnes could not assuage; she was afraid of being charged with "childish frivolity, or stupid insensibility," so she kept her "bright ideas and cheering notions" to herself. Her father also became depressed:

> In vain my mother strove to cheer him,
> > by appealing to his piety,
> > > to his courage,
> > > > to his affection for herself and us.
> That very affection was his greatest torment:
> > it was for our sakes he had so ardently longed to increase his fortune—
> > it was our interest that had lent such brightness to his hopes,
> > > and that imparted such bitterness to his present distress. (8)

He was particularly upset to see his wife reduced to household labor. He was tortured by

> the very willingness with which she performed these duties,
> the cheerfulness with which she bore her reverses,
> and the kindness which withheld her from imputing the smallest
> > blame to him . . . (9)

The pattern of parallelism and antithesis continues, but this summary is enough to make the point. This passage from *Agnes Grey* is just as rhetorical as the passages from *Little Dorrit,* but the rhetoric is very different. Anne Brontë is writing in a neoclassical manner, marked by balanced constructions, parallelism, synonymous doublets, and antithesis. (Her style in *The Tenant of Wildfeld Hall,* however, is more romantic.) Dickens's rhetoric creates a feeling of heightened emotion, but Brontë's manner is more distant, intellectual, and analytic. Neither style is transparent; each asks for attention—but where Brontë guides our thoughts, Dickens guides our feelings.

Rhetorical Figures in *Jazz*
The language of Toni Morrison's *Jazz* is highly rhetorical; Morrison uses many of the traditional rhetorical figures, but she also uses—and foregrounds—figures that don't appear in the handbooks.

The novel tells two main stories, one set inside the other, along with some other related incidents. The outside story takes place in 1926; the three main characters are a married couple, Joe Trace and Violet Trace, and a high-school student, Dorcas, whom Joe loves and kills; at the end of the story a friend of Dorcas, Felice, fills the slot vacated by the death of Dorcas: "I saw the three of them, Felice, Joe, and Violet, and they looked like a mirror image of Dorcas, Joe, and Violet" (2004, 221). The inset story takes place many years earlier, from the 1880s into the 1890s; the main characters are Golden Gray, a young man of mixed race who has been raised white, and a young black woman, called Wild, who lives by herself in the woods of Virginia. As it turns out, the nurse who raised Golden Gray, True Belle, is Violet Trace's grandmother, and Wild is (probably) Joe Trace's mother, so the two stories are connected. There is much to discuss about the position of the narrator and the moral issues raised by the events, but in this section, I want to examine some aspects of Morrison's style.

Morrison uses many of the traditional rhetorical figures. I have found instances of oxymoron: "sad and happy" (3; also 28); chiasmus: "I walked and worked, worked and walked" (126; also 76); epistrophe: "It made her bold. Even as a nine-year-old in elementary school she was bold" (61; also 155); and epizeuxis: "At last, at last, everything's ahead" (7; also 15, 35, 100, 103). There is one extended congeries (10), and one sentence that I would consider a suspended period (138). Morrison uses tricolon, sometimes combined with other figures, such as alliteration (50), parallel structure (32), or anaphora (4, 15; see also 11, 29, 31, 34, 113). There are several instances of local palilogia ("cracks" on 22–23; "cold," "drums," and "marching" on 53–54; "rope" on 58–60), and a few instances of polyptoton, where a root is used in two different parts of speech: "the hurt hurt her" (54), "the anticipation it anticipates" (65). Repetition sometimes is varied: "Some nights are silent" becomes "this totally silent night" (59); "a kind of skipping, running light traveled her veins" (19) becomes "The memory of the light, however, that had skipped through her veins came back now and then" (22); "And they thought men were ridiculous and delicious and terrible" (70–71) becomes "So they looked right at him and told him any way they could how ridiculous he was, and how delicious and how terrible" (71).

Thus we see many of the traditional figures in *Jazz:* oxymoron, epizeuxis, chiasmus, epistrophe, congeries, tricolon, anaphora, palilogia, periodic construction, polyptoton, and anadiplosis—and one could add more, such as alliteration, antithesis, erotesis, polysyndeton, zeugma, simile, and metaphor. Morrison clearly has the whole rhetorical tool kit at her disposal, but for the most part she uses these figures rather sparingly. Most of these traditional figures occur just once or twice or a few times; there is nothing like the profusion of figures we find in *Little Dorrit,* and nothing like the carefully balanced and complex syntax we find in *Agnes Gray.* A sensitive reader of the novel will probably feel that the enumerating of the traditional figures misses the essence of Morrison's style—or styles.

For *Jazz* is not written in a single style. I'm not sure how many styles should be distinguished, but a few stand out. First there is the style of the characters speaking to each other. There isn't a lot of dialogue in the novel, but what there is mostly represents African American Vernacular English. In the following passage Joe Trace is trying to convince his neighbor Malvonne to let him use her apartment for his trysts with Dorcas:

> "A favor you might say."
> "Or I might not say?"
> "You will. It's a favor to me, but a little pocket change for you."
> Malvonne laughed. "Out with it, Joe. This something Violet ain't in on?"
> "Well. She. This is. Vi is. I'm not going to disturb her with this, you know?"
> "No. Tell me."
> "Well. I'd like to rent your place."
> "What?"
> "Just a afternoon or two, every now and then. While you at work. But I'll pay for the whole month."
> "What you up to, Joe? You know I work at night."

Here Morrison represents some of the features of African American Vernacular, such as the omission of the present tense verb "to be" ("While you at work"; "What you up to, Joe?"), or the use of "a" rather than "an" before a vowel ("a afternoon"), as well as other features of speech, such as the broken sentences that show Joe's discomfort: "Well. She. This is. Vi is."

A second style is found in extended monologues: in Section Eight, Dorcas tells no one in particular about breaking up with Joe; this monologue may be, at least in part, her last thoughts after Joe has found her with her new boyfriend, Acton, and has shot her:

"He's here. Oh, look. God. He's crying. Am I falling? Why am I falling? Acton is holding me up but I am falling anyway. Heads are turning to look where I am falling. It's dark and now it's light. I am lying on a bed. Somebody is wiping sweat from my forehead, but I am cold, so cold. I see mouths moving; they are all saying something to me I can't hear. Way out there at the foot of the bed I see Acton. Blood is on his coat jacket and he is dabbing at it with a white handkerchief." (192)

In Section Five we hear Joe deliver a long monologue about Dorcas, and in Section Nine, we hear Dorcas's friend Felice deliver a long monologue, which covers a lot of territory, including Felice's own family, her friendship with Dorcas, what Felice knew about Dorcas and Joe, and about the night of the shooting. The language in these monologues is colloquial, but not dialect; but when Felice quotes other people, then she does use dialectical forms.

A third style is found when the narrator is talking to the reader about the characters. Here is the narrator's description of Violet, near the beginning of the story: "She is awfully skinny, Violet; fifty, but still good looking when she broke up the funeral. You'd think that being thrown out of the church would be the end of it—the shame and all—but it wasn't. Violet is mean enough and good looking enough to think that even without hips or youth she could punish Joe by getting herself a boyfriend and letting him visit in her own house" (4). This style is colloquial and conversational, but not African American Vernacular.

A fourth style is found in lyrical passages spoken by the narrator:

Daylight slants like a razor cutting the buildings in half. In the top half I see looking faces and it's not easy to tell which are people, which the work of stonemasons. Below is shadow where any blasé thing takes place: clarinets and lovemaking, fists and the voices of sorrowful women. A city like this one makes me dream tall and feel in on things. Hep. It's the bright steel rocking above the shade below that does it.

When I look over strips of green grass lining the river, at church stee-
ples and into the cream-and-copper halls of apartment buildings, I'm
strong. Alone, yes, but top-notch and indestructible—like the City in
1926 when all the wars are over and there will never be another one. The
people down there in the shadow are happy about that. At last, at last,
everything's ahead. The smart ones say so and people listening to them
and reading what they write down agree: Here comes the new. Look
out. there goes the sad stuff. The bad stuff. The things-nobody-could-
help stuff. The way everybody was then and there. Forget that. (7)

All of these styles have a certain conversational tone, which is established through the use of sentence fragments and colloquial diction. This
conversational tone is established at the very beginning of the novel: "Sth,
I know that woman. She used to live with a flock of birds on Lenox Avenue. Know her husband, too. He fell for an eighteen-year-old girl with one
of those deepdown, spooky loves that made him so sad and happy he shot
her just to keep the feeling going. When the woman, her name is Violet,
went to the funeral to see the girl and to cut her dead face they threw her
to the floor and out of the church" (3). The book begins with a word which
is not a word at all: "Sth, I know that woman." "Sth" is more a sound than
a word; it is not listed, for instance, in the *Oxford Dictionary of Canadian
English,* which does list "ow," "arf," "argh," and "tsk." Many critics have
commented on the initial "Sth" in *Jazz,* but they don't agree about its
meaning or function. Tracey Sherard (2000, 67) takes "Sth" to be "the
sound of a train slowing down and exhaling steam," or a representation
of the sound of a phonograph. Nick Pici (2000, 31) says that it "recalls the
sound of a ride cymbal." Eusebio Rodrigues (1993, 733) gives the sound
to another part of the drum kit—"'Sth' is "like the muted soundsplash of
a brush against a snare drum"—but then he adds that "a woman's voice
cautions in a whisper." According to Zoltán Abádi-Nagy, the initial "sth"
"definitely identifies a woman, it is something only women say"; the
sound "is meant to catch the reader's attention," but it is "also a word of
disapproval" (2008, 29).

The sound of a train, a phonograph needle sliding into the groove, a
ride cymbal, a brush on a snare drum, a woman's cautious whisper, a word
to catch the reader's attention or to signal disapproval—I would say the
interpretation is up for grabs. But whatever the meaning, the emphatic

position of this non-word sound suggests that Morrison wants us not just to see her words, but also to hear them. I have found two other instances of onomatopoeia in the book: when Dorcas was a young girl in East St. Louis, her house was burned during a riot and her parents were killed; in this section "Sst" represents the sound of a match being lit and starting a fire (61); and when Joe shoots Dorcas, the gun goes "thuh" (130). Sound, and especially music, is a continuing theme of the novel, as indicated by the title itself and by the many references to music throughout.

"Sth, I know that woman." Who is "I"? The first- and second-person pronouns are particularly characteristic of conversation: we know who is "I" and who is "you" only from their position within the discourse; they have no meaning independent of the person speaking and the person spoken to, and they shift back and forth in dialogue: I am "I" to myself but "you" to you. The narrator of *Jazz* assumes that she (he?) is known and does not need to be identified—but the identity of the narrator is a point of critical controversy. (I would suggest that the narrator is the book personified.) The phrase "that woman" also suggests that the woman in question has already been mentioned, perhaps by the narrator's now silent interlocutor. We seem to be in the middle of a conversation.

"Know her husband, too." This is the first of many sentence fragments in *Jazz*. The characters use fragments regularly, and so does the narrator. The grammar of conversation is often fragmentary; people talking to each other face-to-face depend on the context to fill in the blanks. In written texts, however, sentences are usually complete grammatical constructions. Even Huck Finn, whose grammar is hardly standard, generally uses complete sentences. In literature written before the twentieth century incomplete sentences are generally used for special effects, and usually in the mouths of characters rather than narrators, as we saw in chapter 1. (The beginning of *Bleak House* is an interesting exception, or, in Classical literature, the beginning of *Leucippe and Clitophon*.)

The grammar of this fragment—"Know her husband, too"—is clear: the subject has been dropped, but it can easily be supplied from the first sentence—"Sth, I know that woman." In general Morrison's fragments are easy to understand. On page 5 we read that Violet gathers information about Dorcas, the girl her husband fell in love with and killed: "Maybe she thought she could solve the mystery of love that way. Good luck and let me know." The phrase "good luck," of course, is a normal conversational form, though it can have different meanings depending on the tone of voice; the full phrase "Good luck and let me know" means more or less "Fat chance." Later, on the same page, the narrator tells us what Violet has found out about Dorcas: her address, her family, what kind of lip rouge she wore, and what dance steps Dorcas used to do: "All that."

There are countless fragments throughout the novel, and there is no point in attempting a complete list; a few more examples will suffice. On page 7: "A city like this one makes me dream tall and feel in on things. Hep." Also on page 7: "Here comes the new. Look out. There goes the sad stuff. The bad stuff. The things-nobody-could-help stuff." On page 9: "People say I should come out more. Mix." Also on page 9: "Word was that underneath the good times and the easy money something evil ran the streets and nothing was safe—not even the dead. Proof of this being Violet's outright attack on the very subject of a funeral ceremony. Barely three days into 1926." Sometimes a series of fragments act as a kind of moving spotlight: "The City is smart at this: smelling good and looking raunchy; sending secret messages disguised as public signs: this way, open here, danger to let colored only single men on sale woman wanted private room stop dog on premises absolutely no money down fresh chicken free delivery fast" (64; see also 10, 33, 78). Fragments are not recognized in traditional rhetoric, but the fragments in *Jazz* are clearly a deliberate feature of Morrison's rhetoric, and they surely deserve notice and interpretation.

"He fell for an eighteen-year-old girl with one of those deepdown, spooky loves that made him so sad and happy he shot her just to keep the feeling going." The word "deepdown" is a sort of fused form. Morrison often fuses words together: "winterbound" (10); "citysky" (36); "white-people" (39); "whiteboy" (55); "sonofabitch" (94); "citylife" (107); "mammymade" (109). Fused forms can also be found, for example, in William Faulkner's *Absalom, Absalom*—"nothusband" (9); "notpeople" (10); "notlanguage" (10)—and in Katherine Anne Porter's *Ship of Fools*—"Oh, nonono, waitwait my love forgive me" (454). All of these are to be pronounced as single words. A fused form suggests a fused meaning, rather than the combination of two independent meanings: compare the phrase "blue bird" to the word "bluebird." A related figure is formed by a hyphenated string of words: "The things-nobody-could-help stuff" (7); "The cream-at-the-top-of-the-milkpail face of someone who will never work for anything" (12); "Resisting her aunt's protection and restraining hands, Dorcas thought of that life-below-the-sash as all the life there was" (60); "head-of-a-seamstress-head" (71); "A nice, neighborly, everybody-knows-him man" (73); "a story of a used-to-be-long-ago-crazy girl" (167). Sometimes Morrison uses fragments, fused forms, and hyphens together: "Bluesman. Black and bluesman. Blacktherefore blue man. . . . Where-did-she-go-and-why man. So-lonesome-I-could-die man" (119).

"When the woman, her name is Violet, went to the funeral to see the girl and to cut her dead face they threw her to the floor and out of the church" (3). Parenthetical constructions, such as "her name is Violet," and dislocations, such as "She is awfully skinny, Violet" (4) give a feeling that the sentences are not planned and edited, but constructed on the fly. It should be clear, however, that the improvisation is located in the narrator, not in the author, who has carefully planned the telling of the story so that it will appear unplanned.

The sense of improvisation can also be felt at larger levels of construction. The narrative is a kind of jumble of associations, as if the storyteller gets going on one thread, then drops it for another, while introducing people and incidents without explanation, only to pick up later a thread begun earlier, delivering little essays and sermons along the way. Many passages in the novel are incomplete and perhaps confusing on first reading; only on second reading do all the pieces fall into place.

The book as a whole is divided into ten (unnumbered) sections, which may as well be chapters. Each section or chapter in turn is composed of smaller units; some of these are marked by a row of asterisks or by space, but some breaks are not indicated by typography. I would divide the first chapter into eleven subsections, and the second chapter into ten. Often there is no clear progression, either of chronology or incident, from one subsection to the next. For instance, the book begins (pages 3 to 6) with Violet's scandalous behavior at Dorcas's funeral—this is perhaps the pivotal event of the whole story. This section ends with a line of three asterisks. The second subsection (pages 7 to 9, beginning "I'm crazy about this City") is a digression in general terms about the narrator's view of the City. The third subsection (pages 9 to 11), marked off by space, at first seems to return to the main story ("Armistice was seven years old the winter Violet disrupted the funeral"), but it quickly turns into another digression about life in the City at the time of Dorcas's funeral ("and veterans on Seventh Avenue were still wearing their army-issue greatcoats"). The next subsection (pages 11 to 14) now does return to the main story; this subsection is not marked by typography, but the transition is clearly indicated ("But up there on Lenox, in Violet and Joe Trace's apartment, the rooms are like the empty birdcages wrapped in cloth"). Other subsections are flashbacks: for instance, subsection eight (page 17) recounts a time when Violet just sat down in the street, while subsection nine (pages 17 to 22) recounts the time Violet was accused of stealing a baby.

The narrator often drops hints that become intelligible only later. In the seventh subsection of the first chapter, for instance, the narrator mentions True Belle, Violet's grandmother, and Golden Gray (without naming him):

> Not the kind of baby hair her grandmother had soaped and played with and remembered for forty years. The hair of the little boy who got his name from it. Maybe that is why Violet is a hairdresser—all those years of listening to her rescuing grandmother, True Belle, tell Baltimore stories. The years with Miss Vera Louise in the fine stone house on Edison Street, where the linen was embroidered with blue thread and there was nothing to do but raise and adore the blond boy who ran away from them depriving everybody of his carefully loved hair. (17; see also 97, 99–103)

Most of this is incomprehensible until the sixth chapter, when we finally read the story of Golden Gray and Wild.

The central event of the story, Joe's love affair with Dorcas, is narrated in bits and pieces over the whole extent of the novel. Dorcas is introduced on the first page, but without a name or any individual characterization: "He fell for an eighteen-year-old girl with one of those deepdown, spooky loves that made him so happy he shot her just to keep the feeling going. When the woman, her name is Violet, went to the funeral to see the girl and to cut her dead face they threw her to the floor and out of the church" (3). Dorcas is next mentioned, in a flashback, at the end of the first chapter: "Long before Joe stood in the drugstore watching a girl buy candy, Violet had stumbled into a crack or two" (23); then Violet (in the midst of another discussion) asks Joe about the girl: "Got a mind to double it with an aught and two or three others just in case who is that pretty girl standing next to you?" (24). Joe and Dorcas actually meet in the second chapter, when Joe is delivering beauty supplies:

> When he called on Sheila to deliver her Cleopatra order, he entered a roomful of laughing, teasing women—and there she was, standing at the door, holding it open for him—the same girl that had distracted him in the drugstore; the girl buying candy and ruining her skin had moved him so his eyes burned. Then, suddenly, there in Alice Manfred's doorway, she stood, toes pointing in, hair braided, not even smiling but welcoming him in for sure. For sure. Otherwise he would not have had the audacity, the nerve, to whisper to her at the door as he left. (29)

Dorcas now disappears from the story for a while, but in the third chapter the narrator brings us back to Joe's delivery of the beauty supplies: "The peppermint girl with the bad skin answered the door" (69). Here for the first time we learn her name, and here for the first time Joe speaks to her (69, 70). And here the narrator comments: "I always believed that girl was a pack of lies. I could tell in her walk her underclothes were beyond her years, even if her dress wasn't. Maybe back in October Alice was beginning to think so too. By the time January came, nobody had to speculate. Everybody knew" (72). Here and in the following pages the story is gradually filled in, but still just in bits and pieces, until the fifth chapter, which includes Joe's long monologue. Even this monologue is somewhat fragmented. Joe starts to talk about the first time he saw Dorcas—"All I know is I saw her buying candy and the whole thing was sweet" (121–22)—and then the first time he spoke with her, when he was delivering cosmetics to her aunt's apartment—"When I got to the apartment I had no name to put to the face I'd seen in the drugstore, and her face wasn't on my mind right then. But she opened the door" (122). Then the monologue veers off in another direction, as Joe tells about his childhood and his life before he met Dorcas (123–29). Dorcas returns in a new subsection, marked by a line of asterisks: "She had long hair and bad skin" (130). The shooting itself comes in the second paragraph of this subsection: "Right after the gun went thuh! and nobody in there heard it but me and that is why the crowd didn't scatter" (130). But even in the next paragraph the story turns back on itself, as Joe tells about his search for Dorcas, the search which ends with her murder.

This chapter ends without an ending; the sixth chapter turns the narrative back in time to the story of Golden Gray and Wild; and the seventh moves back and forth in time in a series of alternating short sections:

the young Joe searches for Wild (176–80)

the old Joe searches for Dorcas (180–82)

the young Joe searches for Wild (182)

the old Joe searches for Dorcas (182)

the young Joe searches for Wild (183)

the old Joe searches for Dorcas (183–84)

the young Joe searches for Wild (184)

In the eighth chapter Joe finds Dorcas: "There she is" (187). Most of this short chapter (after a couple of pages from the perspective of the narrator) is taken up by Dorcas's monologue: "He is coming for me. I know he is because I know how flat his eyes went when I told him not to" (189); "He is coming for me. And when he does he will see that I'm not his anymore" (191). Dorcas has a new boyfriend, someone her own age: "I'm Acton's and it's Acton I want to please" (191). Joe finds her at a party with Acton and shoots her: "He's here. Oh, look. He's crying. Am I falling? Why am I falling? Acton is holding me up but I am falling anyway" (192). Joe shot Dorcas in the fifth chapter—""Right after the gun went thuh! and nobody in there heard it but me and that is why the crowd didn't scatter" (130)—and now he shoots her in the eighth: "Am I falling? Why am I falling" (192).

And he shoots her also in the ninth chapter. Here Felice presents another version of the shooting and its circumstances, in bits and pieces. The first hint of a different view of the shooting comes in a throw-away line in Felice's monologue: "My mother wants me to find some good man to marry. I want a good job first. Make my own money. Like she did. Like Mrs. Trace. Like Mrs. Manfred used to do before Dorcas let herself die" (204). This hint is left unexplained for the moment, but the next paragraphs tell a little more: Felice feels bad that Joe is so broken up about Dorcas: "Cried all day and all night. Left his job and wasn't good for a thing. I suppose he misses Dorcas, and thinks about how he is her murderer. But he must not have known about her. How she liked to push people, men" (205). "I didn't go to the funeral. I saw her die like a fool and was too mad to be at her funeral" (205). And a few pages later Felice tells Joe and Violet her version of the shooting:

> "Dorcas let herself die. The bullet went in her shoulder, this way." I pointed. "She wouldn't let anybody move her; said she wanted to sleep and she would be all right. Said she'd go to the hospital in the morning. 'Don't let them call nobody,' she said. 'No ambulance, no police, no nobody.' I thought she didn't want her aunt, Mrs. Manfred, to know. Where she was and all. And the woman giving the party said okay because she was afraid to call the police. They all were. People just stood around talking and waiting. Some of them wanted to carry her downstairs, put her in a car and drive to the emergency ward. Dorcas said no. She said she was all right. To please leave her alone and let her rest. But I did it. Called the ambulance, I mean; but it didn't come until morning after I had called twice. The ice, they said, but really because it was colored people calling. She bled to death all through that woman's bed sheets on into the mattress, and I can tell you that woman didn't like it one bit. That's all she talked about. Her and Dorcas' boyfriend. The blood. What a mess it made. That's all they talked about." (209–10)

This account seems to blame Dorcas for her own death; does it therefore absolve Joe? It was Dorcas' decision not to go the hospital; but Felice did call an ambulance, which didn't arrive in time. It's not easy to pin down who exactly is responsible for what. A little later Felice tells Joe, "Even if you didn't kill her outright; even if she made herself die, it was you," and Joe agrees: "It was me. For the rest of my life, it'll be me" (212).

Dorcas's funeral occurs at the very beginning of the story, but the story of her affair with Joe and her death is spread out from the beginning to the end; much of the story doesn't make sense when it is told, and it is up to the reader to piece it all together. The narrative is carefully constructed to give the appearance of carelessness.

Composition in fragments thus runs from the level of sentence up to the creation of episodes and to the narration of the story as a whole. But to complement these fragments, perhaps to control them, Morrison also uses links of various sorts, again from the small to the large. In traditional rhetoric, a link from the end of one clause or sentence to the beginning of the next is called anadiplosis: "From the weeds to the carriage, from the carriage into this cabin" (154); "The illegal liquor is not secret and the secrets are not forbidden" (187); "Alice swore she wouldn't, but she did, pass it on. She passed it on to her baby sister's only child" (77). Some links cross from the end of one paragraph to the beginning of the next, in a figure we can call paragraph anadiplosis:

> Would a kindhearted innocent woman take a stroll with an infant she was asked to watch while its older sister ran back in the house, and laugh like that?
> The sister was screaming in front of her house. . . . (20)

> So Violet sprinkles the collars and cuffs. Then sudses with all her heart those three or four ounces of gray hair, soft and interesting as a baby's.
> Not the kind of baby hair her grandmother had soaped and played with and remembered for forty years. (17)

> Fifth Avenue was put into focus now and so was her protection of the newly orphaned girl in her charge.
> From then on she hid the girl's hair in braids. . . . (54)

Sometimes two subsections are linked; In the first chapter the second and third subsections are linked by Violet's name and the word "funeral"; the fifth and sixth subsections are linked by the word "rest"; the ninth and tenth subsections are linked by the word "cracks"; and so on.

The most striking links in *Jazz* are chapter links: each of the unnumbered sections ends with a word or an idea which is repeated at the beginning of the next section. The link from the first to the second chapter is "birds"; from the second to the third the link is "freezing" and "cool" to "cold"; from the third to the fourth the link is "hat"; from the fourth to the fifth the link is "spring" and "City"; from the fifth through the sixth the link is "state of mind"; from the sixth to seventh the link is "Golden Gray watched" and "Golden Gray stiffened himself to look at that girl"; from

the seventh to eighth the link is "But where is *she?*" to "There she is";
from the eighth to the ninth the link is "heart" to "Sweetheart"; and from
the ninth to the tenth the link is "pain." The technique is clear, though the
links are not mechanically exact.

Some of the chapter breaks divide what could have been unbroken
discourse connections. Thus the end of the first chapter—"He is married
to a woman who speaks mainly to her birds. One of whom answers back
'I love you.'"—is completed by a fragment at the beginning of the second chapter—"Or used to." The end of the second—"From freezing hot
to cool"—is completed by the beginning of the third—"Like that day in
July." The hat at the beginning of the fifth is the same as the hat at the end
of the fourth. And so on. Thus we see that the links are not just repetition
of a word of phrase; in general they mark discourse continuity across a
typographical division.

Perhaps the most interesting of these links, however, significantly
changes this pattern. The end of the seventh chapter asks a question—"But where is *she?*"—which seems to be answered at the beginning
of chapter 8—"There she is."—but the references of the two pronouns
are different: the "she" at the end of the seventh is Wild, the wild woman
found by Golden Gray in the inset story, while the "she" at the beginning
of the eighth is Dorcas. As Jean Wyatt notes, "the pronoun 'she' conflates
the two figures, formally reproducing the conflation of mother and lover
in Joe's mind" (2017, 49). The structure of this link implies the connection
between the main story and the inset story.

Chapter links are found in many novels—in Austen's *Emma,* for example: Volume I, from Chapter II to Chapter III ("Mr. Woodhouse");
from Chapter III to Chapter IV ("Miss Smith" and "Harriet Smith"); from
Chapter IV (skipping over the intrusive Chapter V) to Chapter VI ("Mr.
Elton"); from Chapter VI to Chapter VII ("Mr. Elton . . . London"); Chapter VII to Chapter VIII ("Harriet"); and so on; in Volume II, from Chapter
I to Chapter II ("Jane Fairfax"); from Chapter II to Chapter III ("Emma
could not forgive her"); and so on. The links in *Emma* are less obtrusive
than the links in *Jazz,* but they do create a sense of cohesion and connection from one chapter to the next.

I suspect that most readers don't pay much attention to the links in
Emma, and they have received no critical attention that I know of. The
links in *Jazz* are much more obvious, and critics *have* noticed them.

Wyatt (2017, 54; following Rubenstein 1998, 154) argues that these links derive from the call-and-response form of African American music and oratory. I am not convinced that these links have much to do with call-and-response form; the two parts of a link are repetition rather than a call and a response. Links are a regular feature of narrative technique; in *Jazz*, I think, they help to establish continuity in a fragmented narrative style.

Morrison also uses rings of various sizes, and these also help to create continuity. When Joe delivers the cosmetics to Alice Manfred's apartment, the reaction of the women to him forms a kind of paragraph ring: "They were women his age mostly, with husbands, children, grandchildren too. Hard workers for themselves and anyone who needed them. And they thought men were ridiculous and terrible. . . . So they looked right at him and told him any way they could how ridiculous he was, and how delicious and how terrible. As if he didn't know" (70–71). The beginning and the end of the first chapter form a ring: at the beginning, "the parrot that said 'I love you'" (3) and at the end, "He is married to a woman who speaks mainly to her birds. One of whom answers back: 'I love you'" (24). Of course there can be no link to the beginning of the first section, since nothing precedes it, but the ring in a way does what the link would have done. (This ring also provides the link to the next chapter.)

The whole of the fourth chapter is a ring. This chapter includes several events at several different times, but everything in effect takes place while Violet is sitting in the drugstore drinking a malt:

> The hat, pushed back on her forehead, gave Violet a scatty look. The calming effect of the tea Alice Manfred had given her did not last long. Afterward she sat in the drugstore sucking malt through a straw wondering who on earth that other Violet was that walked about the City in her skin and saw other things. (89)
>
> Committed as Violet was to hip development, even she couldn't drink the remaining malt—watery, warm, and flat-tasting. She buttoned her coat and left the drugstore and noticed, at the same moment as that Violet did, that it was spring. In the City. (114; see also 93, 97, 111).

There are also rings from the beginning of the book to the end. We learn at the beginning that Violet is not a legally licensed beautician, but she goes to the legally licensed beauticians to find out about Dorcas (5); then toward the end we learn that Felice found out about Dorcas and Joe from the licensed hairdressers (202). At the beginning of the story, the narrator predicts the end: "What turned out different was who shot whom" (6), and at the end we learn that the narrator was wrong: "So I missed it altogether. I was sure one would kill the other. I waited for it so I could describe it. I was so sure it would happen" (220). Also at the beginning we learn that Violet let her birds go (3), and at the end Violet buys another bird (223–24); these rings provide a kind of closure. Perhaps the story needs this triple ring because otherwise it is somewhat inconclusive. In general, the extensive repetitions of various kinds—palilogia, links, rings, and so on—hold together what is otherwise a collection of fragments.

In this chapter I have looked at three styles, in *Little Dorrit, Agnes Grey,* and *Jazz.* All of these are highly rhetorical, but in very different ways. Dickens throws in figure after figure to create a florid verbal texture; Brontë uses figures of balance and contrast rather than sensation; and Morrison's style is conversational and fragmented. In the next chapter I will examine two of the tropes, metaphor and simile.

6

Metaphor and Simile
in Homer, Chandler, and James

The Tropes

Chapter 4 presented an account of some rhetorical schemes, how they can work and what they can mean in specific narrative contexts; chapter 5 examined schemes in Charles Dickens, Anne Brontë, and Toni Morrison. This chapter is concerned with tropes, particularly metaphor and simile. My sample authors will be Homer, Raymond Chandler, and Henry James. As usual, I am not much interested in theoretical questions, except insofar as they grow out of or illuminate practical problems. But a few theoretical points about the tropes should be mentioned at least, if only to clear the ground.

First, the distinction between the schemes and tropes is not entirely clear. Some rhetoricians don't make the distinction, and those that do don't always agree about which figures to put in which category. Still, the two categories seem to have solid cores, even if there is some overlapping and some fuzziness around the edges. Schemes, by and large, involve the form of a sentence or two, including repetitions and omissions, while tropes involve a change of meaning. It is often possible to draw a diagram of a scheme— thus chiasmus is "A B B A," anadiplosis is "... A | A ...," and epanalepsis is "A ... A." Tropes are not defined by form, and so they generally can't be diagrammed; they are understood semantically rather than formally. Thus anaphora, the repetition of a word or phrase at the beginnings of successive clauses (A ... A ... A), is a scheme, since the repetition doesn't change the meaning of any of the repeated words. Polysyndeton, the repetition of conjunctions (A and B and C and D), also counts as a scheme, since the conjoined words don't change their meaning, and a sentence with polysyndeton has the same truth value as the sentence without polysyndeton. But when Achilles addresses Agamemnon as "You wine sack, with a dog's eyes, with a deer's heart" (*Il*.1.225), the literal meaning of the sentence isn't true; the words must mean something other than, or something in addition to, their literal meaning, and the figure is metaphor, which is a trope.

This distinction, however, fails to recognize that some schemes do change meaning. In a previous chapter I argued that the figure chiasmus (AB/BA) can reverse the dominance of the two items mentioned: thus the phrase "the philosophy of history" suggests that philosophy dominates history, while "the history of philosophy" suggests the opposite. Even a figure such as polysyndeton can have an effect on the meaning of a sentence, though the meaning of no individual word is changed, as I showed in a previous chapter with an example from *Ship of Fools*. Still, there is a kind of rough-and-ready usefulness in the distinction between schemes and tropes, if we don't worry too much about fuzziness. Some figures do seem to be more schematic, and others do seem to be more semantic. In any case, no important point in the discussion here will depend on a precise distinction between the schemes and the tropes.

There are many differing lists of the tropes and the schemes, and no list is universally accepted. Modern historians of rhetoric have given careful accounts of the various lists (see, for instance, Mack 2017), but the details don't matter for our purposes; it is enough to note that one list or another has included among the tropes metaphor, metonymy, synecdoche, simile, litotes, antonomasia, onomatopoeia, catachresis, metalepsis, hyperbole, irony, allegory, acyrologia, antiphrasis, and a number of others. Similes are not always counted as tropes: there is no change of meaning in the simile "Achilles is like a lion," whereas in the metaphor "Achilles is a lion," the word "lion" must mean something other than its usual meaning. There are good reasons, however, for keeping metaphor and simile in the same category. Some of these tropes seem to involve relatively unimportant changes of meaning—antonomasia: the use of an epithet rather than a proper name; metalepsis: a present effect attributed to a remote cause, while leaving out the intervening steps, so birth is the cause of death; acyrologia: use of an inexact or incorrect word, what we might today call a malapropism; antiphrasis: irony using a single word, such as calling a political opponent "my friend"—but any figure can be interesting if it is used in an interesting way.

Some rhetoricians preferred short lists of tropes. The Humanist rhetorician Peter Ramus (1515–1572) reduced the list to just four: metonymy, irony, metaphor, and synecdoche, though subdivision would bring in some of the others. In modern times, Kenneth Burke (1969, 503–517) called these four—metaphor, metonymy, synecdoche, and irony—the "Four Master Tropes." Roman Jakobson and Morris Halle (1971, 90–96) have argued that the two principal mechanisms of language are metaphor and metonymy, and furthermore, that poetry is particularly metaphoric while prose is metonymic. And Jeanne Fahnestock (1996, 14) notes, in a lovely gradatio, that "the tendency from the eighteenth century on has been to reduce rhetoric to the figures, the figures to the tropes, and the tropes to metaphor."

Of all the figures metaphor certainly has received the most attention. The theoretical literature on metaphor is enormous and varied.[1] I will comment on just a few theoretical points that are relevant to my topic.

Metaphor and simile are closely related. Both are comparisons and therefore both express or imply two terms to be compared. To take a very crude example, if we say (in a simile) that Achilles is like a lion, or (in a metaphor) that Achilles is a lion, we are seeing Achilles in terms of a lion. Using the terminology introduced by I. A. Richards, Achilles is the tenor of the metaphor or the simile and the lion is the vehicle. Both metaphor and simile assume that the best way to talk about something is to talk about something else. Some theorists suggest that these figures elucidate an unknown tenor by reference to a known vehicle—we know that a lion is fierce, and the fierceness of the lion tells us about the fierceness of Achilles—but we will see many examples that don't work that way.

A metaphor is not simply an abbreviated simile, a simile from which "like" has been omitted. There are many ways to express a metaphoric thought (see Brooke-Rose 1965). For instance, a metaphor can be a direct equation of the tenor and vehicle, usually using a copulative verb ("Achilles was a lion in battle"); but a metaphor can express the vehicle while leaving the tenor implicit ("The lion attacked Hektor"); or a metaphor can use the verb "to make" rather than a copulative ("Wrath made Achilles a lion in battle"); a metaphor can be expressed in a genitive construction ("The fire of wrath turned Achilles against the Trojans"); a metaphor can be expressed by an adjective ("The merciless spear of Achilles"); or a metaphor can be expressed by a verb ("Achilles' wrath blazed against the

Trojans"). It may be possible to translate these into similes, but usually with loss of effect. Similes also come in more than one form: for example, not just A is like B, but also A is as X as B, where X is an adjective ("Achilles is as fierce as a lion"), or a hypothetical simile ("Achilles fought as if he were a lion").

These metaphors and similes seem to be based on a point of similarity—both Achilles and the lion are fierce. The comparison has three elements: Achilles, the lion, and the point of comparison, fierceness. The point of comparison is called the *tertium comparationis*—the third element of the comparison. Often, especially in metaphor, the tertium comparationis is not stated; it has to be deduced from the comparison and its context. The tertium comparationis, however, does not exhaust the meaning of the metaphor: the metaphor does not just say that Achilles is fierce: it says that Achilles is fierce the way that a lion is fierce. The lion in its potential fullness is brought into the meaning of the comparison. This additional meaning can have various aspects—a cognitive aspect, a sensory aspect, and an emotive aspect—and these aspects themselves can merge or interact.

Eva Feder Kittay (1987, 22–23) proposes six points that characterize what she calls a "perspectival theory" of metaphor:

1. Metaphors are sentences, not isolated words.
2. A metaphor consists of two components.
3. There is a tension between these two components.
4. These components need to be understood as systems.
5. The meaning of a metaphor arises from an interplay of these components.
6. The meaning of a metaphor is irreducible and cognitive.

When Kittay says that the components need to be understood as systems, she means that both the topic (her term for what Richards calls the tenor) and the vehicle belong to semantic fields, and the interaction that makes the metaphor is an interaction not just of two words, but of two semantic fields. In a sense this must be trivially true, since words don't have meaning in isolation, but only in their relations to other words; but in another sense Kittay's model brings metaphor close to allegory as a system of metaphorical comparisons. In Kittay's model, a metaphor involves more than a single tertium comparationis: the comparison is not based on a single point of similarity, but on a comparison of systems.

According to Kittay (1987, 37), "The cognitive significance of metaphor arises from its capacity to restructure or to induce a structure on a given content domain": that is, more or less, the structure of the semantic field of the vehicle is used to restructure the semantic field of the topic. "Such structuring or restructuring will yield many implicated propositions, some literal some metaphorical. But no one statement from this implication will capture the full meaning of the metaphor"—and thus the metaphor cannot be simply paraphrased.

Kittay understands metaphor as fundamentally cognitive. I am not sure what cognitive means in this context. Often cognitive, or a similar term, is contrasted with emotive—so thinking is contrasted with feeling. Some theorists take metaphor to be fundamentally cognitive, but others take it to be emotive. According to Richards, "There are two totally distinct uses of language" (Richards 1925, 261): "A statement may be used for the sake of the *reference,* true or false, which it causes. This is the *scientific* use of language. But it may also be used for the sake of the effects in emotion and attitude produced by the reference it occasions. This is the emotive use of language. We may either use words for the sake of the references they promote, or we may use them for the sake of the attitudes and emotions which ensue" (Richards 1925, 267). Richards thus contrasts the emotive with the scientific, and in general he would place metaphor on the emotive side. But William Empson argues that "theorists on language, it seemed clear, were threatening to affect the ordinary practice of criticism when they claimed that literary metaphors are Essentially Emotive" (Empson 1967, 1–2). In other words, metaphors must be allowed to have a cognitive function.

Metaphor, according to Robert A. Nisbet (1969, 4), is "much more than a simple grammatical construction or figure of speech": "Metaphor is a way of knowing—one of the oldest, most deeply embedded, even indispensable ways of knowing in the history of human consciousness. It is, at its simplest, a way of proceeding from the known to the unknown. It is a way of cognition in which the identifying qualities of one thing are transferred in an instantaneous, almost unconscious, flash of insight to some other thing that is, by remoteness or complexity, unknown to us." The cognitive value of metaphor has been a central concern of much recent work on metaphor. In an important book and article (Lakoff and Johnson 1980a and 1980b), Lakoff and Johnson argue that "conventional metaphors are pervasive in our ordinary everyday way of thinking, speaking, and acting" and that "most of our ordinary conceptual system is metaphorical in nature" (Lakoff and Johnson 1980b, 453 and 454). For example, many common ways of speaking follow the metaphor that ARGUMENT IS WAR: thus "Your claims are indefensible"; "He attacked every weak point in my argument"; "His criticisms were right on target"; "I demolished his argument"; "I've never won an argument with him"; and so on (454). Another conceptual metaphor is TIME IS MONEY: "You're wasting my time"; "This gadget will save you hours"; "I don't have the time to give you"; "How do you spend your time these days?"; "That flat tire cost me an hour"; "I've invested a lot of time in her"; and so on (456).

The cognitive value of metaphor can be seen in many scientific models. Thus an electrical current can be understood through the metaphor of the flow of water through a pipe, where the amps are like the volume of the water and the volts are like the pressure of the water. One older model of atomic structure takes its form from the solar system: the nucleus is at the center, where the sun would be, and the electrons orbit around it, as the planets orbit around the sun. And Robert Nisbet (1969, 7) argues that the metaphor of organic growth pervades thought on social change: "When we say that a culture or institution or nation 'grows' or 'develops,' we have reference to change in time, but to change of a rather special and distinctive type. We are not referring to random and adventitious changes, to changes induced by some external deity or other being. We are referring to change that is intrinsic to the entity, to change that is held to be as much a part of the entity's nature as any purely structural element." Nisbet adds that this kind of organic change is directional; it is cumulative; it is irreversible; it has stages; and it has purpose. All of these aspects of organic growth are taken metaphorically to be characteristic of social change.

It is quite wrong, in my opinion, to erect a firm boundary between thinking and feeling, or to equate cognition with scientific thought. Many metaphors seem to combine the cognitive and emotive, though perhaps in an unequal distribution. This combination of qualities can be illustrated by three examples, two from Henry James and one from the ancient Greek poet Sappho.

In a famous metaphor from his Preface to *Roderick Hudson*, James compares writing to embroidery and himself as a young writer to an embroiderer; the figure is by no means limited to a single point of comparison:

> A young embroiderer of the canvas of life soon began to work in terror, fairly, of the vast expanse of that surface, of the boundless number of its distinct perforations for the needle, and of the tendency inherent in its many coloured flowers and figures to cover and consume as many as possible of the little holes. The development of the flower, of the figure, involved thus an immense counting of holes and a careful selection among them. That would have been, it seemed to him, a brave enough process, were it not the very nature of the holes so to invite, to solicit, to persuade, to practise positively a thousand lures and deceits. The prime effect of so sustained a system, so prepared a surface, is to lead on and on; while the fascination of following resides, by the same token, in the presumability *somewhere* of a convenient, of a visibly appointed stopping place. (1965, 5)

Once James has established the basic comparison, he then imagines the details: the vast fabric which is embroidered is the vast canvas of life, and the process of embroidering involves passing his needle—perhaps his pen?—though countless holes, in order to produce flowers and figures; the vast extent of the fabric with its countless holes leads the embroiderer on and on; but the artist must somehow find an end.

And here is a metaphor from the very beginning of *Roderick Hudson:*

> Rowland Mallet had made his arrangements to sail for Europe on the 1st of September, and having in the interval a fortnight to spare, he determined to spend it with his cousin Cecilia, the widow of a nephew of his father. He was urged by the reflection that an affectionate farewell might help to exonerate him from the charge of neglect frequently preferred by this lady. It was not that the young man disliked her; on the contrary he regarded her with a tender admiration, and he had not forgotten how when his cousin brought her home on her marriage he seemed to feel the upward sweep of the empty bough from which the golden fruit had been plucked, and then and there accepted the prospect of bachelorhood. (23)

This metaphor has (at least) two points of comparison: the golden fruit, I suppose, represents Cecilia, while the upward sweep of the branch represents Mallet's feeling of loss. Curiously, however, it is not the upward sweep of the branch that removes the golden fruit from Mallet's grasp: the plucking of the fruit—by Mallet's cousin—creates the upward sweep, but the fruit itself is no longer on the branch. The power of the figure resides, I believe, in the reader's ability to make an internal image of the feeling of the sweep of the bough as the fruit is plucked. The physicality of the internal image is essential to the force of the metaphor; I would call it an emotional whoosh. What counts most in the figure is not the loss but the feeling of loss. Indeed, James makes the point that Cecilia is now a widow: the golden fruit is now available, if Mallet wants it: "He no longer felt like marrying her; in these eight years that fancy had died a natural death." Mallet's bachelorhood is a result of the upward sweep of the branch, that is, of the feeling of loss, which is somehow deeper than the specific loss of Cecilia. The point of the comparison, I would suggest, is in the feeling; certainly James wants the reader to understand, but what is to be understood is an experience, and he conveys that understanding through the representation of a physical sensation.

This feeling of loss is replicated in the shape of the whole story: Mallet falls in love with Mary Garland, the fiancée of Roderick Hudson, a promising young sculptor. Mallet makes it possible for Hudson to go with him to Europe for training, but there Hudson is corrupted. Mary Garland comes to Europe as well; Mallet, in a spirit of self-denial, tries his best to make Hudson reform. Hudson finally realizes that Mallet is in love with Mary; then Hudson dies—or perhaps he kills himself—on the penultimate page. The book ends with Mary back in Northampton, "where Rowland visits his cousin Cecilia more frequently than of old. . . . Cecilia, who having her shrewd impression that he comes to see the young lady at the other house as much as to see herself, calls him whenever he reappears the most restless of mortals. But he always says to her in answer, 'No, I assure you I am the most patient!'" (349–50). The ring composition here brings the initial metaphor back to the reader's mind; now the golden fruit is Mary Garland, but it is still out of reach, and Mallet remains a bachelor; James quite deliberately refuses the satisfaction of marriage. The whole of the story is the upward sweep of the bough, and the context of interpretation of the metaphor involves the whole story.

This apple metaphor can be compared to an ancient apple simile found in a fragment (105[A] in the Lobel-Page edition) from the Archaic Greek poet Sappho (my translation):

Such as the sweet apple reddens on the tip of the branch,
the tip of the tippest, and the applepickers missed it,
no indeed they didn't miss it, but they weren't able to reach it.

This fragment is all we have of a longer poem. The consensus of scholarship, I believe, is that this fragment comes from a wedding song. Perhaps, some would say, the bride is being compared to the apple; perhaps she was a little late in getting married, and the poet wants to say that she was not neglected, but hard to reach. The bridegroom is fortunate to have picked the apple no one else could reach. As R. Drew Griffith (1989, 61) suggests, "The poem's performance at a wedding shows the bridegroom has won the bride no one else could, so emphasis on the comparative lateness of her marriage also praises him." If this interpretation is correct, then this metaphor seems to be a mixture of the emotive and the cognitive. The bride is like a ripening apple—the verb perhaps carries the hint of a blush—and the apple pickers are the young men looking for brides. The metaphor is partly sensory—we are supposed to imagine the taste of the succulent ripening fruit, and also perhaps to feel the straining of the apple pickers as they try to reach for it—and these sensations lead to emotion, but it is also cognitive—as we are supposed to re-evaluate the value of this particular late-marrying bride.

It is not necessary, however, to erect a strong boundary between the cognitive and the emotive. "The essence of metaphor," according to Lakoff and Johnson (1980b, 455) "is understanding and experiencing one kind of thing or experience in terms of another." If emotion comes from experience and if understanding is cognitive, then I would argue that experience is the basis for understanding; experience without understanding is incomplete, while understanding without experience is unfounded. Philosophy and literature are not really so far apart. Plato often begins or ends a philosophic dialogue with a story; perhaps philosophy begins in experience and ends in myth.

My interest here is not a general theory of metaphor and simile, but an examination of these figures in literature. Rhetorical figures in literature are usually more complex than the examples typically found in theoretical studies; they often take their meaning from the larger context in which they are situated; they often stimulate some kind of sensuous mental imagery; and often they are designed to evoke an emotional response.

Metaphor in Homer's *Iliad*

Homeric epic is famous for its similes, and we will look at these in some detail in a moment, but Homer uses metaphor as well. In book 24 of the *Iliad,* Hektor has been killed, and Achilles is dragging his body around behind his chariot. Apollo, however, protects the body so that it is not disfigured. The gods meet in council and most of them feel that Achilles has gone too far; as Apollo says, Achilles has destroyed pity. Zeus sends a messenger to tell Priam, Hektor's father, to go to Achilles with ransom for the body. Priam asks his wife, Hekabe, what he should do, and she says

> "Ah me, where has that wisdom gone for which you were famous
> in time before, among outlanders and those you rule over?
> How can you have the will to go to the ships of the Achaians alone
> before the eyes of a man who has slaughtered in such numbers
> such brave sons of yours? The heart in you is iron.
> For if he has you within his grasp and lays eyes upon you,
> that man, savage and faithless, will neither pity you
> nor respect you." (*Iliad* 24.201–8)

"The heart in you is iron." "σιδήρειόν νύ τοι ἦτορ." Here we have a metaphor, a simple metaphor. At first it may seem obvious what Hekabe means, but metaphors do not interpret themselves. If Priam's heart is iron, it must be hard—hardness being one of the most prominent sensuous qualities of iron. Hardness, then, would be the tertium comparationis. But there is more to be said. Whatever quality Hekabe is ascribing to Priam's heart, it is not a good thing. He used to be wise, but no longer. His iron heart is putting him in danger. His action is foolish and reckless. His heart is inflexible. It would be far better if his heart were not iron.

But Priam does go to ransom his son's body. Zeus, meanwhile, has sent a messenger to Achilles; the sea-goddess Thetis, Achilles' mother, has told him he must give up the body, and Achilles has agreed to do so. Priam comes to the camp of the Achaians and supplicates Achilles. He grasps

Achilles' knees and kisses his hands:

"Honour then the gods, Achilles, and pity me
remembering your father, yet I am still more pitiful;
I have gone through what no other mortal on earth has gone through;
I put my lips to the hands of the man who has killed my children."
  (*Iliad* 24.503–6)

Achilles' first reaction is grief—grief for his companion Patroklos, killed
by Hektor, and grief for his father, whom he will never see again. Then he
takes Priam by the hand and sets him on his feet, and addresses him:

"Ah, unlucky, surely you have had much evil to suffer in your spirit.
How could you endure to come alone to the ships of the Achaians
before the eyes of a man who has killed in such numbers
such brave sons of yours? The heart in you is iron.
Come then, and sit upon this chair, and you and I will even let
our sorrows lie still in the heart for all our grieving." (*Iliad* 24.
  518–23)

"The heart in you is iron." "σιδήρειόν νύ τοι ἦτορ." Not only are these
words identical in the two passages, but with minor variations three lines
are the same:

"How can you be willing to go to the ships of the Achaians alone
before the eyes of a man who has slaughtered in such numbers
such brave sons of yours? The heart in you is iron." (*Iliad* 24.203–5)

"How could you endure to come alone to the ships of the Achaians
before the eyes of a man who has slaughtered in such numbers
such brave sons of yours? The heart in you is iron." (*Iliad* 24.519–21)

One difference seems particularly significant: Hekabe asks, "How can you
have the will?" (πῶς ἐθέλεις), while Achilles asks, "How could you endure?" (πῶς ἔτλης).

When Achilles says that Priam's heart is iron, he cannot mean just
what Hekabe meant. Achilles looks at Priam in wonder and admiration.

It is not foolish recklessness that Achilles sees, but courage. His heart is hard because it can endure great pain. The *tertium comparationis* is endurance. The words in these two passages are the same, but the metaphor is different, because the person speaking is different, and because the context is different. When Hekabe speaks, the context brings out the hardness of iron, and when Achilles speaks the context brings out the durability of iron. The repetition of the passages allows, or forces, a comparison of the two qualities of iron, the two qualities of Priam, from Achilles' perspective and from Hekabe's. Thus the meaning of the metaphor depends on the context, and the context selects the qualities in the vehicle which are appropriately compared to the tenor or topic.

Some Homeric Similes

Homer uses simile much more than he uses metaphor. Homeric similes have been extensively imitated by other poets and extensively debated by scholars.[2] There are roughly two hundred similes in the *Iliad* and roughly fifty in the *Odyssey;* here I will be able to comment on just a few. Some Homeric similes are long, complex, and problematic; others are short and to the point. At the beginning of the *Iliad,* when Apollo comes to send a plague against the Greek army, Homer says simply, "He went like night" (*Il.*1.47). Exactly what this image means I am not sure—but it must be foreboding. The emotion comes before the sense, which has to be interpreted from the emotion; but first comes night, with all its connotations. In book 4 of the *Iliad,* a Trojan warrior, Pandarus, has shot an arrow at Menelaos, but Athena deflects it: "She brushed it away from his skin as lightly as when a mother brushes a fly away from her child who is lying in sweet sleep" (*Il.*4.130–31). This elegant short figure links an action to an emotion.

The world of the *Iliad* is in some ways very narrow: the characters are almost exclusively divinities and elite mortals; the major events of the story take only a few days; and the scene is just a city and a battlefield. The similes bring a wider world into the narrative. Many similes refer to the world of nature, either animate or inanimate: a warrior may be likened to a lion (*Il.*3.21–27, *Il.*11.547–55, etc.), or a horse (*Il.*6.506–14 and *Il.*15.263–70), or a donkey (*Il.*557–64). In book 2, the Achaean army as it gathers to hear the leaders is compared to swarms of clustering bees (*Il.*2.87–93); in book 16, the Myrmidons, led by Patroklos, enter the battle like wasps

(*Il.*16.259–67); and in book 17 Athena gives Menelaos strength to defend the body of Patroklos (*Il.*17.569–73):

> She put strength into the man's shoulders and knees, inspiring
> in his breast the persistent daring of that mosquito
> who, though it is driven hard away from a man's skin, even
> so, for the taste of human blood, persists in biting him.
> With such daring she darkened to fullness the heart inside him.

Other similes place an ordinary mortal in a natural setting; here Diomedes retreats as Hektor advances (*Il.*5.596–600):

> Diomedes of the great war cry shivered as he saw him,
> and like a man in his helplessness who, crossing a great plain,
> stands at the edge of a fast-running river that dashes seaward,
> and watches it thundering into white water, and leaps a pace backward,
> so now Tydeus' son gave back and spoke to his people.

All of these similes, and many others, show a remarkable precision and accuracy of observation.

Other Homeric similes describe ordinary human occupations, tasks that would probably be quite foreign to the elite world of the warriors and heroes. A number of similes describe hunters (*Il.*15.271–78) or farmers, often as they try to protect themselves or their domestic animals from predators (*Il.*547–54); in other similes we find ivory dyeing (*Il.*4.141–47), leather tanning (*Il.*17.389–95), working with wool (*Il.*12.432–36), reaping grain (*Il.*11.67–71), and metal working (*Od.*6.229–35).

In a famous passage from the *Odyssey,* the Phaiakian bard Demodokos sings about the very end of the Trojan war: the Trojan horse has been brought into Troy, and the Achaians stream out of their hiding place and sack the city (*Od.*8.521–31):

> So the famous singer sang his tale, but Odysseus
> melted, and from under his eyes the tears ran down, drenching
> his cheeks. As a woman weeps, lying over the body
> of her dear husband, who fell fighting for her city and people
> as he tried to beat off the pitiless day from city and children;

she sees him dying and gasping for breath, and winding her body
about him she cries high and shrill, while the men behind her,
hitting her with their spear butts on the back and the shoulders,
force her up and lead her away into slavery, to have
hard work and sorrow, and her cheeks are wracked with pitiful weeping.
Such were the pitiful tears Odysseus shed from under his brow.

This simile puts Odysseus in the position of one of the Trojan women, one
of the victims of the Achaean army; are we supposed to imagine that Odysseus himself has some feeling for the victims of the war? Or is this just
an extreme example of an extended vehicle that has twisted back on the
tenor beyond the intention of the poet? In any case, the simile reminds the
audience of the experience of the defeated.

At the beginning of book 20 of the *Odyssey* Homer presents two similes to describe the thoughts and feelings of the hero. Odysseus, still disguised as a beggar, is trying to sleep, but his sleep is troubled by his anger
at the suitors and at the handmaids who are their mistresses; he considers jumping up and killing the handmaids right then, and his heart "was
growling within him" (*Od*.20.14–16):

And as a bitch, facing an unknown man, stands over
her callow puppies, and growls and rages to fight, so Odysseus'
heart was growling inside him as he looked on these wicked actions.

He represses his anger, but still he twists and turns on his bed (*Od*.20.
25–30):

And as a man with a paunch pudding, that has been filled with
blood and fat, tosses it back and forth over a blazing
fire, and the pudding itself strains hard to be cooked quickly;
so he was twisting and turning back and forth, meditating
how, though he was alone against many, he could lay hands on
the shameless suitors.

These similes are vivid; the images are easy to see with the mind's eye, and
they provide material correlatives for Odysseus's inner feelings. Their effect is emotive rather than cognitive.

Other similes are more abstract; in this passage Hera hurries from the battlefield to Olympus (*Il*.15.80–83):

As the thought flashes in the mind of a man, who, traversing
much territory, thinks of things in the mind's awareness,
'I wish I were in this place, or this,' and imagines many things,
so rapidly in her eagerness winged Hera, a goddess.

And here Hektor is running from Achilles (*Il*.22.199–201):

As in a dream a man is not able to follow one who runs
from him, nor can the runner escape, nor the other pursue him,
so he could not run him down in his speed nor the other get clear.[3]

Many Homeric similes seem to be either inappropriate or excessive; a simile may hinge on one point of comparison between the tenor and the vehicle, but then the comparison leads out to a more extensive description of the vehicle, which may not apply to the tenor in any obvious way. As A. Shewan (1911, 281) notes, "A scene is before the poet in every detail. He revels in details, whether relevant to the comparison or not, that serve to make his presentation of the matter concrete and vivid. When any such feature suggests a new comparison, he seizes it and states it without hesitation." The virtues of such a simile may not reside in any systematic comparison between the two terms, but rather in the vividness of the image that is created.

Here, for instance, is the first of several lion similes in the *Iliad;* the Greeks and the Trojans have marched out to battle—the first battle depicted in the epic. Alexandros (also known as Paris) jumps out in front of the Trojan warriors and challenges the best of the Greeks to fight man-to-man. Menelaos sees him and takes up the challenge (*Il*.3.31–28):

Now as soon as Menelaos the warlike caught sight of him
making his way with long strides out in front of the army,
he was glad, like a lion who comes on a mighty carcass,
in his hunger chancing upon the body of a horned stag
or wild goat; who eats it eagerly, although against him
are hastening the hounds in their speed and the stalwart young men:

thus Menelaos was happy finding the godlike Alexandros
there in front of his eyes.

Menelaos is like a lion; it is a commonplace in the Homeric epics that lions
are fierce fighters, and so presumably this simile suggests that Menelaos
is also a fierce fighter. In addition, the lion is glad, and so is Menelaos. So
much seems fairly clear. It is much less clear, however, how the rest of
the comparison functions. The lion is glad because he has come across a
carcass, that is, an animal that is already dead: in this simile the lion is a
scavenger rather than a predator. Are we supposed to take the dead animal to represent Alexandros? If so, who killed him? Evidently not Menelaos, since the lion finds the animal already dead. Perhaps Menelaos is
already thinking of Alexandros as a carcass and so his emotion anticipates
the victory he expects. The hounds and the stalwart young men pursuing
the lion are presumably the Trojan warriors—but Alexandros has made
a challenge to fight man-to-man, and as the story continues Alexandros
and Meneloas fight a duel, with no intervention from other warriors.
These details of the simile seem to be not just in excess of the comparison,
but even contrary to it.

In book 16 of the *Iliad,* most of the Greek leaders have been wounded,
and the Trojans are attacking the Greek ships. Patroklos urges Achilles to
re-enter the battle; Achilles refuses, but he agrees to send Patroklos and
the Myrmidons in his stead. Patroklos arms himself in Achilles' armor,
and Achilles arrays the Myrmidons (*Il*.16.156–66):

> But Achilles went meanwhile to the Myrmidons, and arrayed them
> all in their war gear among the shelters. And they, as wolves
> who tear flesh raw, in whose hearts the battle-fury is tireless,
> who have brought down a great horned stag in the mountains
> and devour him, till the jowls of all run with blood;
> and they go in a pack to lap from a spring of black water,
> with their narrow tongues, the black water
> at the edge, belching up bloody gore; and the spirit
> in the heart of each one is untremulous, but the belly is glutted;
> as such the lords and leaders of the Myrmidons
> around the brave henchman of swift-footed Achilles
> swarmed.

As Walter Leaf (1902, ad loc.) points out, the Myrmidons are just now putting on their arms, preparatory to battle, so it is odd to compare them to wolves who have already devoured their prey. "The natural history of 163 is wrong," he says, "for a glutted wolf is a thorough coward." Leaf argues that the lines should be excised as an interpolation "from some poem where they were more appropriately applied to an army returning from battle." By Leaf's standards, however, many of the Homeric similes would have to be removed.

Steven Nimis (1987, 23–42) argues that the problems in this simile are in themselves part of its meaning. The simile describes a kind of (negative) feast. Feasting is an important type scene in the epic, and this simile of the wolves uses the elements of the scene, but converted: "The operation which gives internal coherence to the wolf simile is its consistent conversion of the positive aspects of human feasts into negative aspects" (25). The wolves (and animals generally) eat meat raw, but humans cook their meat—the epic includes many passages which describe in detail the ritual cooking of meat for sacrifice and feasting (e.g., *Il*.2.421–33). Warriors eat meat in order to gain courage in battle (*Il*.9.705–6); in the simile, the battle-fury of the wolves comes first, the feast comes afterward. Humans sacrifice domestic animals on an altar, but the wolves kill and devour a wild stag on the mountains. Even the vocabulary serves to point the contrast: Homeric formulas for a human feast use the word "dainumi" (δαίνυμι)—but in this simile the wolves "devour" the stag—the verb is "dapto" (δάπτω), which is applied only to animals. The savagery of the wolves' meal is shown by the blood on their jowls; Homeric heroes, by contrast, apportion their food according to strict rules of decorum: "they ate, nor was anyone lacking a fair portion" (δαίνυντ', οὐδέ τι θυμὸς ἐδεύετο δαιτὸς ἐίσης: *Il*.1.468, etc.). The wolves finish their meal with a drink of black water, from the edge or on the surface of a spring; a human feast ends with a libation of wine poured from cups (*Il*.1.470–71, etc.). Homeric warriors eat until each has had his fill: "but after they had put away their desire for eating and drinking" (αὐτὰρ ἐπεὶ πόσιος καὶ ἐδητύος ἐξ ἔρον ἕντο: *Il*.1.469, etc.); but the wolves glut themselves until they belch up the bloody gore. In sum, "The simile represents a coherent picture not in terms of the 'natural history' of wolves, but in terms of how heroes conduct a feast. The simile is a conversion of the descriptive system of the meals of heroes" (32).

But what is the point of this conversion? There are five extended descriptions of sacrifice and feast in the *Iliad:* in book 1, when the Greeks give Chryseis back to her father (*Il.*1.458–71); in book 2, just before the first battle described in the poem (*Il.*2.421–31); in book 7, when the Greek leaders meet to discuss strategy (*Il.*7.316–23); in book 9, when Achilles welcomes the ambassadors who attempt to convince him to return to battle (*Il.*9.205–22); and in book 24, when Priam comes to Achilles to ask for the return of Hektor's body (*Il.*24.621–28). Each is different from the others (though they share some formulaic lines), but all in one way or another serve to create some feeling of community, however brief or precarious.

In book 19, however, feasting becomes a point of contention. Patroklos has been killed (in book 16) and Hephaistos has made new armor for Achilles (in book 18); Achilles wants to go straight into battle without eating—he will eat after the battle, he says (*Il.*19.205–14; 305–8), but not before. Odysseus argues at length that the army cannot fight until they have eaten. This whole episode, with several speeches back and forth, takes some two hundred lines (*Il.*19.155–355); clearly this is an important moment. Achilles in effect is rejecting the kind of community which the feasts are intended to symbolize. He has taken on the savagery of the wolves in the simile: in the final battle, as Achilles is about to kill Hektor, he says, "I wish only that my spirit and fury would drive me / to hack your meat away and eat it raw" (*Il.*22.346–47). Thus the simile takes its meaning from the inversion of the formulaic feasts in the epic and gives its meaning to Achilles' battle fury.

At the very end of the *Iliad,* Priam comes to Achilles to ask for the return of Hektor's body. (When Priam arrives, Achilles has just finished eating dinner.) Priam—tall Priam, as Homer says—grasps Achilles' knees in the traditional gesture of supplication and kisses the hands that had killed Hektor and so many of Priam's other sons (*Il.*24. 471–80). Achilles looks at him in wonder (*Il.*24.480–84):

> Tall Priam came in unseen by the others, and standing near
> with his hands he took Achilles' knees and kissed the hands,
> terrible manslaying, which had killed many of his sons.
> As when dense disaster comes on one who in his own land
> has killed a man, and he comes to the country of others,

to a man of substance, and wonder seizes on those who behold him,
so Achilles wondered as he looked on godlike Priam,
and the rest of them wondered also, and looked at each other.

The point of comparison here is the wonder that seizes the men who look
upon the fugitive as he supplicates the wealthy man and the wonder that
seizes Achilles and his men as they look upon Priam. A modern reader
may be surprised that a murderer can run away and be accepted as a fugitive, but this situation is noted elsewhere in the *Iliad* and in other Greek
stories: Epigeus killed his cousin and was accepted by Achilles' father
Peleus (*Il.*16.570–75); Patroklos killed a man and was accepted by Peleus
(*Il.*23.85–90); Adrastus killed his brother (by accident) and was accepted
as a fugitive by Croesus (Herodotus, *Histories* 1:35). Homer seems to
make no moral judgment here, but nonetheless the fugitive is a source of
wonder, perhaps because he is taboo until he is purified.

The difficulty in the simile is that the roles of the principal characters in the vehicle and tenor are reversed. (According to Richard Buxton (2004, 153), the reversal of roles in the simile was noted as early as
the twelfth century by the Homeric commentator Eustathius.) As Bruce
Heiden says (1998, 2), "the tenor and the vehicle of this comparison are
more notable for their dissimilarity than their resemblance: Priam is not
a murderer; he is not in a foreign land but in his own, the man he supplicates is an enemy." In the vehicle, a violent man supplicates a nonviolent
man; in the tenor, a nonviolent man supplicates a violent man—a man
who has killed his sons, and who could very well kill him. Moreover, since
Patroklos came as a supplicant fugitive to Achilles' father, Peleus, the simile "forges an implicit link between Patroklos and Priam" (Buxton 2004,
154). The simile thus creates a proportion: Priam is to Achilles what Patroklos was to Peleus. There are further complications: in the simile, the
fugitive has left his own land, gone as a suppliant to another land; Priam
has left his city and he has come to the Greek camp, but the Greek camp is
in Priam's land, since the Greeks are invaders of Troy. The direct point of
comparison of the simile is the wonder of the onlookers—those who look
on the fugitive and those who look on Priam. The wonder in the simile
feeds into a later moment: after Achilles and Priam have eaten, each looks
on the other with wonder (*Il.*24.628–32):

But when they had put aside their desire for food and drink,
truly Dardanian Priam wondered at Achilles,
his size and his nature: for he seemed like the gods to look at.
But Achilles wondered at Dardanian Priam,
as he looked on his brave countenance and listened to his speech.

The wonder of the simile is repeated as Priam and Achilles look at each other. Once again we see that the meaning of a simile interacts with the broader context in which it occurs.

There is no simple way to explain the function and effect of the Homeric similes; it is clear, however, that they are more than ornamental. They often bring a wider world of nature and human society into the concentrated focus of the story. Typically they are full of vivid sensory detail, and that detail is often emotionally expressive. The meaning of a simile is not limited to the interaction of the two parts of the figure, the vehicle and the tenor, but extends to the general context of the poem. Interpretation of the similes thus calls on a full range of sensitive reading.

It is perhaps worth noting that whatever problems scholars and critics have found in the Homeric similes hasn't bothered poets very much. Extended similes are easy to find in *The Argonautica* (Apollonius of Rhodes); in *The Aeneid* (Virgil); in *The Pharsalia* (Lucan); *The Thebaid* (Statius); *The Posthomerica* (Quintus of Smyrna); *The Divine Comedy* (Dante); *Africa* (Petrarch); *Orlando Furioso* (Ariosto); *The Lusiads* (Camoens); *The Liberation of Jerusalem* (Tasso); *The Faerie Queen* (Spenser); *Paradise Lost* (Milton); and so on. It would be fascinating to compare the practice of these various poets—but that would be a project for another book.

Similes in Raymond Chandler

Raymond Chandler uses a wide range of rhetorical figures (I have found instances of congeries, tricolon, anadiplosis, gradatio, chiasmus, hyperbole, metonymy, epistrophe, transferred epithet, and zeugma), but he is particularly known for his similes. Here I will examine some similes from *Farewell My Lovely* (FML), *The High Window* (HW), and *The Big Sleep* (BS). Some of the similes are one-liners that are easy to extract from their context without much loss of effect. Here are a few from *The Big Sleep:*

A few locks of dry white hair clung to his scalp, like wild flowers fighting for life on a bare rock. (1988, 6)

The General spoke again, slowly, using his strength as carefully as an out-of-work showgirl uses her last good pair of stockings. (6)

I pushed a flat tin of cigarettes at him. His small neat fingers speared one like a trout taking the fly. (98)

Blood began to move around in me, like a prospective tenant looking over a house. (116)

A few from *Farewell My Lovely:*

There was a sudden silence as heavy as a water-logged boat. (1992, 7)

She was as cute as a washtub. (30)

His smile was as stiff as a frozen fish. (179)

And a few from *The High Window:*

Her eyes were as hard as the bricks in her front walk. (1988, 10)

Her hair was as artificial as a night-club lobby. (27)

We looked at each other with the clear innocent eyes of a couple of used-car salesmen. (45)

Almost all the similes in Chandler's novels are in the voice of the hero, Philip Marlowe, sometimes in narrative passages, but also in dialogue. In Chandler's similes the vehicle is often far-fetched or even contrary to the tenor; the term in traditional rhetoric for a far-fetched metaphor or simile is catachresis. These far-fetched similes, which are both witty and surprising, help contribute to Marlowe's characteristic ironic distance.

Chandler often forms similes with the comparative "like," as in "a sound came out of him like a convalescent rooster learning to crow again after a long illness" (HW 49), but he also uses other grammatical forms, such as "X was as Y as Z," as in "Her eyes were as hard as the bricks in her front walk" (HW 10), or "X was Y enough to . . .," as in "The coffee shop smell was strong enough to build a garage on" (FML 96). The copula can be omitted: "two thin cambric handkerchiefs as fine and white as dry powdered snow" (FML 72). Or the comparative particle "like" can be attached to the vehicle: "a bartender moved mothlike against the faint glitter of piled glassware" (HW 78). In other similes, the copulative verb is "looked" or "felt": "Even on Central Avenue, not the quietest dressed street in the world, he looked about as inconspicuous as a tarantula on a slice of angel food" (FML 4); "He looked as if he had been sitting there since the Civil War and had come out of that badly" (HW 35); "She looked as flustered as a side of beef" (HW 90); Marlowe wakes up after he has been beaten unconscious: "I felt like an amputated leg" (FML 65). Other kinds of verbs also can provide the hinge into the simile: "His long fingers made movements like dying butterflies" (FML 179); "This car sticks out like spats at an Iowa picnic" (FML 60). Or an action can be carried out "as if...": "He spoke almost dreamily, as if he were all by himself, out in the woods, picking johnny-jump-ups" (FML 8). If the comparative words are omitted, the figure tends toward metaphor: "my bank account was still trying to crawl under a duck. I put honey into my voice..." (FML 42); "Two big tears formed themselves in Mrs. Murdock's eyes and slowly made their way down the elephant hide of her cheeks..." (HW 96); "I woke up with a motorman's glove in my mouth..." (BS 26); "She gave me one of those smiles the lips have forgotten before they reach the eyes" (BS 37); "Her eyes ate Carmen with a green distillation of hate" (BS 54).

In many of the similes the vehicle invokes a physical sensation. In the simile "There was a sudden silence as heavy as a water-logged boat" the physical heaviness of the water-logged boat is transferred to the immaterial silence. At one point in *Farewell My Lovely* Marlowe has to climb a long set of concrete steps up a steep hill to get to the house of a prospective client. "It was a nice walk if you liked grunting. There were two hundred and eighty steps up to Cabrillo Street. They were drifted over with wind-blown sand and the handrail was as cold and wet as a toad's belly" (FML 47). Many readers will feel the toad's belly in their hands. A little later Marlowe and his client Marriot drive down the same hill: "For two minutes we figure-eighted back and forth across the face of the mountain and then popped out right beside the sidewalk cafe. I could understand now why Marriott had told me to walk up the steps. I could have driven about in those curving, twisting streets for hours without making any more yardage than an angleworm in a bait can" (FML 59). The twisting of the streets is animated in the twisting of the angleworm, and the futility of the worm's struggles expresses the futility of driving those twisting streets. "The giggles got louder and ran around the corners of the room like rats behind the wainscoting" (BS 41). Our feeling about the giggles, and the giggler, is formed by our feeling about rats. The physicality of these similes adds to their vividness. "The room beyond was large and square and sunken and cool and had the restful atmosphere of a funeral chapel and something like the same smell" (HW 4). The effect here is all in the last word, which completely changes the tone of the comparison.

These similes work by comparing something abstract or immaterial to something concrete; but sometimes the adjective in the first part of the comparison is itself a kind of transference from the concrete to the abstract, so the movement is from the concrete to the abstract and back to the concrete. Thus the phrase "her eyes were hard" is a kind of buried metaphor, since eyes are not themselves physically hard; then the simile "her eyes were as hard as the bricks in her front walk" recovers the physicality of the buried metaphor by comparing it to a concrete vehicle. In *The High Window* Marlowe describes his employer, Mrs. Murdock: "A heart of gold and the gold buried good and deep" (HW 17); the phrase "a heart of gold" is a metaphor that has become a cliché (compare "Your heart is iron" from the *Iliad*); Marlowe creates the figure by restoring the original concrete sense of the vehicle and turning it against the usual abstract meaning of the phrase. Other similes work by reversal or contradiction: to say "she was as cute as a washtub" is to say that she wasn't cute at all.

In many similes the vehicle evokes a mood rather than—or in addition to—a physical sensation: "A check girl in peach-bloom Chinese pyjamas came over to take my hat and disapprove of my clothes. She had eyes like strange sins" (HW 78). "A girl passing me on the way from the elevators back to her work turned and gave me one of those looks which are supposed to make your spine feel like a run in a stocking" (FML 106). "I felt nasty, as if I had picked a poor man's pocket" (FML 136). "The wet air was as cold as the ashes of love" (FML 255). "Dead men are heavier than broken hearts" (BS 26). "Under the thinning fog the surf curled and creamed, almost without a sound, like a thought trying to form itself on the edge of consciousness" (BS 91). "She came back with the glass and her fingers cold from holding the cold glass touched mine and I held them for a moment and then let them go slowly as you let go of a dream when you wake with the sun in your face and have been in an enchanted valley" (FML 187). In these the tone of the vehicle is transferred to the tenor.

I have been discussing similes in isolation, as one-liners, but many of the similes in Chandler work best when they are read in context. Often a simile is part of a description of a person or a place. In the following passage Marlowe is describing his own office:

> I looked into the reception-room. It was empty of everything but the smell of dust. I threw up another window, unlocked the communicating door and went into the room beyond. Three hard chairs and a swivel chair, flat desk with a glass top, five green filing-cases, three of them full of nothing, a calendar and a framed license bond on the wall, a phone, a washbowl in a stained wood cupboard, a hat-rack, a carpet that was just something on the floor, and two open windows with net curtains that puckered in and out like the lips of a toothless old man sleeping. (HW 15)

This description includes a lot of precisely observed detail; then at the end we see a merged image of the motion of the curtains and the puckering of the old man's lips; Marlowe's office becomes something worn out with age. The simile changes the tone and acts as a sort of punchline. A punchline simile can be used in the description of a person:

> A long-limbed languorous type of showgirl blonde lay at her ease in one of the chairs, with her feet raised on a padded rest and a tall misted glass at her elbow, near a silver ice bucket and a Scotch bottle. She looked at us lazily as we came over the grass. From thirty feet away she looked like a lot of class. From ten feet away she looked like something made up to be seen from thirty feet away. Her mouth was too wide, her eyes were too blue, her makeup was too vivid, the thin arch of her eyebrows was almost fantastic in its curve and spread, and the mascara was so thick on her eyelashes that they looked like miniature iron railings. (HW 27)

In the following passage Marlowe describes Elisha Morningstar, an elderly numismatist:

In the swivel chair at the desk sat an elderly party in a dark gray suit with high lapels and too many buttons on the front. He had some stringy white hair that grew long enough to tickle his ears. A pale gray bald patch loomed high up in the middle of it, like a rock above the timberline. Fuzz grew out of his ears, far enough to catch a moth.

He had sharp black eyes which had a pouch under each eye brownish purple in color and traced with a network of wrinkles and veins. His cheeks were shiny and his short sharp nose looked as if it had hung over a lot of quick ones in its time. A Hoover collar which no decent laundry would have allowed on the premises nudged his Adam's apple and a thick black string tie poked a small hard knot out at the bottom of the collar, like a mouse getting ready to come out of a mousehole. (HW 36)

Here is the description of Detective-Lieutenant Jesse Breeze:

He was a big man, rather paunchy, wearing brown and white shoes and sloppy socks and white trousers with thin black stripes, an open-neck shirt showing some ginger-colored hair at the top of his chest, and a rough sky-blue sports coat not wider in the shoulders than a two-car garage. He would be about fifty years old and the only thing about him that very much suggested cop was the calm unwinking, unwavering stare of his prominent pale-blue eyes, a stare that had no thought of being rude, but that anybody but a cop would feel to be rude. Below his eyes across the top of his cheeks and the bridge of his nose there was a wide path of freckles, like a mine-field on a war map. (HW 49–50)

And here Marlowe is describing a rundown part of the city:

Bunker Hill is old town, lost town, shabby town, crook town. Once, very long ago, it was the choice residential district of the city, and there are still standing a few of the jigsaw Gothic mansions with wide porches and walls covered with round-end shingles and full corner bay windows with spindle turrets. They are all rooming houses now, their parquetry floors are scratched and worn through the once glossy finish and the wide sweeping staircases are dark with time and cheap varnish laid on over generations of dirt. In the tall rooms haggard landladies bicker with shifty tenants. On the wide cool front porches, reaching their cracked shoes into the sun and staring at nothing, sit the old men with faces like lost battles.

In and around the old houses there are flyblown restaurants and Italian fruit-stands and cheap apartment houses and little candy stores where you can buy even nastier things than their candy. And there are ratty hotels where nobody except people named Smith and Jones sign the register and where the night clerk is half watchdog and half pander.

Out of the apartment houses come women who should be young but have faces like stale beer; men with pulled-down hats and quick eyes that look the street over behind the cupped hand that shields the match flame; worn intellectuals with cigarette coughs and no money in the bank; fly cops with granite faces and unwavering eyes; cokies and coke peddlers; people who look like nothing in particular and know it, and once in a while even men that go to work. But they come out early, when the wide cracked sidewalks are empty and still have dew on them. (HW 41–42)

This virtuoso description deserves some analysis. The passage begins with a sentence made of short parallel phrases with quadruple final repetition (epistrophe); the emphasis is on the epithets: "Bunker Hill is *old* town, *lost* town, *shabby* town, *crook* town." The next two sentences are long and almost elegiac in their rhythm, but the fourth sentence is again short and it includes two evaluative epithets, "haggard" and "shifty." The paragraph ends with a simile, "old men with faces like lost battles": the lost battles are the men's struggle with life. The first sentence of the second paragraph has a good polysyndeton:

flyblown restaurants and
Italian fruit-stands and
cheap apartment houses and
little candy stores where you can buy even nastier things than
    their candy.

The first sentence of the third paragraph has another striking simile: the women have faces like stale beer. Exactly what that means I don't know: the point of comparison is vague but not therefore less effective. Perhaps the effect is the taste of stale beer in your mouth. The catalog of the residents gives a kind of sociological analysis of the dead ends of American life. The final simile in the passage—"people who look like nothing in particular and know it"—breaks Chandler's usual technique: typically the point of comparison is vivid and shocking; here it is empty. The self-knowledge of the people does not add to their nobility, but rather to their despair. The final sentence brings in a contrasting note—there are people who work, who have lives—but they are few and without connection to the rest.

There are many other wonderful descriptions in Chandler's novels—for instance the description of Moose Malloy at the beginning of *Farewell My Lovely* or the description of the Sternwood mansion and General Sternwood himself at the beginning of *The Big Sleep*. Chandler's descriptions are full of the minute observation of physical detail; the details contribute to a psychological sketch; and there is usually some kind of implicit or explicit evaluation of the person or place described, often capped by a simile. Chandler is very aware of his style—Marlowe also seems to be aware of it, and at times he indulges in a bit of self-parody. Here he is describing the photograph of a show-girl:

I went over and took out the photo that lay all alone in the bottom of the drawer, face up, looking at me with cool dark eyes. I sat down again with the photo and looked it over. Dark hair parted loosely in the middle and drawn back loosely over a solid piece of forehead. A wide go-to-hell mouth with very kissable lips. Nice nose, not too small, not too large. Good bones all over the face. The expression of the face lacked something. Once the something might have been called breeding, but these days I didn't know what to call it. The face looked too wise and too guarded for its age. Too many passes had been made at it and it had grown a little too smart in dodging them. And behind this expression of wiseness there was the look of simplicity of the little girl who still believes in Santa Claus.

I nodded over the photo and slipped it into my pocket, thinking I was getting too much out of it to get out of a mere photo, and in a very poor light at that. (HW 11–12)

Chandler lets the reader in on the gag.

Similes in Henry James's *The Wings of the Dove*

Many of the metaphors and similes in Henry James's *The Wings of the Dove* begin with a single point of comparison, which is often some physical object or action intended to express a mental state; but then the figure is extended to include other points of comparison, in a manner that functions more by thought than by feeling—though again I would suggest that there is no firm line dividing the cognitive from the emotive. These extended figures approach Kittay's model of metaphor as described in the first section of this chapter, and the effect is sometimes quite surprising.

Many of the figures in *The Wings of the Dove* are quite long; I have tried to compress where I can, but part of the effect of the figures is precisely their length. It is sometimes difficult to extract a passage from James's novels for analysis; James has a habit of tying his sentences together with links, and any one sentence only makes sense if it is understood as the continuation of the thought and wording of the previous sentence. And sometimes I am not quite sure what a passage actually means.[4]

The first character introduced in the novel is Kate Croy, a young woman from a family once respectable but now poor and disgraced because of some unstated evil action on the part of her father. She has been taken up by her maternal aunt, Maude Lowder, who is immensely wealthy and moves in high circles in London. Kate lives in Mrs. Lowder's mansion, Lancaster Gate, and Mrs. Lowder brings her into high society. Mrs. Lowder clearly wants Kate to marry well—that is, to marry money and status—but Kate has fallen in love with a journalist, Merton Densher, who is clever but unlikely to make a fortune.

Kate and Densher first meet at a party: "The beginning—to which she often went back—had been a scene, for our young woman, of supreme brilliancy; a party given at a 'gallery' hired by a hostess who fished with big nets" (1964, 48). Kate doesn't know many people there, but she is introduced to "a tall fair, a slightly unbrushed and rather awkward, but on the whole a not dreary, young man"—who seemed about to leave the party until he started to talk with Kate:

> They had found themselves regarding each other straight, and for a longer time on end than was usual even at parties in galleries; but that in itself would have been a small affair for two such handsome persons. It wasn't, in a word, simply that their eyes had met; other conscious

organs, faculties, feelers had met as well, and when Kate afterwards imaged to herself the sharp deep fact she saw it, in the oddest way, as a particular performance. She had observed a ladder against a garden-wall and had trusted herself to climb it as to be able to see over into the probable garden on the other side. On reaching the top she had found herself face to face with a gentleman engaged in a like calculation at the same moment, and the two enquirers had remained confronted on their ladders. The great point was that for the rest of that evening they had been perched—they had not climbed down; and indeed during the time that followed Kate at least had had the perched feeling—it was as if she were there aloft without a retreat. A simpler expression of all this is doubtless that they had taken each other in with interest; and without a happy hazard six months later the incident would have closed in that account of it. (49)

The happy hazard that brought them together again was simply an accidental meeting on the Underground.

The general point of this passage is perhaps not so hard to perceive—two lonely people finding each other in a crowd—but the details are not easy to analyze. Some of the phrasing seems odd: just what does James mean by "other conscious organs, faculties, feelers"? Are the "conscious organs" organs of perception or something more? The meeting of feelers brings to my mind an encounter of insects.

The figure itself I think is Kate's own image later on of what the meeting was like. She imagines that she is in a walled garden; there she sees a ladder and climbs it to look over the wall. When she gets to the top, she sees a gentleman who has climbed the wall from his side. Evidently the two share an impulse that brings them together. This image leaves out all of the other people at the party; perhaps the point is that the other people don't exist for Kate and Merton Densher, who might as well have been alone. But the simile is not done: for the rest of the evening the two strangers stay perched on top of the wall—isolated from the party. "Kate at least had had the perched feeling"—as if we all know what a perched feeling is—"it was as if she were there aloft without a retreat." But this meeting in itself would have been a dead end if they hadn't run into each other on the Underground. This first romantic meeting, which will lead to so much in the rest of the story, is visualized as two people climbing ladders and perching on the top of a wall. The tone of the meeting seems oddly incongruent with the tone of the simile, and the more one visualizes the image, the odder it seems.

An extended simile like this one may seem reminiscent of the epic similes discussed earlier in the chapter; as David Lodge notes (with reference to an extended simile from *The Ambassadors*), "The effect is rather like that of the heroic simile in epic poetry, where the 'tenor' recedes from sight, and the 'vehicle' takes on an independent poetic life" (Lodge 207). But the two styles of comparison are in fact quite different. If Homer allows the vehicle to live an independent poetic life, James often strains to relate all the points of the vehicle to the tenor, as we can see in this and in other examples; sometimes he allows the figure to slip back and forth between the tenor and the vehicle, and sometimes he boldly mixes his metaphors.

Kate and Densher start to meet each other in the park near Lambert Gate. Kate knows, however, that her Aunt Maude will not approve of Densher as a suitor and would forbid their marriage. Aunt Maude is a formidable figure: "It was perfectly present to Kate that she might be devoured, and she compared herself to a trembling kid, kept apart a day or two till her turn should come, but sure sooner or later to be introduced into the cage of the lioness." So far we can see the point of the comparison: Aunt Maude is like a lion, Kate is like a trembling kid. But the simile continues:

> The cage was Aunt Maude's own room, her office, her counting-house, her battlefield, her especial scene, in fine, of action, situation on the ground-floor, opening from the main hall and figuring rather to our young woman on exit and entrance as a guard-house or a toll-gate. The lioness waited—the kid had at least that consciousness; was aware of the neighbourhood of a morsel she had reason to suppose tender. She would have been meanwhile a wonderful lioness for a show, an extraordinary figure in a cage or anywhere; majestic, magnificent, all brilliant gloss, perpetual satin, twinkling bugles and flashing gems, with a lustre of agate eyes, a sheen of raven hair, a polish of complexion that was like that of well-kept china and that—as if the skin were too tight, told especially at curves and corners. (37)

The cage is a room, in which the lioness waits for the tender morsel—Kate. Now James gives a description of the lioness, but this description slips back into the human realm, dressed in satin and wearing gems, with raven hair rather than the tawny coat of a lion. And a secondary image is introduced: her complexion is like china.

James has a habit of referring back to a simile at a later point in the text; thus, when Densher meets Aunt Maude, "he was in the cage of the lioness without his whip—the whip, in a word, of a supply of proper retorts" (62). Evidently James expects the reader on page 62 to remember the figure of the lion from page 37.

On another occasion Kate tells Densher that she never asked Mrs. Lowder for help:

> "After all I never asked her; never, when our troubles were at the worst, appealed to her nor went near her. She fixed upon me herself, settled on me with her wonderful gilded claws."
>
> "You speak," Densher observed, "as if she were a vulture."
>
> "Call it an eagle—with a gilded beak as well, and with wings for great flights. If she's a thing in the air, in short—say at once a great seamed silk balloon—I never myself got into her car. I was her choice." (60)

Here Mrs. Lowder is compared to a vulture, an eagle, and a silk balloon, all in the space of a few lines.

Book 3 introduces two new characters—Milly Theale, a wealthy young woman from New York, and her friend and companion Susan Stringham (also known by her maiden name, Susan Shepherd), a middle-aged widow from Boston. Milly has no family left, and so when she decides to take a trip to Europe she asks Mrs. Stringham to accompany her. Here Mrs. Stringham reacts to Milly's situation and nature:

> a nature that reminded Mrs. Stringham of the term always used in the newspapers about the great new steamers, the inordinate number of "feet of water" they drew; so that if, in your little boat, you had chosen to hover and approach, you had but yourself to thank, when once motion was started, for the way the draught pulled you. Milly drew the feet of water, and odd though it might seem that a lonely girl, who was not robust and who hated sound and show, should stir the stream like a leviathan, her companion floated off with the sense of rocking violently at her side. (81; cf. 76)

Milly is like a great ship—or like a leviathan—while Mrs. Stringham is like a little boat tossed about in its wake.

In another passage Milly is compared to a princess and Mrs. Stringham is compared to the confidant of the princess:

> Milly clearly felt these things too, but they affected her companion at moments—that was quite the way Mrs. Stringham would have expressed it—as the princess in a conventional tragedy might have affected the confidant if a personal emotion had ever been permitted to the latter. That a princess could only be a princess was a truth with which, essentially, a confidant, however responsive, had to live. Mrs. Stringham was a woman of the world, but Milly Theale was a princess, the only one she had yet to deal with, and this, in its way too, made all the difference. (85)

And Milly is called a princess in several other passages:

> For she [Susan Stringham] now saw that the great thing she had brought away was precisely a conviction that the future wasn't to exist for her princess in the form of any sharp or simple release from the human predicament. (88)

> Isolated, unmothered, unguarded, but with her other strong marks, her big house, her big fortune, her big freedom, she had lately begun to "receive," for all her few years, as an older woman might have done—as was done, precisely, by princesses who had public considerations to observe and who came of age very early. (94)[5]

In another passage Mrs. Stringham is compared to a fairy godmother (97). Many of the similes in the novel take the form of elaborate fantasies; they express the feelings of the characters and they also bring a kind of romantic luster to the story.

The two sets of characters—Kate, Densher, Mrs. Lowder, and a few others, on the one hand, and Milly and Mrs. Stringham on the other— eventually cross paths, and Milly and her companion are taken up by Mrs. Lowder and her circle. Kate and Milly in particular quickly become close friends; Mrs. Stringham imagines that Kate has just stepped out of a picture, while Milly is a princess:

The handsome English girl from the heavy English house had been as a figure in a picture stepping by magic out of its frame; it was a case in truth for which Mrs. Stringham presently found the perfect image. She had lost none of her grasp, but quite the contrary, of that other conceit in virtue of which Milly was the wandering princess; so what could be more in harmony now that to see the princess waited upon at the city gate by the worthiest maiden, the chosen daughter of the burgesses? It was the real again, evidently, the amusement of the meeting for the princess too; princesses living for the most part, in such an appeased way, on the plane of mere elegant representation. That was why they pounced, at city gates, on deputed flower-strewing damsels; that was why, after effigies, processions and other stately games, frank human company was pleasant to them. (111)

Toward the end of Volume I, Milly consults an eminent physician, Sir Luke Strett; exactly what her complaint may be is left rather vague (the word "vague" is indeed one of the keywords of the whole novel), and Sir Luke's diagnosis is also left vague; the upshot seems to be that Milly suffers from some serious but unspecified illness, but for the time being at least she can, and should, continue with her regular life—indeed, he tells her she should grasp life with intensity. She leaves Sir Luke's office with a complex feeling of both foreboding and freedom:

> The beauty of the bloom had gone from the small old sense of safety—that was distinct; she had left it behind her there forever. But the beauty of the idea of a great adventure, a big dim experiment or struggle in which she might more responsibly than ever before take a hand, had been offered her instead. It was as if she had had to pluck off her breast, to throw away, some friendly ornament, a familiar flower, a little old jewel, that was part of her daily dress; and to take up and shoulder as a substitute some queer defensive weapon, a musket, a spear, a battle axe—conducive possibly in a higher degree to a striking appearance, but demanding all the effort of the military posture.
>
> She felt this instrument, for that matter, already on her back, so that she proceeded now in very truth after the fashion of a soldier on a march—proceeded as if, for her initiation, the first charge had been sounded. (152–53)

Milly goes wandering through the streets of London, through parts of the city where an elegant young woman would not be expected to walk: "she might, from the curiosity she clearly excited in by-ways, in side-streets peopled with grimy children and costermongers' carts, which she hoped were slums, literally have had her musket on her shoulder, have announced herself as freshly on the war-path" (153).

James, like Homer, compares people to animals—as we have seen, Mrs. Lowder is compared to a lion and a vulture and an eagle; Kate is compared to a panther (171); Milly is compared to a lioness (154). The most extended and perhaps the most significant animal comparison also gives the book its title. Milly and Kate have been talking about Mrs. Lowder's social circle and Milly's place in it. "You won't want us next year," Kate says; "we shall only continue to want you." Milly insists on her friendship with Kate, and Kate replies "Oh you may very well loathe me yet!" Milly remonstrates, "Why do you say such things to me?"; and Kate replies: "Because you're a dove." Milly accepts the description: "She found herself accepting as the right one, while she caught her breath with relief, the name so given her. She met it on the instant as she would have met revealed truth; it lighted up the strange dusk in which she lately had walked. That was what was the matter with her. She was a dove" (171). The whole passage is too long to quote, but the word "dove" or "dovelike" occurs nine times in the next page and a half (and the word "princess" once as well), as Milly ponders what it means to be a dove: "the success she could have as a dove"; "she studied again the dove-like"; "She would have to be clear as to how a dove *would* act" (172). James, in his typical manner, leaves all this rather vague. Here we are dealing with metaphor rather than simile, and perhaps with symbol rather than metaphor—a symbol that is developed later in the story.

Kate cooks up a scheme whereby Densher will marry Milly, who will conveniently die of her mysterious ailment, leaving Densher with enough money to marry Kate; it takes some time for Densher to figure out what Kate is planning, and the consequences of his realization are the climax of the whole story. Meanwhile, the figure of the dove recurs. In the following passage, which takes place in Venice, Kate and Densher are attending a party given by Milly, who is wearing a string of pearls. Kate says to Densher:

"She's a dove," Kate went on, "and one somehow doesn't think of doves as bejewelled. Yet they suit her down to the ground."

"Yes—down to the ground is the word." Densher saw now how they suited her, but was perhaps still more aware of something intense in his companion's feeling about them. Milly was indeed a dove; this was the figure, though it most applied to her spirit. Yet he knew in a moment that Kate was just now, for reasons hidden from him, exceptionally under the impression of that element of wealth in her which was a power, which was a great power, and which was dove-like only so far as one remembered that doves have wings and wondrous flights, have them as well as tender tints and soft sounds. It even came to him dimly that such wings could in a given case—*had,* truly, in the case with which he was concerned—spread themselves for protection. Hadn't they, for that matter, lately taken an inordinate reach, and weren't Kate and Mrs. Lowder, weren't Susan Shepherd and he, wasn't he in particular, nestling under them to a great increase of immediate ease? (304)

James extends the figure with details about the dove: a dove has wings, a dove makes wondrous flights, a dove is tinted tenderly and makes soft sounds. But it is the wings that are really the point: the dove spreads its wings, and the other characters in the story are nestling under these wings for protection.

Milly eventually dies in Venice, alone except for Sir Luke Strett. Densher learns the news of her death from Mrs. Lowder: "Our dear dove then, as Kate calls her, has folded her wonderful wings." But then she adds, "Unless it's more true . . . that she has spread them the wider. . . . For a flight, I trust, to some happiness greater—!" (377). The flight of the dove is now a flight beyond life.

And one last time the image returns, on the very last page, in the final conversation between Kate and Densher. Milly has left her money to Densher so that he can marry Kate. "I used to call her, in my stupidity," Kate says, "—for want of anything better—a dove. Well she stretched out her wings and it was to *that* they reached. They cover us" (403). I suppose Kate means that Milly's money will now allow them to marry. But Densher (who may be in love with Milly's memory) stipulates that he will marry Kate without the money; if she wants the money she can have it, but he won't marry her.

The image of the dove has received much attention from the critics, and justifiably so. For my purposes, the examination of simile and metaphor in their various forms and functions, I note three features of this image: first, it is used in close conjunction with other images; second, it is extended to include several points of comparison; and third, it appears several times, and it gathers meaning with recurrence. All of these features it shares with other tropes in the book.

This image may well be the most important figure in the book, but there are many complex tropes to be found in the novel. It is worth looking at one extended example. Some explanation is necessary to put this passage into context. Milly has traveled to Venice with Kate, Susan Stringham, and Mrs. Lowder. They are quickly taken up by society there, both English and American. Milly is once again a great social success; the narrator says that she "moved slowly to and fro as the priestess of worship," and Susan Stringham compares "this portion of the girl's excursion to the Empress Catherine's famous progress across the steppes of Russia" (260). Their little group also toys "with the plan of a series of American visits" (261). In this passage, as I understand it, Milly and Kate have had enough of the social swirl, at least for the moment; they are relaxing and letting their guard down (somewhat) with each other. (It may be useful to explain one reference in advance: Maurice Maeterlinck [1862–1949] was a Belgian symbolist poet and dramatist, who won the Nobel Prize in Literature in 1911; he was an important literary figure at the time *The Wings of the Dove* was written, but I think his work is less read today. He is brought in to supply a kind of symbolist atmosphere to the situation.) Here is the passage:

It wasn't that Kate hadn't pretended too that *she* should like to go to America; it was only that with this young woman Milly had constantly proceeded, and more than ever of late, on the theory of intimate confessions, private frank ironies that made up for their public grimaces and amid which, face to face, they wearily put off the mask.

These puttings off of the mask had finally quite become the form taken by their moments together, moments indeed not increasingly frequent and not prolonged, thanks to the consciousness of fatigue on Milly's side whenever, as she herself expressed it, she got out of harness. They flourished their masks, the independent pair, as they might have flourished Spanish fans; they smiled and sighed on removing them; but the gesture, the smiles, the sighs, strangely enough, might have been suspected the greatest reality in the business. Strangely enough, we say, for the volume of effusion in general would have been found by either on measurement to be scarce proportional to the paraphernalia of relief. It was when they called each other's attention to their ceasing to pretend, it was then that what they were keeping back was most in the air. There was a difference, no doubt, and mainly to Kate's advantage. Milly didn't quite see what her friend could keep back, was possessed of, in fine, that would be so subject to retention; whereas it was comparatively plain sailing for Kate that poor Milly had a treasure to hide. This was not the treasure of a shy, an abject affection—concealment, on that head, belonging to quite another phase of such states; it was much rather a principle of pride relatively bold and hard, a principle that played up like a fine steel spring at the lightest pressure of too near a footfall. Thus insuperably guarded was the truth about the girl's own conception of her validity; thus was a wondering pitying sister condemned wistfully to look at her from the side of the moat she had dug round her tower. Certain aspects of the connexion of these young women show for us, such is the twilight that gathers about them, in the likeness of some dim scene in a Maeterlinck play; we have positively the image, in the delicate dusk, of the figures so associated and yet so opposed, so mutually watchful: that of the angular pale princess, ostrich plumed, black-robed, hung about with amulets, reminders, relics, mainly seated, mainly still, and that of the upright restless slow-circling lady of her court who exchanges with her, across the black water streaked with evening gleams, fitful questions and answers. The upright lady, with thick dark braids down her back, drawing over the grass a more embroidered train, makes the whole circuit, and makes it again, and the broken talk, brief and sparingly allusive, seems more to cover than to free their sense. This is because, when it fairly comes to not having others to consider, they meet in an air that appears rather anxiously to wait for their words. Such an impression as that was in fact grave, and might be tragic; so that, plainly enough, systematically at last, they settled to a care of what they said.

There could be no gross phrasing to Milly, in particular, of the probability that if she wasn't so proud she might be pitied with more comfort—more to the person pitying; there could be no spoken proof, no sharper demonstration than the consistently considerate attitude, that this marvellous mixture of her weakness and of her strength, her peril, if such it were, and her option, made her, kept her, irresistibly interesting. Kate's predicament in the matter was, after all, very much Mrs. Stringham's own, and Susan Shepherd herself, in our Maeterlinck picture, might well have hovered in the gloaming by the moat. It may be declared for Kate, at all events, that her sincerity about her friend, through this time, was deep, her compassionate imagination was strong, and that these things gave her a virtue, a good conscience, a credibility for herself, so to speak, that were later to be precious to her. She grasped with her keen intelligence the logic of their common duplicity, went unassisted through the same ordeal as Milly's other hushed follower, easily saw that for the girl to be explicit was to betray divinations, gratitudes, glimpse of the felt contrast between her fortune and her fear—all of which would have contradicted her systematic bravado. That was it, Kate wonderingly saw: to recognise was to bring down the avalanche—the avalanche Milly lived so in watch for and that might be started by the lightest of breaths; though less possibly the breath of her own stifled plaint than that of the vain sympathy, the mere helpless gaping interference of others. With so many suppressions as these, therefore, between them, their withdrawal together to unmask had to fall back, as we have hinted, on a nominal motive—which was decently represented by a joy at the drop of chatter. Chatter had in truth all along attended their step, but they took the despairing view of it on purpose to have ready, when face to face, some view or other of something. The relief of getting out of harness—that was the moral of their meeting, but the moral of this, in turn, was that they couldn't so much as ask each other why harness need be worn. Milly wore it as a general armour. (261–63)

A complete analysis of the passage would be out of place here, but a few stylistic features are worth noting before we get to the images. First, the passage as a whole is a ring, marked by words and phrases which appear at the beginning and at the end of the passage; the ring tends to make the passage a somewhat self-contained unit of composition. The ring is not evident until the end of the passage, and indeed it may not be evident on first reading at all. The repeated elements at the beginning and the end of the ring are "face to face"; "put off the mask" and "unmask"; and "harness." Moreover, the phrase "put off the mask" in the first sentence is linked to "puttings off of the mask" in the second. This brings us to the second point of style: the passage is full of links and other kinds of repetitions—too many to note here; I count sixteen or seventeen. And third, we can note some additional figures, such as parallel construction, antithesis, and tricolon.

But the point that interests me here is the deployment of metaphor and simile. At the beginning of the passage Milly and Kate are alone, and they feel that they can put off their masks—masks that they have been wearing in public. The putting off of the masks is a sign of their intimate friendship. These masks, of course, are metaphorical: they are not wearing literal masks. They take off these metaphorical masks when they are, as Milly says, out of harness. The harness is a secondary image: the metaphorical mask is a metaphorical harness, and at the end of the passage the metaphorical harness is figured as metaphorical armor. Furthermore, Milly and Kate flourish these metaphorical masks as if they were Spanish fans. They take off these masks, which they flourish like Spanish fans, when they cease to pretend, but oddly enough, it is when they cease to pretend that what they are keeping back is most in the air. I take "in the air" as a kind of buried metaphor. The point, I suppose, is that even though Milly and Kate are letting down their guard, removing their masks, they are still keeping things from each other; their continued reticence is the greatest reality of the situation.

Their situations, however, are not symmetrical: Milly doesn't know what Kate is hiding—the reader may suspect that Kate's secret is her engagement to Densher—but Kate knows that Milly has a treasure to hide. This treasure is a further metaphor. Milly does have a literal treasure, but this is not in any way hidden. I'm not entirely sure what this hidden treasure is; it is "a principle of pride," it is "a truth about the girl's own conception of her validity"—whatever that means. What Milly is hiding, I suppose, is the seriousness of her illness, but it seems a little odd to call this secret a treasure. At any rate, this principle of pride—a principle that is bold and hard—is like a spring that can be set off by a mere footfall. I suppose the point of this simile is that Kate can't get too close to talking about Milly's illness for fear of setting off Milly's pride. A few sentences later, the conflict between Kate's pity and Milly's pride is more explicit:

"the probability that if she wasn't so proud she might be pitied with more comfort"; presumably what Kate would pity is Milly's illness, which Milly's pride would not want to be pitied. But here we see Kate, a "pitying sister," on one side of a moat that surrounds a tower. The grammar is a little vague, but I assume that the moat and the tower have been built by Milly (taking Milly as the antecedent of "she"). The moat and the tower are of course metaphorical. They are situated in the dusk and twilight of a play by Maeterlinck. The characters in this play are a princess, with all her accoutrements—Milly—and a lady of her court—Kate. This image, notable for its detail, picks up on earlier images of Milly and Kate. Susan Stringham is added as a third figure by the moat in the twilight; Kate and Mrs. Stringham share a predicament; they both grasp the delicacy of a necessary duplicity; explicit comment—the lightest of breaths—would bring down an avalanche.

The images in this passage thus include masks, a harness, Spanish fans, a treasure, a fine steel spring, a moat, a tower, a play by Maeterlinck, a princess, a lady of her court and another follower, an avalanche that could be started by the lightest breath, and armor. (And just before this passage we have seen Milly compared to a priestess and to Catherine the Great.)

The overall sense of the passage I think is reasonably clear on first reading, even if the details don't immediately all fall into place. First, the passage centers on Milly and Kate; Mrs. Stringham's role is peripheral and secondary. Second, there is a contrast between social pretense (the masks) and intimate sincerity (the putting off of the masks); third, within the intimate sincerity there is a further level of pretense: "It was when they called each other's attention to their ceasing to pretend, it was then that what they were keeping back was most in the air." Everything else has to contribute to or at least be consistent with these three points. Thus the moat, which derives from the idea that Milly is a princess, expresses the distance between Milly and Kate even when they take off their masks.

James often begins an image with a more or less buried metaphor; here, for instance, the idea of wearing masks is even something of a cliché. But James then visualizes the masks; once he has visualized them, he can turn them into Spanish fans. Then again, once the idea of hiding something has been introduced, James turns that something into something material, a treasure. The emotional distance between Milly and Kate becomes a physical moat, and this image easily associates with the continuing image of Milly as a princess. And so on. It must have taken considerable mental agility to write such a passage, and it takes considerable mental agility to read it. Many readers are put off by the gymnastics; the cognitive effort may interfere with emotional response. The images are not, however, simply cognitive devices; they typically include something sensory, which often is the starting point of the comparison. This point of comparison then is extended in further detail in a kind of small allegory, as each point of the vehicle is potentially matched with a point in the tenor; this extended matching is what takes the cognitive effort.

I am not interested here in making a judgment on *The Wings of the Dove;* I can understand why some people like late James and why some don't. The point here and throughout this chapter has been simply to examine various similes and metaphors in actual literary practice.

It is perhaps possible to identify a typical simile by Homer, by Chandler, by James—while recognizing that the typical leaves room for variation. Homer's typical simile is extended beyond the point of comparison (though clever reading may find that the further details are in fact relevant); often a Homeric simile describes some little incident—sometimes from the world of nature or from the nonheroic activities of mortals. Chandler's typical simile is short and punchy, almost a wisecrack; his similes often force a change of perspective and judgment. James's typical simile is elaborated, but not in the Homeric manner: James imagines a little scene in detail and then insists that the details all beautifully contribute to the comparison, even if the result borders on the ludicrous; nor does he hesitate to mix his images. Homer's similes tend to bring the quotidian world into the world of the heroes; James's similes often add a note of romantic fantasy.

If there is any general conclusion to be drawn from these various images, it may be that they contribute to vividness, what the rhetoric manuals call *enargeia.* But vividness can be created in many ways. Homer's extended similes often describe a scene with precise physical detail: when Athena puts strength into Menelaos, he is like a mosquito buzzing and biting; when Odysseus is unable to sleep as he ponders his revenge, he tosses and turns like a sizzling sausage. Chandler's similes often include some vivid physical sensation: the handrail on a flight of stairs "was as cold and wet as a toad's belly." I imagine that many readers have held a cold wet railing, not so many have felt a toad's belly; the simile works from the unfamiliar to the familiar in order to make the familiar a more vivid sensation. But some similes are vivid without evoking a physical sensation: in the *Iliad* Hera flies from the battlefield to Olympus "as the thought flashes in the mind of a man, who traversing much territory, thinks of things in the mind's awareness," and in Chandler a hat-check girl in a nightclub has "eyes like strange sins." A typical simile in *The Wings of the Dove* certainly includes physical detail, but in a kind of abstract space, not quite moored to anything real: in the passage analyzed above, we see masks, Spanish fans, treasure, a tower and a moat, twilight and dusk; Milly as the princess is wearing ostrich plumes, a black robe, amulets, as well as vaguely referenced reminders and relics—it is typical of James to leave these reminders and relics rather vague. In the same passage, Kate as the lady of the court wears thick dark braids down her back and draws an embroidered train over the grass. All of these details are included not so much for what they are as for what they suggest. A lion in Homer really is a lion, even when it is being used to tell us about one of the heroes; a princess or a lady of the court in James has just magically stepped out of a picture or a play. I have chosen examples from Homer, Chandler, and James because all three are known for their characteristic use of metaphors and similes. But three authors are a small sample, and no doubt additional examples from other authors will add to our understanding of the formation and meaning of these figures.

Afterword

A good novel is one of the most intricate of human creations, the result of thousands of choices and decisions. In this volume I have named and explicated some of these intricacies. Chapter 1 argues that the language of the novel is not a transparent transcription of reality; chapters 2 and 3 discuss aspects of the narrative situation, from the perspective of the author and narrator and from that of the reader; and chapters 4 through 6 examine many traditional rhetorical devices, both schemes and tropes, as they occur in various novels.

A residual trace of romantic ideology persisting even in our postmodern times would suggest that technical terminology gets in the way of artistic creation and appreciation; writers, according to this view, don't know what they are doing, they are simply inspired; and readers want to be overwhelmed by the artistic experience, they want to get lost in a book. If you're talking about how a clock works, then it's appropriate to use technical terms, but if you use technical terminology to analyze a novel, you're turning it into something mechanical.

Most artists, I would argue, know a good deal about what they are doing, even if they can't articulate that knowledge to themselves or others. Writers may or may not be aware of all the decisions they make; it may be enough simply to feel "That works, I can keep going." Writers vary, and some are more aware of the writing process than others. The psychology of creation is an interesting topic, but perhaps not of direct importance to the literary critic.

Readers vary as well. Some are happy just reading and getting lost in a book; others may find some pleasure in figuring out how the tricks are performed. The experience of reading is a gradual process of accumulating understanding. Each sentence in a novel adds or modifies the meanings created by the writer and achieved by the reader. It's not so much that "large parts of a novel go virtually unread," as Frank Kermode would have it; it's more that understanding can occur without conscious awareness. Awareness, however, may add a dimension to the aesthetic experience. I know that my own pleasure in reading has grown as I have learned more about how novels work.

We can trace at least a part of this process in reading, or rereading, a short text. Here are the first three paragraphs of Katherine Anne Porter's *Ship of Fools*. I present the text without comment and follow with a commentary focusing on the two main topics of this volume, language and the narrative situation:

August, 1931—The port town of Veracruz is a little purgatory between land and sea for the traveler, but the people who live there are very fond of themselves and the town they have helped to make. They live as initiates in local custom reflecting their own history and temperament, and they carry on their lives of alternate violence and lethargy with a pleasurable contempt for outside opinion, founded on their charmed notion that their ways and feelings are above and beyond criticism.

When they entertain themselves at their numerous private and public feasts, the newspapers publish lyric prose saying how gay an occasion it was; in what lavish and aristocratic—the terms are synonymous, they believe—taste the decorations and refreshments, and they cannot praise too much the skill with which the members of good society maintain in their deportment the delicate balance between high courtesy and easy merriment, a secret of the Veracruz world bitterly envied and unsuccessfully imitated by the provincial inland society of the Capital. "Only our people know how to enjoy themselves with civilized freedom," they wrote. "We are generous, warmhearted, hospitable, sensitive," they go on, and they mean it to be read not only by themselves but by the polyglot barbarians of the upper plateau who obstinately go on regarding Veracruz as merely a pestilential jumping-off place into the sea.

There is maybe a small sign of uneasiness in this pugnacious assertion of high breeding, in this and in the methodical brutality of their common behavior towards the travelers who must pass through their hands to reach the temporary haven of some ship in the harbor. The

travelers wish only to be carried away from the place, and the Veracruzians wish only to see the last of them; but not until every possible
toll, fee, extortion, and bribe due to the town and its citizens has been
exacted. It is in fact to the passing eye a typical port town, cynical by
nature, shameless by experience, hardened to showing its seamiest
side to strangers: ten to one this stranger passing through is a sheep
bleating for their shears, and one in ten is a scoundrel it would be a pity
not to outwit. In any case, there is only so much money to be got out of
each one, and the time is always short. (Porter 1984, 3–4)

This passage is realistic in the sense that it isn't fantastic—this is not a
story of once upon a time in some fairy kingdom; it takes place in August
1931, in Veracruz—but it is by no means a transparent transcription of reality. Throughout we note the mind of the narrator, organizing and making judgments. The first sentence is a complex combination of trichoto-
mies and dichotomies. Veracruz is a liminal space, between land and sea,
and more specifically it is a purgatory. A purgatory needs an inferno and
a paradise. There may be an allusion here to Dante's *Divine Comedy,* and
thus a suggestion that this story has epic and cosmological implications;
but the heaven and hell are not specified, and probably unspecifiable—we
can't identify either the land or the sea with either heaven or hell. Veracruz is only a little purgatory, so perhaps it sits between a little heaven and
a little hell (a rhetorician would note the figure "meiosis" or "belittling").
    The characterization of Veracruz is presented as a fact, but it is really
a judgment ascribed by the narrator to the travelers; the narrator is evidently able to generalize confidently about the travelers' feelings, and
also able to generalize about the feelings of the people of Veracruz, who
are very fond of themselves and their town. The narrator looks down with
indulgent superiority on the foibles of the people.
    This first sentence states both a division by threes—land/Veracruz/
sea—and also a division by twos—the travelers/the people of Veracruz.
Indeed, the tripartite division of land, Veracruz, and sea can be seen as
two overlapping dichotomies: the people of the plateau versus the people
of Veracruz, and the people of Veracruz versus the travelers.
    The whole passage could serve as a tutorial on the various types of
doublets. The first sentence states two dichotomies, as it distinguishes (1)
the travelers from (2) the people of Veracruz and then notes that the peo-

ple of Veracruz are fond of (1) themselves and (2) their town. In the second sentence we find four doublets: history and temperament, violence and lethargy, ways and feelings, and above and beyond.

The people of Veracruz live lives of alternate violence and lethargy—the narrator is a sort of recording angel, taking note of each action of the people and assigning it either to violence or to lethargy, with nothing in the middle. The narrator's tone of indulgent superiority is reinforced by the phrase "charmed notion." The notion that the people feel beyond criticism is in itself a kind of criticism.

The second paragraph continues the doublets: private/public, lavish/aristocratic, decorations/refreshments, high courtesy/easy merriment, bitterly envied/unsuccessfully imitated. The people of Veracruz believe that the terms "lavish" and "aristocratic" are synonymous; clearly the narrator does not. This paragraph continues the contrast between the inlanders and the people of Veracruz, who characterize themselves with a string of complimentary epithets, while the people of the plateau are polyglot barbarians. The paragraph ends with a ring, as "little purgatory between land and sea" is mirrored by "pestilential jumping-off place into the sea."

The third paragraph now turns to renew the contrast between the people of Veracruz and the travelers; the pivot of this turn is the doublet "pugnacious assertion of high breeding," which recapitulates the second paragraph, and the "methodical brutality" they display toward the travelers. The second sentence continues in the parallel construction of the next sentence: "The travelers wish only" and "the Veracruzians wish only"; but the wish of the Veracruzians to see the last of the travelers is then qualified by their desire for profit, expressed in a small congeries, "tool, fee, extortion, and bribe." The next sentence is a tricolon crescendo: the town is "cynical by nature, shameless by experience, hardened to showing its seamiest side to strangers"; this is followed by another doublet, marked by the inversion of "ten to one" and "one in ten"; this sentence continues the narrator's indirect judgment of the Veracruzians. The last sentence states another doublet: "only so much money" and "time is always short." The reference to time leads naturally to the beginning of the next paragraph—"In the white heat of an early August morning"—which starts the narrative clock of the story.

This commentary would probably count as what Frank Kermode calls "abnormally attentive scrutiny." Even so it does not exhaust everything that could be said—it does not consider, for example, the prose rhythm and its relation to the rhythm of thought; nor does it consider the relationship between this passage and the rest of the novel.

The rhetorical figures and narrative devices described here are not simply ornamental; they create meaning by organizing thought and guiding moral judgments. I don't mean to discount the ornamental—the creation of beauty has its own value. But language is always meaningful; even nonsense syllables are more than nonsense, if, for example, they mean "nonsense."

It is unlikely that most readers consciously note the kind of detail I have cataloged here. These details are the less manifest portions of a novel that (again following Kermode) are unread. They do not therefore lack effect, as they form and guide the readers' responses over one page or several hundred. Whether or not that effect is worth analyzing on rereading is a personal judgment. I have found that my own appreciation and understanding of a novel is increased by scrutiny. A critical vocabulary helps me focus my attention and helps me communicate what I have seen.

The rhetorical figures are structures mostly the size of a sentence, more or less, but the analysis of narrative composition should also include discussion of larger structures, what one might call Narrative Architecture, from paragraphs all the way up to complete novels. A projected companion volume will treat larger elements of composition, including Segmentation, Ring Composition, One-Day Novels, One-Year Novels, Mirror Plots, Beginning with the Ending, Ending with the Beginning, and various kinds of Retrospects.

Notes

Introduction

1. There are too many of these moments to detail here: I will mention just one. In Volume II, Chapter XVI, Jane has been out in the rain to pick up her letters at the post office. Mrs. Elton, in her interfering way, offers to have her servant pick up Jane's letters for her, but Jane declines this offer. Emma mistakenly thinks that Jane has been corresponding with Mr. Campbell; the rereader will understand that she is attempting to hide her correspondence with Frank. (My thanks to the anonymous Reader for the Press.)

2. For extensive discussion of these terms, see Clark and Phelan 2020.

3. The handbooks do not always agree about the names of the figures; I usually follow Lanham 1991, but without worrying too much about minor points of terminology.

1. The Language of Fiction

1. Watt oddly skips more than a hundred years of literary history (Lyly's *Euphues* was published in 1578; Defoe's *Robinson Crusoe* in 1719); he has also failed to mention a number of relevant fictions of the period, including Thomas Nashe's *The Unfortunate Traveller* (1594); Thomas Deloney's *Jack of Newbury* (1597); John Bunyan's *The Pilgrim's Progress* (1678); and Aphra Behn's *Oroonoko* (1688); notice might also be taken of seventeenth-century translations of picaresque novels. Moreover, language is never simply transparent, and although some writers did adopt a relatively plain style, figuration, sometimes abundant figuration, never disappears.

2. See 191, 195, 212; 208–9, 214; 190, 195, 208, 256.

2. Narrators

1. I have discussed witness narrators in Clark 2010.

2. See Phelan 2017, 49–51, for a discussion of this episode.

3. Readers

1. All translations from the Greek novels are taken from Reardon 1989.
2. See 36, 46, 47, 106, 113, 137, 140, 148, etc.

4. The Use and Meaning of Rhetorical Schemes

1. See Lanham 1991, 154–57.
2. See also 515, 567.
3. My thanks to the anonymous Reader for the Press for this example.
4. See also 184, 360, 518, 520.
5. See also 126, 360, 401, 450.
6. See also 79, 223, 442, 451–52, 454, 465, and for another instance of polysyndeton and asyndeton in the same sentence see 384.
7. I have used the Norton Critical Edition of *The Wings of the Dove;* this prints the text of the 1909 New York Edition, rather than the original 1902 edition.
8. See also 34, 44, 48, 69, 87, 82, 94, 131, 147, 175, 215.
9. See also 48, 65, 71, 75, 77, 82, 83, 86, 152, etc.
10. See also 25, 44, 45, 57, 113, 143, 144, etc.
11. Cohen's English translation here closely follows the French original.

5. Rhetorical Schemes in Dickens, Brontë, and Morrison

1. See also 484, 518, 571, etc.
2. See 69, 144, 145, 208, 351–52, etc.; 73, 145–46, 357, 361–62, etc.
3. See also 144, 612, 796, 835, 844, 867, etc.

6. Metaphor and Simile in Homer, Chandler, and James

1. See, for instance, Brooke-Rose 1965; Ricoeur 1981; Lakoff and Johnson 1980a and 1980b; Kittay 1987; Kövecses 2001.
2. See, for example, Shewan 1911; Coffey 1957; Porter 1972–73; Moulton 1977; Foley 1978; Nimis 1987; Heiden 1998; Buxton 2004; Benediktson 2013.
3. Virgil imitates and extends this simile at the climax of the *Aeneid* (XII.905–914).
4. There is copious critical discussion of James, including good work on James's style and other aspects of his technique—see for example Beach 1954; Chatman 1972; Gale 1964; Holland 1964; Short 1946; Smit 1988; Smith 1973; Tompkins 1970.
5. See also 111, 156, 171, 262, 264, 279.

References

Abádi-Nagy, Zoltan. 2008. "Narratorial Consciousness as an Intersection of Culture and Narrative (Case Study: Toni Morrison's "Jazz")." *Hungarian Journal of English and American Studies (HJEAS)* 14, no. 1 (Spring 2008): 21–33.

Achebe, Chinua. 2009 (1959). *Things Fall Apart*. Toronto: Anchor Canada.

Austen, Jane. 2012 (1816). *Emma*. New York: W. W. Norton & Company.

———. 2003. (1818). *Persuasion*. London: Penguin Books.

———. 2001 (1813). *Pride and Prejudice*. New York: W. W. Norton & Company.

———. 2001 (1811). *Sense and Sensibility*. New York: Modern Library (Random House).

Beach, Joseph Warren. 1954. *The Method of Henry James*. Philadelphia: A. Saifer.

Beckett, Samuel. 1959. *Watt*. New York: Grove Press.

Benediktson, D. Thomas. 2013. "Ring Structures in Homeric Similes." *Quaderni Urbinati di Cultura Classica,* new series, 105, no. 3 (2013): 29–44.

Bernardin de Saint-Pierre, Jacques-Henri. 1989 (1788). *Paul and Virginia*. London: Penguin Books.

Booth, Wayne. 1961. *The Rhetoric of Fiction*. Chicago: University of Chicago Press.

Brontë, Anne. 2019. *Agnes Grey*. New York: Penguin Classics.

Brontë, Charlotte. 2009. *Shirley*. Hertfordshire: Wordsworth Editions Limited.

Brooke-Rose, Christine. 1965. *A Grammar of Metaphor*. London: Secker & Warburg.

Burgess, Anthony. 1986. *A Clockwork Orange*. New York: W. W. Norton.

Burke, Kenneth. 1969. *A Grammar of Motives*. Berkley: University of California Press.

———. 1941. "Four Master Tropes." *Kenyon Review* 3, no. 4 (1941): 421–38. Reprinted in Burke 1969: 503–17; and in Franzosi 2017: 91–101.

———. 1962. *A Rhetoric of Motives*. Berkeley: University of California Press.

Buxton, Richard. 2004. "Similes and Other Likenesses." In Fowler 2004: 139–55.

Camus, Albert. 1972. *La Chute*. Paris: Gallimard.

———. 1991. *The Fall* [*La Chute*]. Translated by Justin O'Brien. New York: Vintage Books.

Cather, Willa. 1972 [1923]. *A Lost Lady.* New York: Vintage Books.

Chandler, Raymond. 1988 (1939). *The Big Sleep.* New York: Vintage Books.

———. 1992 (1940). *Farewell My Lovely.* New York: Vintage Books.

———. 1988. (1943). *The High Window.* New York: Vintage.

Chatman, Seymour. 1972. *The Later Style of Henry James.* Oxford: Basil Blackwell.

———. 1978. *Story and Discourse: Narrative Structure in Fiction and Film.* Ithaca, NY: Cornell University Press.

Clark, Matthew. 2010. *Narrative Structures and the Language of the Self.* Columbus: Ohio State University Press.

Clark, Matthew, and James Phelan. 2020. *Debating Rhetorical Narratology: On the Synthetic, Mimetic and Thematic Aspects of Narrative.* Columbus: Ohio State University Press.

Coffey, M. 1957. "The Function of the Homeric Simile." *American Journal of Philology* 78 (1957): 113–32.

Cohn, Dorrit. 1978. *Transparent Minds: Narrative Modes for Presenting Consciousness in Fiction.* Princeton, NJ: Princeton University Press.

Conrad, Joseph. 2012 (1907). *The Secret Agent.* London: Penguin Books.

DeLillo, Don. 1985. *White Noise.* New York: Viking Press.

Dick, Philip K. 1992. *The Confessions of a Crap Artist.* Vintage Books: Random House.

Dickens, Charles. 1965 (1860–61). *Great Expectations.* Harmondsworth: Penguin Books.

———. 2008 (1854). *Hard Times.* Oxford: Oxford World's Classics.

———. 1980 (1855–57). *Little Dorrit.* London: Penguin Books.

———. 2000 (1836–37). *The Pickwick Papers.* Hertfordshire: Woodsworth Editions Limited.

Eliot, George (Mary Ann Evans). 1985 (1859). *Adam Bede.* London: Penguin Books.

Empson, William. 1967. *The Structure of Complex Words.* Ann Arbor: University of Michigan Press.

Fahnestock, Jeanne. 1996. "Series Reasoning in Scientific Argument: *Incrementum* and *Gradatio* and the Case of Darwin." *Rhetoric Society Quarterly* 26, no. 4 (Fall 1996).

Flaubert, Gustave. 1980. *The Letters of Gustave Flaubert, 1830–1857.* Translated by Francis Steegmuller. Cambridge, MA: Harvard University Press.

Finney, Charles G. 2002. *The Circus of Dr. Lao.* Lincoln: University of Nebraska Press.

Foley, Helene P. 1978. "'Reverse Similes' and Sex Roles in the *Odyssey.*" *Arethusa* 11, no. 1–2 (Spring and Fall 1978): 7–26.

Follet, Ken. 1978. *The Eye of the Needle*. New York: HarperCollins.

Ford, Ford Maddox. 1997 (1915). *The Good Soldier. A Tale of Passion*. New York: Penguin.

Fowler, Robert, ed. 2004. *The Cambridge Companion to Homer*. Cambridge: Cambridge University Press.

Franzosi, Roberto. 2017. *Landmark Essays on Trope and Figures*. New York: Routledge.

Friedman, Norman. 1967. "Point of View in Fiction: The Development of a Critical Concept." In Stevick 1968, 108–38.

Gale, Robert. 1964. *The Caught Image: Figurative Language in the Fiction of Henry James*. Chapel Hill: University of North Carolina Press. PS 2124 G3.

Genette, Gérard. 1982. *Figures of Literary Discourse*. Translated by Alan Sheridan. New York: Columbia University Press.

———. 1980. *Narrative Discourse: An Essay in Method*. Translated by Jane E. Lewin. Ithaca, NY: Cornell University Press.

Gibbon, Edward. 1993 (1776). *The Decline and Fall of the Roman Empire*. Volume 1. New York: Everyman's Library: Alfred A. Knopf.

Golding, William. 2011. *Lord of the Flies*. New York: Perigee (Penguin Group).

Griffith, R. Drew. (1989). "In Praise of the Bride: Sappho Fr. 105(A) L-P, Voigt." *Transactions of the American Philological Association* 119 (1989): 55–61.

Hartley, L. P. 2002 (1953). *The Go-Between*. New York: *New York Review Books*.

Heiden, Bruce. 1998. "The Similes of the Fugitive Homicide, *Iliad* 24.480–84: Analogy, Foiling, and Allusion." *American Journal of Philology* 19, no. 1 (Spring 1998): 1–10.

Hemingway, Ernest. 1997 (1929). *A Farewell to Arms*. New York: Scribner.

Herman, David, James Phelan, Peter J. Rabinowitz, Brian Richardson, and Robyn Warhol. 2012. *Narrative Theory: Core Concepts and Critical Debates*. Columbus: Ohio State University Press.

Holland, Laurence. 1964. *The Expense of Vision: Essays on the Craft of Henry James*. Princeton, NJ: Princeton University Press. PS 2124 H64.

Homer. 1961. *The Iliad of Homer*. Translated by Richmond Lattimore. Chicago: University of Chicago Press.

———. 1991. *The Odyssey of Homer*. Translated by Richmond Lattimore. New York: HarperCollins.

Hughes, Dorothy. 2017. *In a Lonely Place*. New York: New York Review of Books.

Hunter, Stephen. 2017. *G-Man*. New York: G. P. Putnam's Sons.

———. 1993. *Point of Impact*. New York: Random House.

Jakobson, Roman. 1987a. *Language in Literature*. Cambridge, MA: Harvard University Press.

———. 1987b. "Linguistics and Poetics." In Jakobson, *Language in Literature*.

Jakobson, Roman, and Morris Halle. 1971. *Fundamentals of Language*. The Hague: Mouton.

James, Henry. 1965 (1875). *Roderick Hudson*. Harmondsworth: Penguin Books.

———. 1964 (1902). *The Wings of the Dove*. New York: New American Library.

Jordan, John O., ed. 2001. *The Cambridge Companion to Charles Dickens*. Cambridge: Cambridge University Press.

Joyce, James. 1964 (1916). *A Portrait of the Artist as a Young Man*. Harmondsworth: Penguin Books.

Kermode, Frank. 1981. "Secrets and Narrative Sequence." In Mitchell 1981: 79–97.

Kipling, Rudyard. 1987 (1902). *The Just So Stories*. London: Penguin Books.

Kittay, Eva Feder. 1987. *Metaphor: Its Cognitive Force and Linguistic Structure*. Oxford: Clarendon Press.

Köcvecses, Zoltán. 2001. *Metaphor: A Practical Introduction*. Oxford: Oxford University Press.

Krauss, Lawrence M. 2012. *A Universe from Nothing: Why There Is Something Rather than Nothing*. New York: Simon & Schuster.

Lakoff, George and Mark Johnson. 1980a. *Metaphors We Live By*. Chicago: University of Chicago Press.

———. 1980b. "Conceptual Metaphor in Everyday Language." *Journal of Philosophy* 77, no. 8 (August 1980): 453–86.

Lanham, Richard. 2003. *Analyzing Prose*. Second Edition. London: Continuum.

———. 1991. *A Handlist of Rhetorical Terms*. Second Edition. Berkeley: University of California Press.

———. 1974. *Style: An Anti-Textbook*. New Haven, CT: Yale University Press.

Lanser, Susan Snaider. 1981. *The Narrative Act: Point of View in Prose Fiction*. Princeton, NJ: Princeton University Press.

Leaf, Walter, ed. 1902. *The Iliad*. Second Edition. London: Macmillan.

Lobel, Edgard, and Denys Page, eds. 1955. *Poetarum Lesbiorum Fragmenta*. Oxford: Clarendon Press.

Lodge, David. 2002. *The Language of Fiction: Essays in Criticism and Verbal Analysis of the English Novel*. London: Routledge.

Longus. 1989. *Daphnis and Chloe*. In Reardon 1989: 285–348.

Mack, Peter. 2017. "Manuals of Tropes and Figures." In Franzosi 2017: 75–90.

Melville, Herman. 1972 (1851). *Moby-Dick; or, The Whale*. Harmondsworth: Penguin Books.

Mitchell, W. J. T., ed. 1981. *On Narrative*. Chicago: University of Chicago Press.

Morrison, Toni. 2004. *Jazz*. New York: Random House.

Moulton, C. 1977. *Similes in the Homeric Poems*. Göttingen.

Nabokov, Vladimir. 1974 (1947). *Bend Sinister*. Harmondsworth: Penguin Books.

———. 1985. *Pnin*. New York: Vintage Books.

Nimis, Stephen A. 1987. *Narrative Semiotics in the Epic Tradition: The Simile*. Bloomington: Indiana University Press.

Nisbet, Robert A. 1969. *Social Change and History: Aspects of the Western Theory of Development*. New York: Oxford University Press.

Phelan, James. 2017. *Somebody Telling Somebody Else: A Rhetorical Poetics of Narrative*. Columbus: Ohio State University Press.

Pici, Nick. 2000. "Trading Meanings: The Breath of Music in Toni Morrison's 'Jazz.'" *CEA Critic* 62, no. 3 (Summer 2000): 18–38.

Plato. 1961. *The Collected Dialogues of Plato*. Edited by Edith Hamilton and Huntington Cairns. Princeton, NJ: Princeton University Press.

———. 1961. *Euthyphro*. In *The Collected Dialogues of Plato*, 169–85.

———. 1961. *Republic*. In *The Collected Dialogues of Plato*, 575–844.

Porter, D. H. 1972–73. "Violent Juxtaposition in the Similes of the *Iliad*." *Classical Journal* 68 (1972–73): 11–21.

Porter, Katherine Anne. 1964. *Pale Horse, Pale Rider*. New York: Harcourt Brace.

———. 1984. *Ship of Fools*. New York: Little, Brown.

Prince, Gerald. 1987. *Dictionary of Narratology*. Lincoln: University of Nebraska Press.

Rabelais, François. 1955 (1534–1551). *Gargantua and Pantagruel*. Translated by J. M. Cohen. Harmondsworth: Penguin Books.

Reardon, B. P., ed. 1989. *Collected Ancient Greek Novels*. Berkeley: University of California Press.

Richards, I. A. 1925. *Principles of Literary Criticism*. New York: Harcourt, Brace & World.

Ricoeur, Paul. 1981. *The Rule of Metaphor: Multidisciplinary Studies of the Creation of Meaning in Language*. Toronto: University of Toronto Press.

Rimmon-Kenan, Shlomith. 1983. *Narrative Fiction: Contemporary Poetics*. London: Methuen.

Rodrigues, Eusebio L. 1993. "Experiencing 'Jazz.'" *Modern Fiction Studies* 39, no. 3/4, Toni Morrison Double Issue (Fall/Winter 1993): 733–54.

Rubenstein, Roberta. 1998. "Singing the Blues/Reclaiming Jazz: Toni Morrison and Cultural Meaning." *Mosaic: An Interdisciplinary Critical Journal* 31, no. 2 (June 1998): 147–63.

Sherard, Tracey. 2000. "Women's Classic Blues in Toni Morrison's Jazz: Cultural Artifact as Narrator"; *Genders*. https://www.colorado.edu/gendersarchive1998-2013/2000/03/01/womens-classic-blues-toni-morrisons-jazz-cultural-artifact-narrator.

Shewan, A. 1911. "Suspected Flaws in Homeric Similes." *Classical Philology* 6, no. 3 (July 1911): 271–81.

Short, R. W. 1946. "The Sentence Structure of Henry James." *American Literature* 18 (1946): 71–88.

Small-McCarthy, Robin. 1999. "From 'The Bluest Eye' to 'Jazz': A Retrospective of Toni Morrison's Literary Sounds." *Counterpoints* 96 (1999): 175–93.

Smit, David W. 1988. *The Language of a Master: Theories of Style and the Late Writing of Henry James.* Carbondale: Southern Illinois University Press.

Smith, William F., Jr. 1973. "Sentence Structure in the Tales of Henry James." *Style* 7 (1973): 157–72.

Stanzel, F. K. 1986. *A Theory of Narrative.* Translated by Charlotte Goedsche. Cambridge: Cambridge University Press.

Sternberg, Meir. 1987. *The Poetics of Biblical Narrative. Ideological Literature and the Drama of Reading.* Bloomington: Indiana University Press.

Sterne, Laurence. 1964 (1759–1767). *The Life & Opinions of Tristram Shandy, Gent.* New York: Holt, Rinehart & Winston.

Stevick, Philip, ed. 1968. *The Theory of the Novel.* London: The Free Press (Collier Macmillan).

Stewart, Garrett. 2001. "Dickens and Language." In Jordan 2001, 135–51.

Sutherland, James R. 1965. *On English Prose.* Toronto: University of Toronto Press.

Tatius, Achiles. 1989. *Leucippe and Clitophon.* In Reardon 1989, 170–384.

Thomas, Francis-Noël, and Mark Turner. 1994. *Clear and Simple as the Truth: Writing Classic Prose.* Princeton, NJ: Princeton University Press.

Tompkins, Jane P. 1970. "'The Beast in the Jungle': An Analysis of James' Late Style." *Modern Fiction Studies* 16 (1970): 185–91.

Trollope, Anthony. 2004 (1858). *Dr. Thorne.* London: Penguin Books.

———. 2004 (1861). *Framley Parsonage.* London: Penguin Books.

———. 1984 (1855). *The Warden.* Harmondsworth: Penguin Books.

Twain, Mark (Samuel Clemens). 1912 (1884). *Huckleberry Finn.* New York: P. F. Collier & Son.

Vonnegut, Kurt. 1980. *Player Piano.* New York: Random House.

Watt, Ian. 1983. *The Rise of the Novel.* Harmondsworth: Penguin Books.

White, E. B. 1973 (1945). *Stuart Little.* New York: Harper & Row.

Woolf, Virginia. 1977 (1931). *The Waves.* London: Granada Publishing.

Wyatt, Jean. 2017. *Love and Narrative Form in Toni Morrison's Later Novels.* Athens: University of Georgia Press.

Index

Printed in the USA
CPSIA information can be obtained
at www.ICGtesting.com
LVHW091409291223
767659LV00005B/591